SUPPRESSED, FORCED OUT AND FIRED

SUPPRESSED, FORCED OUT AND FIRED

How Successful Women
Lose Their Jobs

Martha E. Reeves

Quorum Books
Westport, Connecticut • London

Library of Congress Cataloging-in-Publication Data

Reeves, Martha E., 1951–
    Suppressed, forced out and fired : how successful women lose their jobs / Martha E.
Reeves.
        p.   cm.
    Includes bibliographical references and index.
    ISBN 1–56720–356–6 (alk. paper)
    1. Sex discrimination in employment—Case studies.   2. Women—Employment—Case
studies.   I. Title.
    HD6060.R44   2000
    331.13'3—dc21   99–056363

British Library Cataloguing in Publication Data is available.

Library of Congress Catalog Card Number: 99–056363
ISBN: 1–56720–356–6

First published in 2000

Quorum Books, 88 Post Road West, Westport, CT 06881
An imprint of Greenwood Publishing Group, Inc.
www.quorumbooks.com

Printed in the United States of America

The paper used in this book complies with the
Permanent Paper Standard issued by the National
Information Standards Organization (Z39.48–1984).

10 9 8 7 6 5 4 3 2 1

Contents

Acknowledgments

$\blacklozenge\blacklozenge$

I wish to thank the ten women who shared their experiences, which formed the basis of this book. I also want to thank Steve Jeffries, Wendy Richards, and Judi Marshall for their suggestions to improve the manuscript. Linda Wirth at the International Labour Organization provided me with valuable information. I am grateful to my children, Alex and Chris, who were patient with me as I juggled my work, their needs, and the research for this project. Finally, I wish to thank Alexander Rosenberg for his support and encouragement.

CHAPTER 1

Introduction

◆◆

Even in an age of equal opportunity legislation and workplace initiatives to make work more flexible and agreeable to women, women still occupy the lower rungs of the corporate ladder. Today's corporations spend a portion of their training budgets communicating employment law to managers, particularly laws concerning racial and sexual discrimination and how to prevent it, yet discrimination in the workplace continues. In spite of legal remedies in the United States (Title VII of the Civil Rights Act of 1964 and the Equal Pay Act of 1963) and in Britain (the Sex Discrimination Act of 1975 and the Equal Pay Act of 1970), inequities and power differences between men and women persist.

By examining the stories of ten middle and senior women managers, this book uncovers some of the mechanisms that make this entrenched discrimination possible. The women, after much investment in their careers, were forced out of their organizations. Through their experiences we come to understand how talented women are marginalized and eventually dismissed from organizations. As these women took exception to their treatment, their circumstances worsened. Their expressed concerns over equity were met with sexual harassment, bullying, and other forms of workplace intimidation. The women profiled in this book were employed in common fields such as human resources, finance, management consulting, marketing, engineering, and sales. They came from both the manufacturing and service sectors, representing companies in the financial services, retail, printing, aerospace, and food-processing areas. Having reached a level in their careers marked by a substantial amount of authority and responsibility, they expected to continue moving upward in their organizations. They managed staff, had responsibility for budgets, made decisions, and identified with a peer group of men of substantial rank. Many of them had made an effort to enhance their skills through attainment of a postgraduate qualification such as an MBA degree.

Career counseling companies, outplacement organizations, governmental agencies, national newspapers (where a few cases were highlighted), and managers of organizations in which the women worked helped me locate women who had been displaced from organizations. When I initially undertook this research, I simply wanted to find out how women experience job loss and how they adjust to change; I was not looking for or expecting to uncover gender discrimination. However, the stories of the inequities the women faced became so compelling and similar among the women that I could not ignore them. In addition, looking back to my own career in management with several organizations in both England and the United States I found the incidents of subtle (and not so subtle) inequalities in the workplace described by these women all too familiar. I had experienced the same type of communication stumbling blocks and all-male camaraderie that so often excludes women. I had found it difficult to break into all-male networks, gain access to information that seemed available to my male colleagues, and in meetings to be listened to as men listen to men. My own experiences and those of the women in this book have led me to examine whether or not real progress has been made since the early 1970s. Even though the 1990s has been a decade characterized by equal opportunity lawsuits, have the ways of discrimination simply become more subtle, covert, and underground?

In conducting this research, I tried to obtain a multicultural sample of women, but found this extremely difficult. At senior and middle management levels, the outplacement firms I contacted had only white females on their registers. The number of minority women who reach the upper levels of an organization becomes scarce as one moves further up the management hierarchy. Some of the individuals I tried to speak to had been held to "gag" clauses as part of their legal settlements, preventing them from discussing any of the details of their cases. I conducted lengthy interviews with each woman and in every case met with each individual several times. Over the course of two years data was collected. As requested, the names of the women, their bosses, and other key individuals in their stories and in their companies have been changed to maintain anonymity. Many of the women expressed fear of reprisal from their respective companies for disclosing information about people and events and expressed concern about finding employment if they became labeled "a fired employee."

In addition to interviews, I collected documents and information the women were given by their employers when they were dismissed. These materials included legal documents, grievance procedures, and dismissal policies. The documents, as well as the women's opinions about them, provided insight about the legal and bureaucratic framework through which the women were terminated. Three women—Diane, Elizabeth, and Mary—gave me lengthy diaries of their experiences leading up to their dismissals and Mary provided e-mail correspondence that she had written to a friend during her ordeal. Several of the women gave me copies of their performance reviews. These proved to be valuable additions to the interviews because they were written during or shortly after important events in their work lives.

A LOOK AT SOME OF THE QUESTIONS

The case studies address several questions that are important to women as they navigate their careers. These questions and others will be discussed in detail in Chapters 4–7 through the case studies of the individual women. The case studies and the statistical material in Chapter 2 raise at least 13 questions, and perhaps more, that this book attempts to address.

Do women recognize systematic discrimination or do they view their failure to succeed as their own fault or the fault of one, sexist boss?

It is important for women to stand back and observe organizational dynamics and to work together to call attention to inequities. Women have a tendency to be hard on themselves and to look for their own shortcomings before looking outside themselves. Several of the women in this book blamed themselves for being fired, constantly replaying what they should have done to avoid termination. Some attributed their terminations to one individual, ignoring patterns and policies that disadvantage all women and some were blind to the general lack of progress of women within their organizations. While it is important to look inside oneself for answers, this introspection can obscure systematic discrimination.

Do men in organizations recognize their own biases? Are men consciously or unconsciously discriminating against women?

If senior management hopes to eradicate gender discrimination, its key players need to find out whether discrimination happens consciously or unconsciously. A recent disclosure by the president of MIT suggested that gender discrimination on the MIT campus against women faculty members is definitely present, but largely unconscious (Wilson, 1999). Cases of women faculty members not receiving resources or promotion have the appearance of isolated cases, rather than being part of system-wide discriminatory patterns. It was not until women faculty members compiled data on individual departments and their practices that discrimination was recognized by the administration as a problem.

Why do some women make it above the glass ceiling? Does this prove that the glass ceiling no longer exists?

Occasionally, women have managed against the odds to make it to the very top of organizations. Is this because of the individual aptitude and personality attributes of the woman or because the organization has a strong commitment to the advancement of women? Or a combination of the two? Some literature suggests that more compliant, noncontroversial women move more quickly to the top. In the case of Carly Fiorina, recently named president of Hewlett-Packard Co., certainly commitment, long service with the company, and talent made her a contender for the job. In addition, her predecessor, Lewis Platt, had a life-changing experience that made him an advocate for women's progress within his company. His wife, Susan, died of cancer, leaving him with two small children. He became more understanding of women as he juggled the responsibility for his children and maintained a high-powered career. Platt commissioned an outside consultant to conduct interviews with women in the company to find out why so many women managers were leaving the organization. Next, Platt instituted a program to raise awareness about women's issues in the workplace and to give everyone the option of more flexibility to ease the pressures of work and family life (Abelson, 1999). Is Carly Fiorina an exception to the glass ceiling rule as the result of one man's personal experience or is she the beginning of a trend of women senior managers?

Does women's progress vary between Western countries? If there are differences between the United States and Great Britain in terms of the advancement of women, to what can they be attributed?

Women have had more success in advancing their careers in the United States than elsewhere in developed economies. Although women are entering the workplace in large numbers everywhere in the Western world, their success (especially in terms of breaking into the ranks of middle and senior management) varies by country. What sociocultural and legal differences exist between the United States and the United Kingdom that have helped women advance more quickly in the United States?

Are women held to a different personality standard than men?

Are women judged by the same criteria in terms of their personality or are they expected to be less aggressive and more passive than men? While everyone in the workplace is expected to be generally optimistic and even-tempered, is it more acceptable for men to display anger, criticize, and raise their voices beyond a normal volume? Because women are thought to be more nurturing than men, when they display emotion, become angry, or criticize others do they risk being labeled as "out of control," "uncooperative," or "aggressive"? How women carry themselves, their demeanor, and their behavior in the workplace seem to warrant constant observation by others whereas men's behavior is less scrutinized. How does being held to a different personality standard affect women at work?

Does being perceived as "assertive" hurt or help women in their careers?

If the expectation for women is to be pleasant and noncontroversial, when they are perceived to be too outspoken, too negative, or too assertive does this perception hold talented women back? If an assertive style holds a woman back, how can she ensure that she gets credit for what she does? How can she move up the ranks of the hierarchy without pushing?

Are women held to the same performance standards as men?

Many surveys suggest that women feel that they are held to higher standards than their male counterparts. In fact, some men have reported that women work harder than they do. In addition to working harder than men for the same rewards, are women judged by different criteria? Recall Ann Hopkins, the Price Waterhouse consultant, who was denied a partnership in the firm because she wasn't feminine enough, didn't wear make-up, and didn't wear jewelry (Lacayo et al., 1988). Are women's careers still dependent on outward appearances that have little to do with their work performance? To become noticed, a woman often has to take on visible, often risky assignments. However, a failure, a misstep, or an ill-conceived project can often damage a woman's career and suggest that she is too risky a proposition to promote. Do women suffer from their mistakes more than men suffer from theirs?

Do women obtain the same level of organizational support as men?

Support comes in many forms: from extra staff and a realistic budget to being included in male networks. To be successful in organizations women need the same resources as men, including having a sponsor or mentor as one progresses in one's career, being welcomed as part of the decision-making group, and being given means to effectively deliver programs. Why is it that in organizations where men dominate the ranks of senior management, it is not uncommon for this support to be withdrawn from women either consciously or unconsciously, when they begin to need it most? If women are unwelcome as part of an inner circle of influential managers, how do they maintain their equilibrium and perform their jobs effectively?

How important are outward symbols of status?

Many senior management jobs come with status markers such as a large corner office or an upscale company car. When women are given titles such as "director" or "vice president" that puts them on a par with men, why are they denied symbols of status? Is it to keep them in their "true" place? Many women do not place importance on status symbols and material objects and because they are unaware of their importance, they may not realize that being denied them is a way of signaling to other women and men their inferior status. To be treated differently is damaging in at least two ways. First, a woman's confidence is eroded. She may become distracted or angry when denied what men get as a matter of course. Second, others in the organization will notice that she is being treated differently and this will affect their perceptions of her. Why don't women recognize this signal immediately? What happens when a woman manager finally realizes what is going on?

Do communication styles between men and women differ and, if so, is this damaging to women?

Researchers in workplace gender dynamics and communication patterns suggest that men communicate for dominance (Tannen, 1995) and that women are less argumentative than men (Schullery, 1998). For example, their contributions in a meeting are intended to assert their position within a hierarchy. By contrast, women communicate to understand or to be understood and are less aware of positioning themselves within a hierarchy. Women are more tentative in their language and actively seek others' opinions as an effort to include others in the discussion. Rather than having a positive impact, these language characteristics make women appear unsure of themselves. Does this difference in communication style hold women back or is it merely a stylistic difference that women can work around?

Do performance appraisals count for anything?

Organizations invest a lot of time and energy on annual performance evaluations that theoretically should help individuals in their careers. As an organizational tool, appraisals can highlight people with potential, serve as a record of their achievements, and can help individuals progress up the organization. In addition, they should map out opportunities for growth. But what if positive appraisals are ignored or incorrect, or unfavorable ones introduced? If appraisals are not the measure of success in organizations how then do women gauge how they are doing and by what criteria should they measure their own performance?

Is it wise to complain about unfair treatment?

Grievance procedures in organizations are intended to be an unbiased procedure to adjudicate differences between the organization and the employee. How do grievance procedures work in organizations? The women profiled in this book believed in justice and expected the formal grievance process in their organizations to be above board. However, when they complained about equal pay, sexual harassment, or a promotion that was promised but denied, these women found themselves in a catch-22 situation; if they did not complain their situations would not improve and if they did complain, they risked losing their jobs. What is the real function of a formal grievance process? Are organizations concerned with due process in these proceedings?

Both men and women are fired, but are they terminated in the same way?

These stories profiled in this book suggest that the process of termination is long and painful for women. It often begins with the unjustified suggestion of poor performance and, if the woman will not go quietly, ends with a campaign of intimidation. Although little research has been done on the differences between men's and women's terminations, some research suggests that men are fired quickly and civilly without intimidation tactics (Gould, 1986). Exactly how do women experience termination?

THE STRUCTURE OF THIS BOOK

The first several chapters of the book are organized to provide a factual account of how women have been subordinated in the workplace (Chapter 2) and to explain the various, competing explanations for women's lack of progress at the middle and senior management levels in organizations (Chapter 3). In Chapter 2, how horizontal and vertical segregation have prevented women from reaching their potential is explained and the employment patterns and earnings of women in Western economies is traced. It is clear that in male-dominated industries, such as financial services, banking, accountancy, and insurance, women have encountered an impenetrable glass ceiling. In all organizations and business functions, progress for women has been primarily at the lower levels of management where women cannot influence or alter the norms and culture of organizations. In Chapter 2, the reader is introduced to workforce statistics and studies that have uncovered gender discrimination. Chapter 3 surveys a range of theories that try to explain women's subordination; these include human capital theory, Marxian theory, dual systems theory, and patriarchy theory. The early chapters in the book provide a context for what follows: the individual case studies describing workplace subordination and eventual dismissal. Chapter 4 introduces the ten women featured in this book by explaining their career histories, ambitions, and values and by describing the facts surrounding their dismissals.

Katherine, age 33, held a variety of positions in the financial services arena, including running a brokerage and managing a marketing function. She had managed staff and complex operations including compliance with financial services regulations. Diane, age 52, had extensive experience in finance with a variety of companies. She had obtained both an MBA degree and credentials in accounting. She had conducted due diligence procedures on other companies during acquisitions, oversaw the installation of large computer systems, managed staff, and been responsible as a finance director for the financial accounts of several companies. Elizabeth, age 30, had worked her way up within a large management consultancy and had established her own client base. She was knowledgeable in a variety of areas including employment law, supervision and management, and diversity issues in the workplace. At the time of her resignation, she was the top producer within her group. In addition, Elizabeth was in the process of earning a Master's degree. Madge, age 54, was a seasoned human resource professional with over 20 years of experience. She was employed by a large retail clothing chain. At the time of her dismissal, she had responsibility for health and safety; client service functions; personnel systems such as recruitment, promotion, and hiring for all sites; and compensation systems. She was also a member of the board of directors along with the other male directors. Lesley, age 50, had earned a PhD in physics and had become the head of a large engineering group for an electronics company. She managed 250 engineers and complex projects involving staff and subcontractors. Under constant pressure to reduce costs, meet deadlines, and maintain quality, Lesley's group was also awarded an international quality standard, the ISO 9000. Patricia, age 39, worked for many years as a marketing manager. Like Lesley, she had obtained further education in her field—an MBA degree. While working for a graphics company, she developed the marketing strategy for four major divisions of the company, managed staff, and managed a large budget. Karen, age 41, had held positions as a value engineer and as a total quality manager. Employed by a printing company, she was the only woman in the senior management ranks. Her job involved recommending quality improvements and ensuring that quality standards were maintained within the company's printing processes. Fiona, age 41, had also invested time and energy in her career. She had earned an MBA degree and had held positions within the financial services arena including regional manager, manager of employee communications, and manager–sales management development. She managed staff and budgets, and was responsible for all training and selection of sales management personnel. Mary, age 45, had earned an MBA degree and worked in the manufacturing sector as director of training. She managed a department of 50 people who provided training in both technical and soft skills. Her role was complex because she was responsible for the head office and field sites across many locations in the United Kingdom. Caroline, age 50, had held a series of more influential positions in management consulting. She had managed large projects with *Fortune 500* companies and had won million-dollar contracts. With an MA in industrial relations and many years experience in managing client relationships and developing programs, she was an asset to the firm. In spite of the credentials and experience of these women, their careers were derailed.

Chapter 5 details the obstacles common to each woman as she tried to successfully navigate her way through the organization. Chapter 6 provides more details of the events leading to these women's dismissals. It records their inability, despite a variety of methods, to save themselves from victimization, humiliation, and ultimate termination. These women encountered broken promises of job advancement and intrusive and inappropriate supervision over their work. As they filed grievances or complained, there were allegations of poor performance and they were isolated from their peer group and finally "let go." Chapter 7 explores how the women's personalities interacted with the patriarchal institutions in which they found themselves. The very qualities that had made them successful climbing the lower rungs of the management ladder seemed to work against them at the higher reaches of management. Many of these women were not aware that systematic discrimination occurred in their organizations until after they left. This lack of awareness handicapped them.

In Chapter 8, some conclusions about the future of women in business are discussed. This book suggests that there are still serious impediments facing women in business despite statistics that suggest weakening of the glass ceiling effect. Both theory and the experiences of the women in this study suggest that long-term progress in the positioning of women in business will only change as a result of the weakening of the patriarchy on many different fronts. The focus is on the strategies that will work for women and strategies that women should avoid. Final discussion returns to the questions of whether a glass ceiling is inevitable for women or whether through sociocultural changes real progress can be expected for women in contemporary business organizations.

CHAPTER 2

Women's Subordination in the Workplace

◆◆

Quantitative evidence and some empirical studies establish the pattern of workplace inequality for women in Western economies. In the higher levels of professional and managerial work horizontal segregation (the exclusion of a particular group of people from the highest paid and most responsible positions within the employment hierarchy) of women becomes most noticeable. Discrimination in the workplace takes place in many areas; for example, recruitment and promotion are two human resource systems that overwhelmingly favor men over women. An internal labor market in organizations creates a pool of eligible men and ineligible women. In addition, more aggressive forms of discrimination exist in the harassment of women and in their isolation from organizational activity. In general, the organizational experiences of men and women demonstrate that indeed men enjoy advantages from which women are either formally or informally barred.

INCOME AND SEGREGATION IN THE WORKPLACE

By 1995 women comprised 43% of the labor force of working age in the United Kingdom (Sly, 1996, p. 92). This level is characteristic for countries in the European Union (United Nations, 1995). Women make up 40% of the European Union labor force and 47% of the employed working population, although the employment of women is higher in Britain and lower in the countries of southwest and southeast Europe. In the United Kingdom over 70% of women of working age were economically active in 1995 (Sly, 1996, p. 91).

These high rates of employment represent a significant change over a relatively brief period. In 1951, only 22% of married women in the United Kingdom worked outside the home (Hakim, 1979). In fact 90% of the increase in the labor force between 1971 and 1990 was the result of women joining the workforce (Department of Employment, 1990, pp. 186–195). This trend continued; from the summer of 1993 to the summer of 1994, men's employment increased by nearly 200,000 while women's employment increased by 250,000. From the summer of 1994 to the summer of 1995, men's employment increased by nearly 200,000 while women's employment increased by 300,000 and from the summer of 1995 to the summer of 1996, men's employment increased by nearly 100,000 while women's employment increased by double that figure, 200,000 (Department of Employment, 1997). Projections for women in the workforce are higher than for men; by 2006, the labor force is expected to increase by 1.2 million of which 900,000 are expected to be women (Department of Employment, 1997). Similar patterns of female employment have occurred in the United States. In 1996, there were 7.7 million women employed in executive, administrative, and managerial occupations. The number of women employed in these categories increased by 39% between 1988 and 1996, while the number of men in the same categories increased by only 16% (U.S. Department of Labor, 1997).

In some industries the expansion of female employment has been exponential. In British banking the size of the male labor force grew by 40% in the period 1948–70, while the number of women employed in banking expanded by 270%. In 1985 more than 60% of English clearing bank employees were female (Collinson, Knights, and Collinson, 1990, p. 19).

In 1982 Chiplin and Sloane concluded that available evidence shows conclusively that average earnings for women are well below those of men in every country where statistics on earnings classified by sex are published. In countries such as the United States, the United Kingdom, Canada, and Australia women tended to earn on average less than 60% of male average earnings. In the United States, median weekly earnings of female managers are well below those of male managers. In 1996, females employed in executive, administrative, and managerial occupations earned on average 67% as much as their male counterparts (U.S. Department of Labor, 1997). According to a United Nations study, the United Kingdom was at that time among the most unequal of Western nations in discrepancy between male and female earnings. The United Kingdom's 50% proportion of female to male earnings compares with an 80% proportion in Sweden. The same report records that the gap narrowed less in Britain over the period of the 1970s than elsewhere (United Nations, 1995). In Britain women earned about two thirds the average male salary for as long as records have been kept until about 1974, when their percentage began to rise to about 73% (Ellison, 1989). By 1996, sample surveys conducted by the U.K. Labour

Force Survey suggested that women in full-time hourly employment had reached 79% of male earnings (Sly, 1996). In management grades, however, the differences between men's and women's earnings are greater. Among executives, administrators, and managers, women earned an average of 68% of male salaries (Russell, 1995).

Thus, despite the large number of women working, in 1995 women in Britain were earning only about three quarters of the hourly wage of male workers, and their average gross weekly earnings were only two thirds that of men. More than 43% of women are employed only part-time, and 84% of all people of working age employed part-time were women (Sly, 1996, p. 94). There has been a disproportionate percentage of men and women in full-time permanent employment; 86% of men's employment is full-time permanent compared with 52% of women's employment, and 39% of women's employment is part-time permanent compared with 6% of men's (Department of Employment, 1997).

The proportion of women securing unemployment benefits was marginally below that of men in the latter half of the 1980s, but this figure excludes women ineligible for unemployment benefits because their spouses were employed. Moreover, unemployment among women fell much less rapidly over the period 1985–90 than male unemployment. In the European Union, male unemployment dropped by almost three million, while women's unemployment fell by a fifth of that figure despite their almost equal participation in the labor force (Eurostat, 1991). Similar figures are reported for the United Kingdom in the period 1993–95 (Sly, 1996, p. 97).

In the United Kingdom, work is heavily segregated by sex. A survey conducted in 1980 by the Department of Employment found that about 80% of men worked only with other men and 60% of women worked only with women. By the mid-1990s this pattern had hardly changed. As Sly (1996, p. 96) reports, "In many traditionally male occupations, women are still poorly represented: engineers, technologists (6%), computer analysts (18%) and skilled craft trades, especially in construction and engineering (10%). . . . While women have made some progress in many managerial and professional occupations they still only represent 32% of managers and administrators, 34% of health professionals and 27% of buyers, brokers and sales representatives." Other occupations are disproportionately female: 81% of health care workers, 69% of education employees, 60% of retail trade and restaurant workers, and 73% of employees in clothing manufacturing are women (Sly, 1996, p. 97).

This so-called vertical segregation—in which men and women are separated at all levels of the employment hierarchy—has remained little changed in the U.K. workforce for a century. Bagguley and Walby (1988) have traced changes in vertical segregation over the period 1971–81. Their data show a significant decrease in the number of men who are employed in settings that are 90% or more male, but a smaller decrease in settings

70% or more male. Changes in the pattern of women's segregation are similar. This pattern is mirrored throughout the industrial world. In 1980, according to one analysis of 503 U.S. occupational categories, 19% were female intensive (60% or more female), while 48% were male intensive (80% male) (Holden and Hansen, 1987, p. 218).

HORIZONTAL SEGREGATION AT THE SENIOR MANAGEMENT LEVEL

Horizontal segregation is the exclusion of a particular group of people from certain levels of the employment hierarchy. Here there appears to be some significant change in the male-female dichotomy. Although men predominate at the level of managerial, professional, and supervisory positions, the percentage of women in these positions has increased, in some cases sharply, over the last 20 years, albeit from very low levels. While the U.K. Census of Populations reports that only 22% of managers were women in 1981 and only 11% of professionals were female, the number of women in the highest grades of the "Standard Industrial Classification" minimum list headings doubled in the period 1971–81. By the end of the decade the number of women managers had risen to 27%, but the percentage described as middle and senior managers was 4% and less than 2% were senior executive–level managers (NEDO, 1990). A similar pattern exists in the United States where senior management positions are gender and race segregated. Although women hold 43% of executive, administrative, and managerial positions, they constitute only 3% to 5% of top executive positions. Surveys of *Fortune 500* companies found that 95% to 97% of senior managers, vice president level and above, were men. Furthermore, a 1989 survey reported that 97% of top male executives were white (U.S. Department of Labor, 1997).

Even in occupations that are vertically segregated, such as nursing, in which 90% of the labor force is female in the United Kingdom, only about half of the senior managers are women (Sly, 1996). In Sly (1996, pp. 96, 97), it was noted that 81% of all employees in U.K. health care organizations are women but only 34% of health professionals are women. Although 44% of the U.K. workforce is female, in 1995 only 32.5% of managers and administrators, 11.5% of science and engineering professionals, 2.2% of skilled engineering trades, and 29.8% of machine operators were women. On the other hand, 67.2% of clerical occupations and 96.7% of secretarial occupations were filled by women. Vertical segregation is coupled in several of these categories with horizontal segregation. For example, 63% of sales occupations are female, but within this category only 26.5% of sales representatives or buyers are women, while 73.3% of all other occupations in this category are filled by women (Sly, 1996, table F, p. 110).

In the U.K. civil service and in local government, in which more than half the employees are women, the percentage of principal officers is below 10%, while less than 4% of senior managers are women. In 1988 only four local government chief executives were women and only about 50 chief officers were women (Equal Opportunities Commission, 1988).

A survey of 420 companies in Western Europe conducted in 1982 revealed that the majority had never employed a women manager, while only 8% of managers in the United Kingdom, 9% in France, and 13% in Portugal were women. Indeed, 15% of managers of these 420 companies admitted that they would never consider appointing a women to a management post. Although 91% of respondents agreed that women could serve as managers in their firms, almost none had made any provision to recruit women to management (Adler and Izraeli, 1988, pp. 168–185). Fifteen years later, only about half of a set of European Union organizations with over 200 employees surveyed by Hegewisch and Mayne (1994) targeted women for recruitment.

There is good reason to believe that this underrepresentation of women in senior management is not a pipeline problem. In Britain the number of women in university rose from 12% to 27% in the 1970s, and by 1981 over 40% of students in the United Kingdom's largest university management department were women (Davidson and Cooper, 1983). Yet by 1992, only 18.3% of managers in the United Kingdom were women and only 8.3% of senior managers were women (Davidson and Cooper, 1992). In the United States, the number of bachelor of business degrees awarded to males between 1970 and 1996 increased 21% while the number awarded to females during the same period increased 994% (Post Secondary Education Opportunity, 1998).

Accountancy provides another profession in which vertical segregation appears to have abated, but horizontal segregation continues. A survey of the six principal accountancy bodies by the Chartered Institute of Management Accountants (Boyer, 1995) found that 36% of students in these bodies were women. The report concludes that barriers to women's entry to accounting have been removed. However, the report goes on to reveal that 14% of accountants registered with these bodies in 1995 were women. While this is almost a tripling from the figure in 1980, it compares with a participation rate of 30% for women physicians and 31% for women in law professions. More important, the survey reveals that men are still twice as likely as women to become directors and partners. According to the report's analysis, if women were doing as well as men in accountancy, then at least one of every three or four appointments in accountancy should be female. But the actual figure is one in six female members of the Chartered

Institute, and less than one in nine female members of the Chartered Association of Certified Accountants reaches a senior post.

RECRUITMENT AS THE SOURCE OF SEGREGATION

In the early 1980s the Equal Opportunities Commission in Britain financed a study to "explore whether, and if so how, the recruitment process can contribute to the perpetuation of traditional segregated patterns of 'men's' and 'women's' work" (Collinson et al., 1990, p. 3). The project provided a detailed case study of recruitment and promotion as it operated in a sample of 45 companies in the period after the implementation of the 1970 Equal Pay Act and the 1975 Sex Discrimination Act. The Sex Discrimination Act made it unlawful to discriminate on grounds of sex and marriage in offering employment, and in general terms of employment. The Equal Opportunities Commission had concluded by the early 1980s that these acts had been relatively ineffective, and sought to examine why. The results of this study were reported in Collinson et al. (1990); they secured data from companies engaged in banking, mail order sales, insurance, high tech, and food manufacturing.

It is well known that there is a strong preference for informality in the recruitment process, which has the effect of making practices unaccountable as well as fostering the intentional and unintentional persistence of discrimination. Formalizing recruitment processes is difficult because of the marginal position of personnel managers in most business organizations. As the Collinson et al. (1990) case studies show, the attempt by personnel officers to introduce formal recruitment and promotion policies was resisted by line management, which insists on autonomy and independence in the selection of staff: "As the self appointed organizational bread winners, line managers typically dismissed formalization as a bureaucratic encumbrance impeding their ability to recruit and manage production effectively. Formal procedures were seen as unnecessary, time consuming and costly" (p. 108). On the other hand, personnel managers are unwilling to challenge line managers because of a concern with their own professional credibility. The result, according to Collinson et al. (1990), is the persistence of occupational segregation and promotional discrimination despite a legal climate of legislatively enforced formalized procedures.

Even when personnel managers are able to exercise control over recruitment they reproduce the previous pattern of discrimination in new appointments, while rationalizing these decisions; typically personnel managers blamed the women applicants, society as a whole, or excused unlawful practices as necessary to "control the labour process and to stabilize production" (Collinson et al., 1990, p. 111). Alternately, they endorsed discrimination because of its alleged positive consequences and/or denied that the practices constituted discrimination (p. 131).

Collinson et al. devote considerable discussion to one industry:

Job segregation pervades the insurance industry. Life-assurance in particular has come to be characterized by a sex-segregated process in which men are employed as inspectors (i.e. salespeople) working externally "in the field" whilst women occupy most of the down graded clerical positions and are restricted to internal office work. (1990, p. 136)

In this industry the informality of the recruitment process facilitates sexual segregation and the heavy dependence on an internal labor market, in which current employees are preferred, together enforce a strong horizontal segregation. An internal labor market is one in which eligibility or at least strong preference for available vacancies is accorded to current employees. Such markets reduce training, transaction costs, and uncertainties about suitability but exclude potentially more well-qualified candidates who are not current employees. An internal labor market in which women are already underrepresented, or in which available women lack skills because of a pattern of discrimination already in place, will neither supply nor demand women for positions of a kind they do not already hold; therefore, strong horizontal segregation continues.

The authors of this study conclude: "Overall, the research findings reveal that despite anti-discrimination legislation in the mid-1970s, a substantial number of employers, many of whom publicly subscribe to equal opportunities, are still 'managing to discriminate' on the grounds of sex through a variety of recruitment practices" (Collinson et al., 1990, p. 192).

In 1992, a landmark decision in a U.S. case forced State Farm Insurance to pay $250 million for denying 814 women jobs as insurance agents. Although given many chances to settle for a lesser amount, State Farm executives stood their ground. During the case, a spokesperson for State Farm was reported to have said that State Farm did not know where to find women to apply for the insurance agent role (Reuters, 1997).

THE MALE CULTURE, HARASSMENT, AND ISOLATION

"More than 20 years after the initial United Kingdom sex discrimination legislation, employment statistics confirm that the labour market is still segregated by gender." So begins the Hammond (1994, p. 305) report on the work of "Opportunity 2000," an initiative begun in 1991 and sponsored by a consortium of private sector and government enterprises "to bring women fully into the mainstream of organizational life" (p. 306). Membership in this initiative is voluntary, but requires payment of a fee and commits the agency to set goals for the enhanced participation of women by the year 2000, to publish these goals, and to monitor and report on their progress regularly. Opportunity 2000 also provides material for boards, chief executives, human resource directors, and equal opportunity officers as well as line managers.

Organizations participating in Opportunity 2000 have undertaken a variety of new work practices, including enhanced maternity leave, job sharing, child care, special health care provisions, and pensions especially designed to retain women managers. Many of these initiatives have been collected into "best practice" resources that can be adopted by other participating companies. Despite its evident benefits for woman managers, Opportunity 2000 cannot effectively address the deep structural obstacles to gender equality in management.

In recent years the availability of day care and flexible working schedules has become more widespread through initiatives like Opportunity 2000 throughout Western industrial economies. While these accommodations have reduced the difficulties faced by women in management, they are, on the one hand, relatively easy to provide and, on the other hand, do not constitute a serious threat to the "male-dominated management culture" widely reported by women seeking places in senior management. In a set of papers based on a series of seminars of Opportunity 2000 members in 1995, several conclusions were reached. Organizations need to support and develop senior women for top jobs, manage contract and project-based workers, and "employers will need to examine their culture, especially at senior levels, if they are to retain women" (Court, 1995, p. 16). The seminars further indicated that organizations are rebranding and repackaging their equal opportunity policies and programs to avoid a backlash and to disguise and make more palatable their intent. For example, Unilever packaged its diversity and equal opportunities training as "team work training" (p. 23). Of far greater impact than flexible working hours, career break schemes and child care provisions are certain invisible obstacles to success. Sexual harassment, isolation, and other forms of differential treatment in the workplace are harder to eradicate because they are not easily identified by others.

Sexual harassment is constituted by either, or both, a demand for sexual favors in exchange for some employment-related benefit or the imposition of a hostile work environment in which unwelcome sexual attention is persistent. As MacKinnon (1979) points out, sexual harassment involves the imposition of unequal power to impose requirements or improper treatment on another. As Hadjifotiou (1983) suggests, recourse by men to sexual harassment underwrites the subordinated labor market position of women. However, sexual harassment also appears to be common at the higher levels of management.

Figures on the frequency of sexual harassment show that women in many different areas of life report it as a common occurrence. Davidson and Cooper (1992) report that 59% of women working in the United Kingdom report incidents of sexual harassment. However, only about 14% of workplace incidents are reported. Sexual harassment is usually repeated, lasts for long periods, and is focused on younger women who are more frequently single or divorced and have an above-average level of education. Women in management jobs report more sexual harassment than others (Gutek and Dunwoody, 1987). In a 1992 U.K. survey of sexual harassment conducted by an American university, over one third (34%) of those reporting harassment were managers, 27% were office or clerical workers, and 20% were professional or technical workers. Women aged 25 to 30 were the most frequent age group to be targets for harassment. It appears that individuals with a sense of power or control over women most frequently are the perpetrators of harassment; the majority of harassers were peers or managers at least one level removed from the harassee's immediate supervisor. Of individuals who requested an investigation of their complaint, 70% said this action "had made no difference or made things worse" (University of St. Thomas, 1993). A typical problem with reporting sexual harassment within organizations occurs when the grievance procedure uses the chain of command. Women are confronted with potentially having their claim dismissed by either their line manager or a manager one level removed; either individual may be the perpetrator of the harassment or may feel a need to protect the accused. Unlike the teasing, gestures, and catcalls characteristic of other work environments such as the shop floor, women in management experience hostile and threatening sexual comments and nonsexual treatment interpreted by these women as showing that they are outsiders. Lach and Gwartney-Gibbs (1993) consider these incidents a form of retaliation against female employees for threatening male economic and social power. The differential distribution of men and women in authority hierarchies across all institutions in which sexual harassment is reported tends to confirm this theory strongly.

Collinson and Collinson's (1996) study of patterns of harassment in a British insurance company provides a series of illustrations of this phenomenon. They undertook a qualitative analysis of five women in life insurance sales management, a nontraditional area of female management. Four of these women were the most senior females in their divisions and three were never to reach the position of manager within the sales function. Typically women in nontraditional work will be at greater risk of harassment, in part, according to Collinson and Collinson (1996, p. 32), because "men will often try to reassert their control over women who have managed to break away from their traditional subordinated labour market position." These women are perceived as intruders and men employ sexual harassment in order to keep them from a male preserve (Collier, 1995).

Collinson and Collinson summarize their findings as follows:

Women life assurance sales managers suffered extensive sexual harassment. Despite performing their jobs extremely well, the women received no support from senior managers. Separated off from one another, they found it extremely difficult to respond in effective ways; their individualized responses were reinterpreted by men as justifying the women's subsequent exclusion from life assurance sales management. These dynamics produced a vicious circle of sexual harassment in which the brief presence of a few women in insurance sales had the unintended effect of reinforcing rather than transforming the prevailing masculine culture. (1996, p. 45)

A comparison to other data lead Collinson and Collinson to conclude that this vicious circle has wider applicability, and supports the feminist argument that sexual harassment can be used by men to try to exclude women from nontraditional work.

Among available theoretical accounts for the frequency of sexual harassment, especially among more senior women in management appointments, the most well supported is the sociocultural model (Tangri, Burt, and Johnson, 1982). This view proposes that sexual harassment is the result of authority relations, reflected in organizational structure, that provide men with normatively supported opportunities to impose aversive conditions on women. High-status agents are often entitled by their position to make demands on lower-status individuals. Sexual harassment may be viewed as an exercise of that right. Evidence suggests that informal power structures in management exclude women; even cases in which men and women have the same degree of *de jure* power offer opportunities for sexual harassment as a means of enforcing power differences (Brass, 1985). Sexual harassment also appears to be common among employees at the same level of authority when there is perceived competition between males and females for high status, especially in previously all-male positions, and women occupying such positions are reported as having less actual power than men (Ragins and Sundstrom, 1989). Cleveland and Kerst (1993) report that since women are required to establish a record of effectively working with men, males are able to extract sexual favors in return for cooperation.

Another well documented asymmetry more subtle than that reflected in sexual harassment is differences in men's and women's access to networks and the isolation of women from sources of informal support and resources. This is not merely a matter of the quite literal "old boy" network excluding women, but of its very existence being hidden from them. Kram and Isabella (1985) have noted the importance of such networks, which are similar in their support to those provided by mentors, meeting professional and social support needs. Ibarra's (1992) study of access to informal networks indicated that men's networks are more organizationally central and far more same-sex male in composition than women's groups, and are more likely to be based on work experience and professional activities.

There is also a smaller number of mentors available for women. Burke and McKeen (1989) have noted that there are many barriers to the provision of mentors for women: tokenism and stereotyping, which make women unattractive as proteges; suspicion of cross-gender relations; women's use of non-male cultural strategies; and the circular problem of the small number of women already in senior management positions.

The cumulative effect of the lack of mentors and exclusion from networks establishes a degree of isolation, sometimes intended but almost universal even when unintended. This isolation makes the successful participation of women in management more and more difficult as their positions in an organization rise. These impediments are often recognized by women who face them as aspects of a "male culture" in the workplace. This culture has been taxonomized by Maddock and Parkin (1993) into several different variants: the gentlemen's club, in which women may participate so long as they sustain conventional gender stereotypes; the "barrack-yard," a quasi-military bullying culture characterized by authoritarian males and the subordination of junior employees, especially women; the "locker room," which also excludes senior women or denigrates them to enhance male solidarity; and gender-blind cultures, which make no accommodation to women's needs for physical security or family responsibilities. Each of these widely recognized structures affects the climate within which women must seek opportunities in management and they underlie the treatment these women are accorded.

COMPARATIVE ORGANIZATIONAL EXPERIENCE

In 1975 Miller, Fry, and Labovitz revealed significant inequities between men's and women's experiences in organizations. Their study measured differences in access to support networks within organizations, differences in job strain, and work satisfaction among more than 300 respondents in five different settings, including one commercial enterprise.

Miller et al. observed, "women face consistent disadvantages in their experiences in organizations . . . in interpersonal attractiveness, social isolation, job satisfaction and work strain" (1975, p. 336). Miller et al. first determined differences between men and women in their survey on three dimensions:

1. access to organizational networks (as measured by interpersonal attractiveness, perceived influence, respect, and knowledge) and isolation (as measured by contact with persons of influence)

2. job strain (as measured by reported concerns over job clarity, autonomy, progress, and tension)

3. job satisfaction

Having established significant differences between men and women in these three areas among managers in five professional organizations and businesses, Miller et al. considered whether inequalities in these three areas could be attributed to gender-neutral categories such as official position, occupational rank, or education. They noted that

if the differences observed on these variables do not decrease markedly when official position, occupational rank, and expertise are controlled, this would indicate that more is involved than the possession of vital organizational resources. By inference, it would indicate that the organizational structure, and particularly its mechanism for distributing rewards, functions to preserve men's vested interests by allowing interpersonal barriers to exist which could not be anticipated by the rationalistic (i.e. non-discriminatory, p. 366) view of organizational influence. In fact, in some situations women might find their problems intensified with increasing expertise and status because they represent a greater threat to male dominance than those who occupy statuses traditionally defined as women's positions. (Miller et al., 1975, p. 367)

Miller et al. also recognize that, however objectively discriminatory, the expectations of women in management may be significantly lower than those of men. If so, measures might not reveal significant differences in felt access to networks, job strain, or satisfaction: "What is important is that a structure that is objectively inequitable would be imperfectly mirrored in personal reactions if such a mechanism were operating. We will be sensitive to this possibility" (p. 367). However, their data show significant differences among informants on all three of these dimensions.

Miller et al. collected data from over 300 subjects, approximately half were women, in a school system, two survey research institutes, a food processing concern, and several alcohol rehabilitation clinics. The 335 respondents constituted 90% of the employees of these organizations. Each organization was characterized by formal and informal criteria of expertise, in which there was a close correspondence between authority and control, and in which status and hierarchy were legitimated by most employees. In these organizations, 6% of women had supervisory authority over other employees, compared with 29% of men, while 15% of women had professional occupations compared with 53% of men. Employing a variety of questionnaires, data was acquired on subjective measures of attractiveness/isolation, measured in perceived friendships and influences as well as information sources; job strain as indicated by subjective reports of clarity, autonomy, progress, and tension; and job satisfaction.

The findings of this study were unambiguous. "Men enjoy an advantage on each of the measures of interpersonal attractiveness" (Miller et al., 1975, p. 372). They are four times as likely to be perceived as influential and three times more likely to be identified as sources of respected judgment.

Men had greater access to persons in authority, but women had equal access to persons whose work-related judgment was respected. Strikingly, when Miller et al. controlled for education, occupational rank, and authority, they concluded that "the disadvantages that women face are more pronounced for those who have advanced education, high occupational rank, and superior authority" (p. 372). The same finding arises for differences in job strain: while women in lower educational categories report somewhat less job strain than men,

The important point, however, is that on all four dimensions of job strain the situation changes in the highest educational category (which includes 21 women . . . who have had graduate work). The modest advantages of women in the lower educational categories disappear, on the dimensions of clarity and progress, and where autonomy and tension are concerned, the pattern that favors men begins to reappear. Having graduate training is apparently the key. Among the men who have crossed this important barrier, concern is generally lower, but for women with post-graduate training the level of concern is higher. Once the critical point corresponding to college graduation is surpassed, women begin to pay a price for their advancement that men apparently do not have to pay. (Miller et al., 1975 p. 377)

In general the findings suggest that "an inequitable system that affects the work experiences of all women creates much greater pressures for those whose achievements confront the basic pattern of discrimination directly . . . [W]omen who have moved into organizational position and occupations that allow some access to decision making and policy formation threaten the very core of male dominance" and concludes, "A more detailed conceptualization would now stipulate that only certain kinds of females will be the primary targets of discrimination, namely those with high status, expertise or authority" (Miller et al., 1975, p. 378). Although this study is now at least a working generation old, there is little quantitative evidence at variance with its conclusions.

Despite the increased number of women in senior management positions in large commercial institutions over the last two decades, men in these organizations retain traditional attitudes about the role of women and seem unaware of the need for provisions to enhance women's access to management positions (Newell, 1993). By contrast, survey research in the 1980s highlighted quite different attitudes toward work among women in the workforce. A majority of women felt that married women have a right to work if they wish. The most traditional view of women's role as homemaker came from older, nonworking women without children; the least traditional view of women came from young, full-time working women (Dex, 1988). Women in Britain say they work for a variety of reasons including a desire for income; a need for social interaction, self-fulfillment, and challenge; and a desire to escape from routine household tasks (Dex,

1988). A survey of 387 female office workers found that the three most important aspects of a job for women are interesting and fulfilling work, a good boss, and the chance to improve one's career (Marks, 1984).

THE GLASS CEILING AND THE SUBORDINATION OF WOMEN IN MANAGEMENT

Horizontal segregation at the upper levels of the labor market has been labeled the "glass ceiling" by Morrison et al. (1987, 1992).

Holding constant such variables as age, experience, credentials, and marital status, women are consistently underrepresented in senior management, they are paid less than men in the same positions, and the disparity grows as promotions are made. Although 43% of the U.K. workforce in 1995 was female, women constituted only 4% of middle managers and less than 2% of executive level managers (Sly, 1996). In banking, a sector in which 64% of the workforce is female, women comprise less than 2% of the nonclerical positions, compared to 37% of males. In traditional female occupations such as nursing, only 8% of principal officers were women and less than 5% served in higher grades. Even local government, which is over 60% female, was led by only four women chief executives and about 50 chief officers (NEDO, 1990).

Morrison et al.'s work (1987) was the result of a three-year study, which examined the experiences of women who had attained management positions. These women identified several work experiences critical to their success: acceptance by their organizations, support and encouragement, training and development opportunities, and challenging work in visible assignments. However, these women claimed that constraints increased and support decreased as they moved higher up the employment ladder. Morrison et al. reported that many of their subjects complained of exhaustion and contemplated employment changes. A subsequent study (Morrison, et al., 1992) reported that many of the original subjects had made no progress in their management hierarchies.

Morrison et al.'s original study (1987) noted several conditions for success by women managers, including strong desire, risk taking, willingness to be decisive and set high standards, a pattern of successful accomplishment, sponsorship by superiors, an easy working style, and an ability to adapt. The study found that women by and large required these traits to a greater degree than men in order to succeed in a male-dominated environment. Besides the pressures of a job, women must also deal with the pressure of being tokens and handle family responsibilities in ways men do not. Women who wanted too much for other women or for themselves were likely to meet with obstacles.

Besides overcoming negative stereotypes and appearing neither too masculine nor too feminine, the demands on successful women Morrison et al.

(1987) identified are, in fact, mutually incompatible and thus overdetermine failure. It is impossible to both take risks and amass a record of invariably successful performance; an authoritative style is hard to reconcile with a relaxed working style; it is difficult to be ambitious while not demanding equal treatment; and assuming individual responsibility and taking credit for one's accomplishments is difficult while being the protégé of a senior manager.

In a subsequent work Morrison (1992) developed a model for successful career development in management, which involved three elements: challenge, which requires managers to learn new skills to perform at higher levels; support, understanding, and acceptance, which enables managers to make their work part of a rewarding life; and recognition and resources to continue to motivate the manager to achieve corporate and personal goals. For women, the demands of challenge usually swamp the other two components of the model. Daily assignments that are part of the challenge go undetected by males, support systems are inadequate, and barriers to advancement in the form of stereotypes, men's discomfort, and sexism reduce levels of reward. The result is failure, exhaustion, and bail-out by women managers. Moreover, as McCall et al. (1988) document, certain job assignments (for example, line as opposed to staff positions) that provide significant challenges are not provided to women. Morrison and Von Glinow (1990) note that women often do not receive reward or recognition commensurate with responsibility. More often than men, their titles are "acting" and their promotions less rewarded. Support in the form of mentoring is in shorter supply for women than for men (Ragins, 1989). Similarly, women are excluded from informal networks critical for information, advice, and sponsors. Lipman-Blumen (1984) found that women use formal processes to seek promotion, whereas men rely on informal processes, such as the "old boy" network, to gain access to better jobs in corporate America.

The glass ceiling has become a commonplace term to describe the experiences of women in contemporary management. But it is only part of the architecture of the modern commercial bureaucracy. It is important to recognize that the organizations in which women managers find themselves are not gender-neutral ones; they erect obstacles to equal treatment in many directions, not just upward into senior positions. The contemporary business office is gendered in the sense that "advantages and disadvantages, exploitation and control, action and emotion, meaning and identity, are patterned through and in terms of a distinction between male and female, masculine and feminine. Gender is not an addition to ongoing processes, conceived as gender neutral" (Acker, 1990, p. 146). Although the explicit lines of organization in most bureaucracies make no mention of gender, work activities reveal a clear gendered substructure. Men are superiors, women subordinates; men make decisions, women execute them; men perform "instrumental roles," women have "expressive" functions. The public patriarchy of the office reproduces the private patriarchy of the family (Acker, 1990, p. 142). If most secretaries are female and most managers male, the female manager enters into what is now a firmly established hierarchy of male dominance, in which her existence is an anomaly. Since the office is organized for instrumental—means and ends—rationality and the minimization of uncertainty and anarchy, nonrational forces affecting work must be minimized. Scott (1986, p. 151) points out that the gender-neutral job, from which sexuality, emotions, and procreation have been abstracted, obscures while it reproduces established gender relations reflecting male dominance.

In these contexts, what Perrow (1986) calls "premise controls" operate. Among senior managers direct bureaucratic controls are hard to impose. Instead subordinates channel normative restrictions by limiting the range of options they will present as available given the organization's culture. Perrow suggests that social class, ethnic origin, and social networks are so important because—they make it more likely that certain kinds of premises will exist (Perrow, 1986). Perrow does not include gender in his list of premise controls, but it is an extremely powerful one. The values internalized by the procedures of an organization must be embraced by its successful managers. As women find their way into management positions, they need to adopt norms that implicitly require their own subordination while explicitly expressing gender neutrality. This conflict between gender and occupation—between subordination and authority—works as strongly as the glass ceiling to ensure horizontal segregation at the higher levels of management.

The organizational culture of management shifts sources of power predominantly to males, even at levels to which women have attained. This concentration of power outweighs equal opportunity, affirmative action, and antidiscrimination regulations to prevent fundamental change in the culture (Still, 1994, p. 4). Power stems not only from formal authority, but from control of resources, information, and technology within an organization. For example, as Brosman and Davidson (1994) note, the introduction of computerization in a workplace may manifest all three of these dimensions of male power concentration.

In modern business organizations, power is provided by participation in networks from which women are often excluded by temporal and physical barriers, failure to know the informal rules of the game, or discomfort in a majority male milieu. Women's subordinate position does not provide them with anything that male colleagues need by way of resources, information, or technology; therefore, women are in no position to offer incentives to males to allow them into such networks (Kottis, 1993).

In a series of Opportunity 2000 seminars, women-only networks were identified as a means for women to further the equal opportunity agenda.

The seminars, however, uncovered that these networks are fraught with problems unless the organizational culture changes in a way that truly rewards and values women. To be effective, networks need to involve senior-level women. At Unilever, for example, there are few women at senior levels and women managers at these levels feel nervous about appearing to be receiving preferential treatment. "Establishing networks without a strategy for implementing more widespread change can just increase the level of frustration" (Court, 1995, p. 22).

Moreover, the importance of power in commercial organizations is invisible to many women, even successful women managers. Interviews by White, Cox, and Cooper (1992) reveal that women attribute their success to ambition and luck, not to an understanding of or ability to exploit sources of power. Arroba and James (1987) attribute the failure of women to exploit political power to a widespread women's belief that they lack political competence, a consequent lack of confidence, and, finally, a distaste for political activity.

GLASS CEILING EFFECTS IN THE INTERNAL LABOR MARKET

What are the specific institutional and cultural impediments to women's breaking the glass ceiling in senior management? Explanations focus on the character of the internal labor market for senior management positions. While there is evident recruitment bias against women in intake, as Collinson et al.'s study (1990) shows, once women secure positions on a management trajectory, there are further obstacles that prevent their arrival above the glass ceiling.

The glass ceiling is protected by a set of standards and criteria for advancement to senior-level positions that disproportionately discriminate against women without reflecting objective needs to be served by these positions. Although prior experience at a variety of positions in an industry is crucial for advancement, women's already horizontally and vertically segregated experiences are devalued as compared with men's. This will be true even for women unencumbered with family and children. For example, in the British civil service graduate management training scheme, women begin to experience a slower rate of promotion at the outset of their careers (Collinson et al., 1990). Similarly, in the United States, a study of male and female MBA graduates from Stanford University found that although 10% of women had become vice presidents by 1992, by comparison 32% of men had. Women occupied 2% of chief executive positions while men held 16% of these positions (Through a glass, darkly, 1996).

In Europe, 20 years after equal opportunity legislation has been adopted, women seem to fare no better than women in the United Kingdom. Although women make up 41% of the European workforce, only 1% of board members are women (Dwyer, Johnson, and Miller, 1996). In New

Zealand the situation is similar for senior-level women. Male members of the accountancy profession are more likely to hold senior positions than female accountants. This trend still persists in the younger age groups where levels of experience and seniority between men and women are minimized (Rainsbury, Sutherland, and Urlich, 1996).

In the United Kingdom, the National Management Salary Survey, published by the Institute of Management and Remuneration Economics, shows a modest increase of women in management positions. Despite these increases, women still lag behind men in earnings. Female managers earned the same salary increases as men, which suggests that discrimination in earnings potential occurs at the entry level (Management Services, 1996).

Senior management positions are stereotyped as requiring character traits associated with men: rationality, lack of emotion, competition, hierarchical decision making, action orientation, and risk taking. This view is widely shared by both men and women managers and management students (Powell, 1990). Women lacking these traits are viewed as unqualified for senior positions. Women who manifestly demonstrate them are criticized for being overly masculine and failing to fit into a business organization (White et al., 1992). This double-bind effectively excludes women from positions of the highest responsibility.

There is some evidence that women's management styles differ from men's, although it is by no means clear that these differences reduce their effectiveness. In fact the contrary may be the case. Vinnicombe (1987) reported differences between men and women in the Myers-Briggs psychometric questionnaire, suggesting that women embrace a more intuitive style of decision making than men. Bartram's application (1992) of Cattell's personality inventory to managers suggests women score higher for anxiety and lower for independence than men. Women are often described as more inclined to encourage participation, motivate by inclusion of others in decision making, and seek to improve the work environment for all subordinates as a means of enhancing effectiveness, by contrast with men whose management styles are more clearly based on power asymmetries and contractual exchanges (Rosener, 1990). Marshall (1995) reports that women are more likely than men to seek satisfaction from their jobs than to view them as means to further promotion.

Rigg and Sparrow (1994) undertook a study to examine whether women differed from men in their approaches to management in identical positions. They interviewed 16 district housing managers in a local authority, 4 female and 12 male, without raising gender issues to determine whether gender issues might emerge from the interviews.

The interview data confirmed that women were seen both by themselves and males as emphasizing team management, being people oriented, and making considered decisions, while men adopted an entrepreneurial or quantitative approach to their positions, were policy or rule governed, and were more detached in decision making. Operating styles were generally participative for women and paternalistic for men; women were said to have a better understanding of ethnic groups and young people. Interviewees' comments about other managers differed significantly by sex. Men described one another, both positively and negatively, in terms less moderate than their description of women managers and they had more to say about other men than about women managers. Women's comments about fellow managers were more nuanced and did not show gender differences.

Although they identify gender differences in management, Riggs and Sparrow (1994) argue that the cooperative/competitive difference they uncovered should not be erected into a stereotype. Men and women are not homogeneously the same but organizational structure tends strongly to reward male attributes, no matter whether they make a greater contribution to organizational effectiveness. This preference is manifested in recruitment and promotion through the employment of these stereotypes to assess qualifications. Thus a position requiring significant decision making may make the disposition of women to consult widely appear to abdicate this responsibility. Powell notes,

Promotion decisions are based in evaluations of the past performance and future potential of candidates. . . . These evaluations are based on beliefs about what the individual is like, which are influenced by whether the individual is male or female. Thus stereotypical beliefs that women are more nurturant or that men are better leaders can have an influence on evaluation far beyond what the actual facts may dictate. (Powell, 1988, p. 65)

In a National Health Service (NHS) survey of senior women managers conducted in 1992, the majority of senior women managers were in stereotypically female roles of family health services, community care, health visitation, and mental health. These roles are seen to need "female" characteristics of warmth and expressiveness, whereas the "high-tech" acute units and regional and district control units are generally reserved for men (Proctor and Jackson, 1994). Two further findings from the NHS study are of interest. First, it seems that women managers are promoted by male managers to symbolize a commitment to change. Women in these situations often manage all-male teams and experience isolation. Their promotions were high risk because their male managers could withdraw their support at any time. Withdrawal of support occurred when women were seen to be having difficulty in their roles, when their boss retired, or when their boss was promoted. This conditional support by men often left women starting over in more junior-level posts. Second, the motives of women seeking promotion outside the geographical area in which they had been successful are questioned. Although men are often promoted to other geographical areas, this advantage is not extended to women. Despite their talent and proven track record, women were unlikely to be offered posts outside their region and were often questioned about why they wanted to move.

While some writers treat these stereotypes as accidental, unintentional, and unrecognized, they have identified the processes by which they protect the glass ceiling from breakage. Kathleen Hemenway (1995) identifies what she calls natural consequences of human nature that may contribute to the glass ceiling, based on psychological research and on anecdotal reports about the glass ceiling. For example, conversational dominance of men makes it difficult for women with a more cooperative conversational style to participate, therefore, their contribution is either minimized or goes unheard. Paternalistic protection of women can exclude them from the most challenging assignments, thereby preventing women from expressing their ambitions. Women's style of waiting to be rewarded instead of seeking rewards disadvantages them in any competition for promotion.

These stereotypes of differential treatment begin as early as primary schooling. Boys' and girls' participation is differently encouraged and evaluated, even by women teachers. Experiments reveal framing and bias effects, of the sort made familiar by Kahneman, Slovic, and Tversky (1982), operate in differential judgments between women and men in hiring and job performance ratings. The same résumé presented for John Smith and Joan Smith results in significant differences in ability ratings, except where the résumé is extremely strong. The same effects have been detected for starting salaries, task assignment, and pay increases. Asked to explain successful performance in a masculine task, experimental subjects cited luck in the case of women and ability in the case of men (Kesler, 1975).

These differences can be attributed to the effects that uncertainty has on judgment. Even when a manager is committed to equal reward for the same accomplishment, judgments of accomplishment generally are uncertain. Judgment under uncertainty inevitably calls into play biases and preconceptions—so-called framing effects—about men and women, which typically lead to devaluing women's contributions. Experiments in which uncertainty is minimized show no such gender biases on the part of male managers. Similar studies showed that subordinates, both male and female, rated women managers' past performance more highly than males', but looking forward rated women's long-term potential as lower than the same males, again showing the role of stereotypes in judgment under uncertainty (Alimo-Metcalfe, 1994).

Another well-known bias effect in selection and promotion results from the reliance on personal networks in securing information about job candidates and promotable employees. It is not simply that rewards are distributed along an "old boy" network. The effect is more subtle. Familiarity with a restricted range of employees will bias a senior manager's memory of available candidates for a position, when scanning a mental network of familiar employees.

One of the most well-known framing effects is the tendency to generalize from a limited range of examples. This tendency is in fact the source of most stereotypes, while at the same time crucial to all aspects of cognition. When we set out general features of a category, for example, managing director or member of the board, we extract features from examples of this category we know. Even when gender, race, age, and appearance are irrelevant to the category, their predominance among the sample from which we construct the category inevitably leads to conscious and more often nonconscious biasing against candidates that lack the irrelevant traits for category membership. Combined with the dearth of senior women managers, this psychological process further reduces the opportunities for those who do not fit senior management stereotypes.

The theory of bias in selection and promotion is supported by research. A study of three London-based organizations and 38 selection interviews demonstrated that male interviewers held gendered perceptions that influenced their evaluation of candidates. They admitted to a preference for candidates "like themselves," had a bias against pregnant women and women whom they perceived to be "too aggressive," referred to female candidates in terms of their physical attractiveness, and used the pronoun "he" when referring to candidates' desired qualifications in the abstract (Rubin, 1997, pp. 27–28).

As White et al. (1992) emphasized, mentoring is crucial to promotion into senior positions. But long-established biases on the part of male managers make them unwilling to mentor or often to share information with women. This introduces still another obstacle to career advancement. Just as mentoring subordinates is crucial to their success, access to information from channels beyond one's immediate superior is important. These channels provide messages about the culture of an organization and its major players, and signals about major changes both technical and organizational, that are crucial to advancement (Mattis, 1990). The tendency of people to network within gender, as opposed to across genders, must perforce limit the channels of information accessible to the minority gender.

Additionally, organizations typically adopt the culture, style, and even the personality of its numerically predominant gender. Because most business corporations are male dominated, their accepted and expected behavioral styles will reflect male models. These styles are often identified by women as creating a hostile work environment, even when men plead that casual conversation, jokes, and casual physical contact are innocent of sexist intent. When institutional practices extend to doing business on the golf course, the squash court, the locker room, or the private club, women are effectively locked out of participation in the organizations to which they ostensibly belong (Maddock and Parkin, 1993).

Most of the psychological and social processes reflect features common to men and women across periods, cultures, classes, and castes. They are not only ineradicable, they are essential to efficient functioning in any well-established institution, within any system of authority, and in most informationally rich environments where decision making is uncertain. They provide the effective mechanism whereby long-standing inequitable practices, expectations, and norms are perpetuated unintentionally, nonconsciously, and without deliberation.

RECENT U.K. STUDIES OF WOMEN IN MANAGEMENT

In 1990 the Hansard Society Commission investigated barriers to the appointment of women to senior occupational positions. The report identified two interrelated barriers to women's progress: the predominance of men at the top of corporate Britain and traditional attitudes toward women. The first, the report asserted, was unlikely to change by increasing the number of women's networks or the number of junior- and middle-level women managers. Too many men at the top encouraged entrenched attitudes about women's subordination (Hansard Commission, 1990).

In 1996 the Hansard Society undertook a follow-up study to see if women had made progress after five years. The results indicated that the presence of women in board rooms increased, but only slightly. In 1989, 80% of firms reported no women on their main boards, as either executive or non-executive directors. By 1995, this figure had dropped to about half of the 120 organizations surveyed. Over the period, women made the least progress as executive board members on main boards, and the most progress as non-executive, subsidiary board members. Women accounted for just 1% of main board members in 1995 and 6% (up from 2% in 1989) of subsidiary board members (McRae, 1996, p. 14). Janet Cohen, director of Charterhouse Bank and a member of a subsidiary board, highlights the diminished status that women have on boards, "There are virtually no women on any boards of the merchant banks, only on the subsidiary boards. The top boards are where the real power lies" (Figes, 1994, p. 49). A Policy Studies Institute Report investigated the reasons why so few women are on British boards. It concluded that the favored candidate of many chairmen [sic] for their board is another company's chief executive or someone with executive board experience. Both will be predominantly male. Attitudes often prevent women from attaining these positions; a science-based company chairman is reported to have said about a well-qualified woman scientist, "I don't want a bright woman on my board" (Howe and McRae, 1991, p. 5). Finally, chairmen [sic] often resort to the "old boys" network for finding suitable board members or use headhunter firms that overwhelmingly put forward male candidates.

Ashridge Management Research Group's survey of the top 200 British companies reported that 25% have women on their boards. Of these board appointments, 19% are executive appointments and 81% are non-executive appointments. Of the companies surveyed only 4% had two or more women on the board (Holton, Rabbetts, and Scrivener, 1993).

In the Hansard Society follow-up report (McRae, 1996), several barriers were identified that impede women's progress. These included

- recruitment practices in which men recruit in their own image, where appointing a woman is considered "too risky," or where men use the "old boy" network
- work cultures that do not encourage women
- lack of role models, mentoring, and networking
- women having to balance family roles with work roles
- attitudinal barriers such as prejudice from other male colleagues and managers, outdated attitudes toward women, and the undervaluation of women's management styles
- women's own limitations, such as lack of commitment, lack of determination to succeed, lack of confidence, and unwillingness to take risks

It is interesting that the survey's respondents, male chairs and male chief executives, cited women's own limitations as the *greatest* barrier to their success and accorded it the highest percentage (29%) of all the barriers (McRae, 1996, p. 14). There appears still to be a tendency to blame women for not reaching the top despite the fact that in this study, as well as in other studies, women are reported to be just as ambitious as men, to work harder than their male colleagues, and to have frequently sacrificed their family life for their careers (Marshall, 1995; Alban Metcalfe, 1989; Nicholson and West, 1988; Hutt, 1985).

Like the Hansard Society studies, the British Institute of Management found that women perceived the greatest barrier to their progress as the "existence of the men's club network" and "prejudice of colleagues." In addition, women perceived their chances for promotion as less than men's. Only 20% of the women anticipated internal promotion as the next step in their careers as compared to 36% of men (Coe, 1992, p. 3). Moreover, there seems to be an attitudinal barrier against women managers that disadvantages them. One third of the women surveyed felt that they do not receive adequate support from male superiors and 13% felt that their organization's attitude toward women was "negative" or "very negative." Only one quarter of the female managers felt their organization's attitude toward women managers was "positive." Only 35% of male managers "strongly agree" that women managers bring positive skills to the workplace and 18% said they would or do find it difficult to work for a woman manager (Coe, 1992, p. 4). Similar data comes from the United States. Catalyst, a business research organization that focuses on women's progress, conducted a study of 1,735 women in 30 major companies. Nearly 40% of the female respondents said that there had been no change in their chances for advancement in the past five years (Catalyst, 1999). Furthermore, women of color in the United States encounter a "concrete ceiling" where reaching the top is impossible. In this study, 47% said they had no support from a mentor or sponsor, 40% complained of the lack of informal networking with influential colleagues, 29% said that there were inadequate numbers of company role models of the same ethnic group as themselves, and 28% reported the lack of high visibility assignments for minority women. Over half of the women in this study cited pervasive stereotypes that they believed held them back (Catalyst, 1999).

Gregg, Machin, and Szymanski (1993) tracked promotion and remuneration levels of women from 400 British companies between 1989 and 1992. They found no evidence that women would progress up the career ladder given time. Instead, they found that women are less likely than their male counterparts to be promoted and the earnings gap between men and women widens the farther a woman moves up the hierarchy.

A housing association study found several barriers to promotion of women in management, many of which pointed to senior management. Mixed messages were delivered from top-level management who said they support equal opportunity but in reality do not spend time supporting or leading the strategy. In addition, top-level management was uneasy about defining explicit objectives or targets for promoting women into management. Finally, top-level management may reinforce the organizational culture, a culture unfriendly to women, by their own behavior (Office for Public Management, 1994).

This unfriendly culture toward women is mirrored in the United States. Over 400 women executives were surveyed to identify the greatest obstacle to their success. Being female and sexism were reported as their key challenges (Korn-Ferry and UCLA, 1993). Several U.S. lawsuits have focused on gender discrimination involving unequal pay and lack of opportunity for women. In 1997, Home Depot agreed to pay $87.5 million to settle a class action sex discrimination suit. The female plaintiffs charged that Home Depot had consistently paid them less than men for equal work, had given them fewer raises than their male counterparts, and had systematically denied them promotion. In 310 of its stores, Home Depot focused on hiring women only at lower levels and keeping them there (Reuters, 1997). In addition, Publix Super Markets, Lucky Stores, and Northwest Airlines have faced similar charges. Publix was forced to pay $81.5 million to its women workers, Northwest Airlines flight attendants were paid $58 million, and Lucky Stores settled for $107 million in a sex discrimination suit (Reuters, 1997).

SENIOR MEN AND WOMEN LEAVING EMPLOYMENT—RECENT STUDIES

Some empirical data suggests that in general women leave management positions at rates in excess of men. The few studies of why men and women leave senior management positions suggest that their reasons and the processes through which men and women do so are quite different.

Besides reports in business magazines like *Fortune* and newspapers (Taylor, 1986), some academic studies have found higher attrition rates among women in senior management. Schwartz (1989) estimates that turnover rates for top-performing women managers are 250% of the rate for male managers. Stroh, Brett, and Reilly (1993) record a 12% difference in female/male turnover rates for a sample of 615 comparable male and female managers who had accepted geographical relocation by 20 *Fortune 500* companies in eight different industries in the two years before the survey. Except for the Stroh et al. study (1993), much data is anecdotal or restricted to a single company, lacks comparative data on male managers, and focuses on non-managerial samples (see, for instance, Cotton and Tuttle, 1986).

Accordingly, Rosin and Korabik (1991) undertook a study to determine whether there are sex differences among managers on a range of personal, organizational, and affective variables that are sometimes viewed as factors in the decision to leave employment. They also examined expressed decisions for leaving employment, especially family concerns. In a prior study Rosin and Korabik (1990) had found that domestic reasons for leaving employment were important only for women who had permanently withdrawn from work, whereas gender, work-related factors such as office politics, and its male-dominated environment were more powerful determinants.

Rosin and Korabik (1991) did not measure actual turnover, but only the intention to do so in a random-sample survey among 303 women and 238 men with MBAs from a large Canadian business school working in the city in which the school is located. All subjects were working full-time, with an average age of 32 years for women and 40 for men. The women had on average received their MBAs at age 28.7 and had 6.7 years of work experience. Males had on average received their MBAs at age 29 and had 11.3 years of work experience. Fifty-four percent of the women and 27% of the men were in middle management, while 20% of the women and 49% of the men were in more senior management positions. Forty-four percent of the women had children and 80% of the men had children. The questionnaire solicited information on leadership, responsibility, and variety in jobs; demands like travel and weekend work; whether job expectations—salary, advancement, influence—were fulfilled; and data on organizational commitment, job satisfaction, and reasons for leaving.

To measure the effects of gender differences in the propensity to leave,

Rosin and Korabik carried out a series of hierarchical multiple regressions on males and females, treating the intention to leave as the dependent variable. This approach revealed significant differences between men and women in marital status, number of children, income, job demands, and expectations as determinants of the intention to leave a job. The data also showed that equivalency in age, education, and experience does not close the salary gap between women and men. Respondents did not differ in the number of hours worked or in other characteristics of their positions, even though women's perceived job demands were lower than men's. The authors commented that "Possibly the women rated their jobs lower in demand due to their own expectations or perceptions. Since women entering a male dominated profession like management are likely to be strongly motivated 'survivors' . . . who expect their work to be highly demanding, a job which meets this expectation might be seen as average in demand" (Rosin and Korabik, 1991, p. 12). However, women in the study were more likely than men to rate their expectations as not having been met. Nevertheless, the regression did not show evidence of gender differences in variables predicting the intention to leave. For both men and women affective reactions, especially commitment and satisfaction, account for most of the variance. Characteristics of the position an employee occupied are also significant for both sexes in the intention to leave. "Since women are new entrants to the field of management and therefore younger and less experienced, they tend to have positions with less responsibility and opportunity. Consequently they may be more likely to leave, particularly if they perceive the barriers they face to be permanent obstacles to advancement" (Rosin and Korabik, 1991, p. 13).

Rosin and Korabik noted some limitations of their study. In particular, the sample is composed only of MBAs. Accordingly, the results may not generalize to more educationally and occupationally diverse populations. They suggest that the failure of their empirical study to find substantive gender differences in the intention to resign "raises the question of how to account for the discrepancy between this outcome and beliefs that women managers are less satisfied and more inclined to leave corporations than men" (Rosin and Korabik, 1991, p. 13). Their likeliest explanation is the persistence of widespread negative stereotyping of women. As Kanter (1977) argued, female attrition may be more noticeable than male attrition, even though it is statistically no different, because it is used to confirm existing stereotypes.

According to Rosin and Korabik, men and women may in fact differ in their decisions to leave jobs for reasons not measured. "For example, the survey received by female respondents included several gender based reasons such as sexual harassment and being in a male dominated environment. Because they were not included in the men's questionnaire, comparisons could not be made" (Rosin and Korabik, 1991, p. 13). Analysis of the women's data, which Rosin and Korabik published elsewhere (Rosin and Korabik, 1992), however, did reveal that being in a male-dominated environment was significantly related to low commitment, poor job satisfaction, and a propensity to leave. They discovered that even though turnover rates for managerial men and women may be similar the dynamics underlying their decisions to resign may be very different.

Brett, Stroh, and Reilly (1994) reviewed research and concluded that there is convincing evidence that female managers leave organizations at higher rates than comparable male managers. They also considered empirical data relevant to three possible explanations for this phenomenon: whether women are bailing out of the workforce to raise families, whether women leave corporations because of discrimination, or whether they leave for better career opportunities in more women-friendly organizations.

By and large Brett et al. (1994) reject the notion that women leave management disproportionately for family reasons. Indeed, family responsibilities have been found empirically to reduce the intentions of female employees to leave their current positions. Rather, they adopted Schwartz's distinction. Among female managers remaining in the workforce Schwartz (1989) distinguished between career-primary and career-and-family women; career-and-family women are willing to trade off some career advancement for shorter hours and free weekends. These women typically report far higher stress levels than male managers (Burke and McKeen, 1994). The source of this stress appears to be in the roles women play as minorities in organizations.

Empirical data suggest, however, that reconciling work and family responsibilities are not the primary cause of stress. Brett et al. (1994) found no turnover studies documenting that women leave corporate positions in the United States for less stressful jobs, although there is evidence that women leave their corporate positions to set up their own companies, especially after hitting the glass ceiling.

Rather, Brett et al. embrace Davidson and Cooper's conclusion (1983) that "structural and systematic discrimination embedded in organizational policies and practices, or the lack thereof, may cause higher levels of stress and ultimately higher levels of turnover for female than male managers" (p. 59). Even among women managers earning more than $170,000 per year, according to a Stroh and Senner study (1994), the two primary reasons for leaving an organization were lack of opportunity for advancement and a male-dominated corporate culture. Stroh et al. (1993) report that among the 615 managers in their survey, work attitudes including satisfaction with the job itself, organization loyalty, and self-loyalty predicted intent to leave for both males and females. Indeed there was significant interaction between self-loyalty and gender. They constructed a self-loyalty index composed of two items: "My loyalty is to my own career and not to any particular company," and "I would be willing to change companies for career advancement." Females turned out to be significantly more self-loyal than males, and this may result in a higher incidence of leaving current employment. Brett et al. concluded:

The results of our study are consistent with the glass ceiling perspective (Morrison et al., 1987) that female managers lack career opportunities in American corporations. Female managers leave their organizations for the same reason that male managers leave—dissatisfaction with career opportunities. In our study proportionately more female managers were dissatisfied and intent on managing their own careers. Those who lacked family responsibilities were particularly likely to leave their current organizations. (Brett et al., 1994, p. 61)

In 1994 and 1995, a study was undertaken to try to understand why women managers leave their organizations (Marshall, 1995). Six general reasons were identified by the women managers.

1. Women found the hostile, male-dominated organizational culture repressive.
2. There was a lack of opportunities and/or an untenable job situation. The women felt undermined, their jobs became unrewarding, or opportunities were denied them.
3. The women experienced conflict and lack of recognition.
4. Stress made the women want to stop working temporarily and change their lifestyle.
5. The women found that their values did not match the kind of person they felt that they had become and, thus, they wanted to explore other aspects of their identity.
6. The women wanted more time fostering important relationships such as those with their husbands or children.

The pattern of interaction described by Marshall's subjects reflects the dynamic of tokenism portrayed in Kanter's *Men and Women of the Corporation* (1977). This account of tokenism is not gender specific but is asserted to obtain whenever a group contains a small number of individuals different from the dominant social type and viewed as symbols of their social category. The visibility of these tokens draws extra attention to their behavior and status; majority group members are made uncomfortable by the contrast with tokens; and judgments of tokens against stereotypes generally preserve the stereotype and label the token as an "exception." Marshall's findings (1995) strongly confirm findings, such as those of Rosin and Korabik (1994) and Brett et al. (1994), that male domination of organizations is the key reason women managers leave jobs.

There are only a small number of empirical studies of termination. These studies suggest that the causes of termination for successful women managers are different from men's cases and that the experiences leading up to termination are different as well.

Burns (cited in Gould, 1986) reported results of a survey questionnaire completed by senior executives in 73 corporations representing diverse industries, ranging in size in sales from $50 million to over $15 billion. More than half were *Fortune 500* companies. Following the survey, Burns conducted interviews with human resource executives from these companies to provide insight into individual terminations. The study found that among those terminated despite better than adequate performance, 70% were fired because of problems getting along with other people, in particular their immediate boss. It was initially thought that most terminations were the undoing of bad hiring decisions. In fact, only 12% had been terminated within the first two years of being hired. In almost every instance, termination took place within 18 months of the terminee's working for a new boss. Burns concluded:

The Executive Termination Study . . . indicated that those executives caught in a conflict with the boss, for the most part, were usually not at odds with the prevailing corporate culture, nor were they organizational rebels or misfits. Insubordination was also not their style. The follow-up interviews revealed that they had been reasonably adept at organizational life and survival. However, at some point prior to the termination there invariably was a deterioration in their relationship with their boss. In the final analysis, with few exceptions, the difficulty was sharply tied to a clash with one individual in the organization—the boss. (cited in Gould, 1986, p. 16)

These clashes were categorized in one of four ways: incompatible personalities, divergent strategies, philosophical differences, or role conflicts. What is significant about this research is that it identifies the predominant cause of termination of successful male managers as a personality conflict with one individual rather than by institutional factors. Gould (1986) outlines the findings about the process of termination for the male managers. Nothing suggests a pattern of systematically aversive treatment of the male manager to be terminated. This finding must be kept in mind when analyzing the process of termination experienced by the women profiled in this book.

Another study relevant to the experiences of senior men and women is Van Velsor and Hughes (1990). Van Velsor and Hughes studied 78 women and 189 men who had lost management positions. According to their findings, "business mistakes" were reported by women to have had more of a negative impact on women's careers than business mistakes that men make. Of the women who reported having had "career setbacks," 20% said they were due to discrimination yet no men reported career setbacks as being discriminatory in nature. Van Velsor and Hughes state:

We should also stress that the majority of mistakes were not major product or business failures. The most common setback these executives had faced was not being able to sell an idea or project. Top management or their boss or colleagues were unswayed by their opinions on a staffing decision, a new sales strategy or a major reorganization. So we know that many of the mistakes the women reported reflect an inability or a perceived inability, to influence decisions or strategy. (1990, p. 32)

Again, this conclusion should be borne in mind when considering the cases discussed in this book.

There is relatively little research on gender, class, or racial correlates of the termination of male managers because the class of managers is largely homogeneous for these factors. The absence of any obvious pattern of discrimination—vertical or horizontal—means there is nothing to explain. However, even were there no reported differences between men and women managers subject to termination, qualitative accounts of women's experiences may reveal patterns of inequity that their bosses have reasons to obscure. The legal climate makes it a wise precaution to at least maintain the appearance of equal treatment and due process in the termination of women managers.

The next chapter assesses a number of competing explanations for the general subordination of women and for workplace inequality. Discussion then turns to ten individual cases of successful women whose terminations tests these theories.

CHAPTER 3

Understanding Women's Subordination

◆◆

A range of theories seeks to explain the patterns of discrimination, inequality, and subordination of women in contemporary society. None of these accounts is fully satisfactory, but one, patriarchy theory, at least seems to be more able to account for the subordination of women, and especially educated, professional women in the modern business corporation. Recording women's experiences and uncovering their meanings is one way to test and to develop patriarchy theory's account of the causes and mechanisms of segregation and other means by which women's subordination is maintained. How much of the horizontal segregation of women is the result of the operation of autonomous patriarchal forces in which both men's and women's choices and actions are constrained? How much of this segregation is the result of men's and women's conscious choices, deliberate strategies, perceptions, interpretations, and constructions of the managerial workplace? These are questions crucial to the testing and development of patriarchy theory and can be answered by a close study of individual cases.

EXPLAINING THE DATA: FROM HUMAN CAPITAL THEORY TO PATRIARCHY

The statistical data and the studies reported in Chapter 2 strongly substantiate the conclusion that the treatment of women in the postindustrial economy perpetuates long-standing gender inequalities, despite significant narrowing of differences relevant to employment, promotion, authority, and pay. The range of inequities in the social and economic position of women even in modern, secular, democratic societies is broad and deep. In spite of two generations during which these inequalities have been recognized and their elimination made the subject of individual, corporate, and governmental policy, they still exist. The pattern of women's subordination is too pervasive to be merely the coincidental by-product of the operation of a large number of unconnected forces in modern society. Indeed, its persistence in the face of apparently countervailing forces tending to homogenize treatment of individuals in the postindustrial economy makes the inequitable treatment of women even more remarkable. This pattern needs to be explained if it is ever to be eliminated.

Women's subordination could be explained with a default theory: human capital theory (Becker, 1964, 1985). This theory identifies the causes of women's subordination in obvious facts about women and modern industrial and postindustrial economy, facts that make the appearance of long-run permanent horizontal segregation merely the by-product of women's free choices and distinctive preferences.

Human capital theory is the application of neoclassical microeconomics to the explanation of patterns of labor force participation. Neoclassical theory treats each individual as an autonomous agent who maximizes his or her own utility. Individuals do this by spending or investing their assets, working to secure more assets, or leaving the workforce for leisure (for example, when wages are below what they will accept or when they have earned enough to satisfy their wants). The theory has no special role for economic classes and none for gender. All economic agents are assumed to be equal. In particular among economic agents—consumers and producers—no socially or economically significant asymmetries of market power exist or, if they do, the market will eventually eliminate these inequalities. For example, standard microeconomic theory tells us that the excess profits of a monopoly will eventually attract the notice of other entrepreneurs who will enter the monopolist's market and end its monopoly.

Why then do women find themselves in less well-paid work, vertically segregated from certain sectors of the economy, horizontally segregated from positions within other sectors, and subject to blatant and subtle forms of mistreatment even within those sectors where their participation is tolerated or encouraged? Neoclassical economic theory gives two sorts of answers. First, most patterns of employment reflect either the willingness of workers to invest in schooling and training appropriate to various jobs or the preferences and tastes of individuals confronted with job choices. Second, where patterns of labor force participation cannot be explained by these considerations, the results reflect economic inefficiencies, which we can expect the market to punish and eventually eliminate (Arrow, 1972).

The theory suggests that women do not participate equally with men in the labor market because they choose not to invest in the same quantities or the same types of education and training as men; because they rank marriage, children, and domestic pursuits as more preferred than men do; and because physical and biological differences between women and men make it economically more efficient for them to work part-time and have shorter careers than men (Mincer and Polachek, 1974; Lloyd, 1975). Human capital theory focuses particularly on differences in the pattern of investment in training and education—human capital—to explain differences in workforce participation between men and women.

Where inequalities in workforce participation cannot be explained by considerations of economic efficiency and differences in preferences and human capital, neoclassical theory applies its policy prescription for the elimination of monopoly: simply wait for it to correct those inequalities. Unequal treatment of women in the workforce, like racial discrimination, is inefficient. It fails to employ human capital optimally. Employers and supervisors who fail to employ the most well-qualified women (or other minority), pay for their sexist (or racist) preferences. They secure a reduced economic return from non-optimally efficient production using less economically efficient resources than are available (Arrow, 1972). Others not burdened with such (irrational) preferences will secure greater economic returns and eventually drive sexist employers from the market by undercutting their prices. Thus, where differences in workplace participation cannot be explained as the result of individual people's tastes and natural skills, it can be expected to disappear over the long run. All we have to do is wait.

This explanation for women's subordination in the economy has so many weaknesses it is hard to take seriously. First, it is burdened with all the weaknesses of neoclassical economic theory: unrealistic assumptions about individual economic rationality, about equality in power between economic agents, about the effects that these inequalities will have on the market (market failure), and about the empirical measurement of its variables (Cain, 1991). Second, to the standard idealizations of economic theory it adds unsubstantiated assumptions about differences in the tastes and preferences of women and men, for example, ambition and interest in child rearing as well as unwarranted claims about differences in their biologically fixed (capital) endowments, such as strength, size, and endurance. If anything, the modern workplace makes these differences increasingly irrelevant to job performance and thus eliminates their explanatory relevance. Third, the expectation that sexism (and racism) should disappear in the long run because it is uneconomical is patently belied by the facts about modern economy (Thurow, 1969). Finally, human capital theory's claim that men and women are characterized by differences in human capital has become weaker over the last generation. A larger number of women have invested in professional qualifications in managerial and technical disciplines. In terms of educational attainment, women have a higher degree of formal education than men; 44% have a postgraduate or Master's degree compared with 28% of men (Coe, 1993). But this difference in educational achievement has not translated into the more efficient pattern of employment human capital theory would lead us to expect. Research has found that for women, unlike for men, a higher level of education does not serve as a vehicle for attaining occupations characterized by greater wage growth with increased experience (Duncan, 1996). Exploring the correlation between earnings differences and productivity-enhancing characteristics, Ferber and Green (1991) concluded that a more significant indicator of wage inequality between men and women was simply the proportion of women in the occupation: the more women in an occupational category, holding human capital constant, the lower average income. Ferber and Green went on to study a small number of a "rare population," namely, women in "top management" (1991, p. 147). They concluded:

One interpretation, consistent with Kanter's (1977) hypothesis, is that members of this extremely small minority tend to be treated not as individuals, but as "tokens." What the majority notices about them is not the particular characteristics that differentiate one from another but rather that they all belong to a group of outsiders. This would account for the fact that human capital differences have virtually no effect on their earnings. (Ferber and Green, 1991, p. 160)

To the extent that modern business proceeds in accordance with the claims of neoclassical economic theory, it is evident that women's subordination reflects some sort of "market failure." In particular, the labor market does not satisfy the conditions on pure competition either between suppliers of labor or employers that would result in equal representation of individuals of equal productivity across the economy. Attempts to explain patterns of discrimination by according preferences for discrimination against women or racial groups to employees and consumers, instead of producers and managers (e.g., Krueger, 1963; Alexis, 1974), may enhance the credibility of an economic approach to discrimination; leaves unexplained, however, the very preferences that drive the subordination of women.

Many economists and social scientists have sought explanations for labor market inequalities by examining structural facts. As seen in Chapter 2, the existence of an internal labor market, in which selection of workers is not directly governed by a competitive market and has an already unrepresentative set of prospective workers, will prevent competition in external labor markets from effacing inefficient patterns of discrimination. Research on imperfections in the labor market that produce inequalities began with the work of Doeringer and Piore.

[E]ven at entry points where it would seem most likely that wage rates and worker productivity should be closely related, employment and wage decisions generally apply to *groups* of workers rather than *individuals*. The group may be defined by characteristics such as age, race, or education as is common at entry points, or by seniority and job classification as in the case of jobs filled internally. When wage determinations are made for groups of workers, the influence of economic constraints—labor costs, productivity, and so forth—is estimated in terms of the *expected value* for the group as a whole and not for individuals. (Doeringer and Piore, 1971, p. 77, italics in original)

In order to explain why the labor market outcomes for women are different than for men, we need to answer the question of why they constitute a homogeneous group to which lower expected values of productivity and/or labor costs are attributed.

Thus, even if women's economic subordination was a case of market failure that human capital theory might analytically accommodate, it would not be so much of an explanation as the uncovering of more facts about women's subordination that demands explanation. Why are there differences in human capital investment between men and women? How are women's preferences for part-time work or unskilled labor or shorter careers formed or domestic and family work formed? How and why are inefficient sexist practices enforced over long periods despite their alleged economic inefficiency? The more that is learned about the character of labor markets, the clearer it becomes that these questions cannot be answered by considerations from economic theory.

Barron and Norris (1991) appeal specifically to the structure of the labor market to account for the differences in the occupational experiences of men and women. They argue that the long-term needs of employers to solve labor productivity problems generate a dualism in the labor market between a primary sector, containing well-paid long-term jobs with promotional prospects, and a secondary sector, characterized by lower pay, job insecurity, and restricted mobility between the sectors. By placing key workers in the primary sector and retaining them over fluctuations in the business cycle, businesses can minimize the impact of such cycles on their long-term growth. Employers can, however, only do so if they can reduce other costs by making a different set of employment decisions in the secondary sector. Determining whether a potential employee is to be consigned to the primary or secondary sector of the employment market involves both informational costs and great uncertainties. Employers deal with groups of employees, as Doeringer and Piore (1971, p. 77) note, and seek out markers or indicators to make employment decisions:

Given the limited information about potential job applicants normally available to recruiters, it may often be difficult for an employer to obtain direct evidence about the likely reliability and stability of a potential employee. Therefore use is frequently made of relatively visible individual characteristics which are thought to correlate highly with these qualities. For purely operational reasons employers rely on formal education and training qualifications and other easily identifiable, personal criteria, such as age, sex, color. (Barron and Norris, 1991, p. 160)

The use of "ascriptive characteristics" such as sex "confines the group so delineated to the secondary sector over the whole of their working lives" (Barron and Norris, 1992, p. 160). Barron and Norris identify five main attributes that consign a group to the secondary labor market: dispensability—ease of removal from a redundant job; easily identifiable social differences from workers in the primary sector such as race or ethnicity; comparatively lower interest in training, education, and job experience; low economism—a weaker concern for economic as opposed to other rewards of work; and low solidarism—the degree of collective organization and action that characterize a group. It is clear that over the long term, and in modern Britain, women as a group satisfy all five of these criteria for relegation to the secondary labor market. Accordingly their segregation into lower-paid, less stable, more part-time, less supervisory work is a consequence of their bearing the ascriptive characteristics by which employers solve their uncertainty problems in the labor market.

This theory treats the five characteristics that employers use to relegate groups to the secondary labor market as explanatory variables. What is needed to explain the differential experience of men versus women in the labor market, however, is an account of why women appear to manifest these five characteristics more predominantly than men. This is an explanatory vacuum filled by patriarchy theory. It is not a vacuum that economic theory can be expected to fill. Shared employer's beliefs about dispensability, social stigmas, education, economism, and solidarism are not themselves the products of market forces, are increasingly incorrect, and require more fundamental social and psychological explanation.

Most important, both pure human capital theory and theories about structured labor markets leave completely unexplained, indeed may be disconfirmed, by phenomena of special importance to the women featured in this book: the treatment of women managers in the so-called "primary sector." The data reported above show that the pattern of allegedly costly discrimination against women is in respects stronger as one moves up the employment hierarchy in training, education, remuneration, and power. Thus, the higher status a women reaches along each of these measures, the greater the likelihood that she will be exposed to sexual harassment and the higher levels of stress she will report in her working situation. Most surprisingly, given the apparently greater degree of commitment to and recognition of the need for economic efficiency at the top of a firm than at the bottom, the pattern of apparently non-optimal exploitation of available female human capital has persisted even as the capital has become increasingly available. A theory of women's subordination must dig deeper into the underlying social mechanisms that result in the economic subordination of women.

Beginning with Kate Millett's *Sexual Politics* (1970), feminist theorists sought a theoretical explanation for the patterns of workplace inequity, segregation, and mistreatment in the concept of patriarchy. Of course, to the degree patriarchal institutions organize an entire society or culture, their effects will be felt far beyond the workplace. Patriarchy is a social and political structure characterized by two principles: male shall dominate female, elder male shall dominate younger. Millett holds that every avenue of power within Western societies is in male hands. The patriarchy is enforced through implicit consent on the part of women. The consent results from socialization in accordance with an ideology that distinguishes male and female temperaments as respectively more and less suited to dominance, that stipulates sex roles and child care responsibilities, all of which are ultimately grounded in claims about biology.

The patriarchy operates through three principal institutions: the family, the society, and the state. Although the family is patriarchy's chief institution for socializing its members, Millett argues, "It is both a mirror of and a connection with the larger society; a patriarchal unit within a patriarchal whole. Mediating between the individual and the social structure, the family effects control and conformity where political and other authorities are insufficient" (1970, p. 33). Beyond the family, the patriarchy's assignment of women to a lower caste is likely to cut across social class differences, thus obscuring gender dominance and producing social confusion. Patriarchy allows for women's role in dominant classes. The advantages of class membership obscure but do not destroy or compensate for subordination to males within the class or even sometimes in nondominant classes.

Millett's account of the way the patriarchy maintains an economic hold over women is of special importance. Traditional patriarchy permits women no independent economic existence, although it accorded them onerous labor. Contemporary patriarchy continues to make women's economic position "vicarious or tangential." At the time Millett wrote *Sexual Politics*, in the late 1960s, only one third of women in the United States were employed and at half the average male income despite a higher level of educational attainment. Adopting a Marxian notion, Millet argued that women function as a reserve labor force, to be employed as needed, while middle-class women have been traditionally discouraged from employment altogether. Discrimination against women was very great.

Although overt physical force that characterized historical patriarchies is less visible, legal systems that restrict abortion, do not punish spousal abuse, obscure the actual incidence of rape or treat it leniently, and tolerate exhibitions of cruelty and victimization enforce patriarchal values with the same effectiveness as suttee (woman willingly being cremated on the funeral pyre of her husband), purdah (seclusion), foot binding, or the veil. Millett traces the patriarchal character of contemporary society back through the cultural and symbolic meanings that stand behind the overt expression of patriarchy in these non-Western practices, meanings that contemporary Western societies retain even as they surrender these practices. Groups Millett calls "primitive peoples" have pejorative myths about the origin of female genitalia, prize virginity, ostracize women during their menstrual periods, almost universally enforce taboos against women touching ritual objects, and widely require them to eat apart, although they require female service, and dominant males are expected to eat first or to eat better food when both sexes do dine together. Patriarchies usually exclude love as a basis for mate selection and "modern patriarchies tend to do so through class, ethnic, and religious factors" (Millett, 1970, p. 50). Millett summarizes the cultural meaning these patriarchal cultures accord the female:

Primitive society practices its misogyny in terms of taboo and mana which evolve into explanatory myth. In historical cultures, this is transformed into the ethical, then the literary, and in the modern period, scientific rationalizations for the sexual politic. Myth is of course a felicitous advance in the level of propaganda, since it often bases its arguments on ethics or theories of origins. (p. 51)

Presumably the cultural meanings pre-Western societies attached to women, which fixed their patriarchal character, outlived these groups and still animate modern societies.

Patriarchy's ideology—the differences in status, temperament, and role expressed in the continued bearing of these myths—is so pervasive that a woman develops "group self-hatred and self-rejection, a contempt for herself and for her fellows—the result of that continual, however subtle, re-iteration of her infirmity which she eventually accepts as a fact" (Millett, 1970, p. 56). This "disesteem" for "themselves and each other" (p. 55), according to Millett, is a group characteristic common to those who suffer minority status and a marginal existence, "here defined not as dependent upon numerical size of the group, but on its status" (p. 55).

Sexual Politics is silent on both the origins of the patriarchy and on what ensures its persistence through so much prehistory and history. Other patriarchy theorists were not so reticent. Shulamith Firestone's *Dialectic of Sex* (1970) offers a more univocal theory of the factors that generate and maintain patriarchies. All aspects of women's subservient position are to be understood as products of sexual, reproductive, and other anatomical differences between men and women. The initial and fundamental institution of the patriarchy is, in Firestone's view, the biological family. The domination of the family by males establishes a sexual class system that expresses itself throughout the rest of social, political, and economic institutions, including those that relegate women to inferior status in work: "the natural reproductive difference between the sexes led directly to the first division of labour based on sex, which is at the origins of all further divisions into economic and cultural classes" (Firestone, 1970, p. 9). The search for reliable males and the vulnerability to which the bearing and care of infants exposes women makes them asymmetrically dependent on males.

Firestone holds that technological developments and access to political power can enable women as a class to reverse the discriminatory arrangements to which they have been subjected. As technology frees women from the biological facts that constrain reproduction and political organizations enable women to gain control of the means of reproduction their subordination can be reduced and perhaps eliminated.

Whereas Firestone identified biological differences as the source of patriarchy, Susan Brownmiller advanced the thesis that male violence is the principal source of women's subordination. Brownmiller (1976) traces the socialization of males into a culture of violence and rape, especially through military training and experience. Other researchers have argued that male violence is a common patriarchal practice, not merely the irrational behavior of a few psychologically deranged men (Bernard and Schlaffer, 1997; Caputi and Russell, 1997).

Patriarchy theorists share in common the claim that society is pervasively structured in conformity with male privilege and hierarchical arrangements. Although they may differ among themselves on the fundamental causes of the patriarchy, patriarchy theorists typically identify distinct features of modern and premodern societies that are explained as effects of the operation of the patriarchy and in particular its greater power to effect social arrangements than other social forces such as economic organization, religion, social class, or political power. For example, the high degree of horizontal and vertical segregation of women in preindustrial, industrial, and postindustrial economies is an empirically observable effect that needs to be explained by a distinct cause or causes. Although the origins of patriarchy are shrouded in the mists of historical or indeed evolutionary time, its persistence must be due to its providing men with the means to secure a disproportionate share of scarce resources, that is, almost everything that humans value. Certainly, across the period of recorded history in the West, East, Arctic, African savannah, or the Asian Pacific, scarcity of resources, whether in the domestic, agricultural, feudal, cottage, or industrial economy, has provided an incentive to concentrate power. The patriarchy has provided the means across climes, cultures, and periods to secure it for men, and in particular older men. The only contexts in which one might expect the patriarchy to weaken its grip on the social order will be those characterized by affluence, the promise of increased affluence, and the decline of scarcity among those commodities prized by men.

Patriarchy theory distinguishes the structures of male dominance and hierarchy from their effects in female subordination, as recorded and measured in observations of social processes. However, social structure is not itself a directly observable cause. Hierarchies of dominance are hard to measure independent of the behavior of individuals they order. Nevertheless, it is a continuing methodological responsibility of patriarchy theorists to seek out independent evidence for the existence of the patriarchy, that is, data distinct from the quantitative record of subordination of women patriarchy is invoked to explain. Finding an originating cause for the emergence and persistence of patriarchy in prehistory is extremely difficult, but identifying the machinery by which it preserves itself in the present is vital.

Millett's (1970) patriarchy theory was not so much a finished theory as a program for developing a detailed autonomous explanatory theory of women's subordination. In the period that followed its publication, feminist scholars attempted to develop it while others sought to supplant it. Of particular interest is the debate about the adequacy of patriarchy theory to explain the facts of women's subordination and segregation in the labor market.

FROM MARXIAN THEORY TO A DUAL SYSTEMS EXPLANATION

Among patriarchy theory's most vigorous critics have been Marxian and Marxist feminist theorists. These theorists subsume the subordination of women to the exploitation of economic classes composed of men and women. For example, Goldthorpe (1983) argued that the unit of sociological analysis is the family, whose status is that of its male income earner. Goldthorpe held that women's economic role was too limited and too variable to affect class status independent of the male head of household. Accordingly, women should not be viewed as a distinct class for purposes of the analysis of social inequality or capitalist exploitation. Similarly, Delphy (1984) divides the family into an oppressing class (males) and an oppressed class (females). Like the proletariat from which surplus labor is extracted as profit in capitalism, men extract surplus value from women's domestic production. Patriarchy thus labels a mode of production to be analyzed alongside other modes: feudalism, capitalism, and socialism. In Delphy's system of patriarchy, men devalue women by assigning them to only domestic roles. This domestic class system subordinating women to men operates in parallel with the more familiar system, but it is far more pervasive and of much longer standing. Both Goldthorpe's and Delphy's analyses have been overtaken by the exponential increase of women's nondomestic labor force participation. Marxian theories can no longer account for their subordination by an appeal to domestic exploitation. Or at least they cannot do so in ways that distinguish their accounts of women's inequality from the patriarchy theorist's.

Other Marxist-feminist theorists have sought to subordinate the sex role to economic class interest outside the home and to explain it as a consequence of Marxian theory's analysis of how control of the means of production determines the relations of production. Women's subordination is the result of inequalities in power over commodities and their production, and the exploitation this inequality in power generates. This subordination is a form of capitalist class exploitation identified in Braverman's widely influential work, *Labour and Monopoly Capital* (1974). Braverman advances an account of the subordination of women in the capitalist economy as mainly the result of changes in the mode of capitalist production. Braverman subsumes women's role in the economy under the Marxian conception of a reserve army of labor, whose existence effectively prevents the proletariat from threatening to withhold labor in order to increase its share of income. As technological progress reduced the demands of the domestic economy on women throughout the industrial revolution, the size of the reserve army has grown. At the same time ever-increasing capital investment in automated production reduces the level of expertise required of labor. This de-skilling and the emergence of de-skilled jobs offering lower wages for workers with less education, less experience, and fewer alternatives results in segregation of women into low-wage, dead-end work.

The empirical facts about women's participation in labor markets make it difficult to treat male domination as just another dimension of capital's exploitation of labor. First, women's employment levels seem to increase during periods of recession as the male portion of the reserve army increases (see, for example, Walby, 1986, p. 167). Second, women's status as a pool of de-skilled labor long antedates capitalist modes of production. More important, capitalism can be expected to work against vertical segregation and other sorts of gender discrimination just because doing so will add to the supply of labor and thus lower wage rates for all workers.

Marxian theories about the exploitation of labor have not been strongly supported by empirical evidence over the century during which they have been developed. The result has been further development of these theories in order to accommodate and better explain the actual course of development in the labor markets of industrialized economies. For example, Edwards, Gordon, and Reich (1982) and Gordon (1989) have introduced further factors into the traditional Marxian account, in particular to answer the question: "Why has the achievement of a working class agenda always remained so distant?" (Edwards et al., 1982, p. 2). Their answer is that the working class, at least in the United States, is segmented, separated into distinct labor markets that "has inhibited the growth of a unified working class movement" (p. 3). According to Edwards et al., labor segmentation has a significant impact on women in the workforce, and this may explain their economic subordination.

This theory of labor segmentation faces several difficulties, both in its account of separated labor markets to explain continued capitalist exploitation and any attempt to ground an explanation of women's economic subordination. The general difficulties are well illustrated by the fate of the four hypotheses that Edwards et al. (1982) consider to be central tests of the adequacy of their theory:

1. Value added per production worker in the largest, most unionized, and bureaucratized "core" corporations in the economy increases relative to that of so-called "peripheral" smaller, non-unionized, service-oriented firms, permitting a higher rate of technological innovation and investment in core firms.
2. Production workers' earnings in core firms increase faster than those in the periphery.
3. The ratio of production workers to total employees in the core industries declines as core firms devote more resources to planning, supervision, and sales.
4. The ratio of layoffs to worker falls in the core industries relative to the periphery.

The U.S. data brought together to support these four hypotheses were ambiguous in the long period leading up to the early 1980s (Edwards et al., 1992, pp. 193–200). The trend in the years since Edwards et al.'s theory appeared has been clearly in the direction opposite to all four of these hypotheses. The older and larger core firms in almost every industry have suffered in competition with smaller, non-unionized, service-oriented firms over this period largely because they have been less able to respond to technological and market changes (Peters, 1988, p. 197). The core firms have had to lay off and make redundant more of their employees, they have had to make recourse to outside sources of planning, their workers' pay has not increased as quickly as that of non-unionized service-oriented firms, and the productivity of their workers has not increased as rapidly.

The weakness of a labor segmentation approach to explaining horizontal and vertical discrimination of women in the workforce is amply illustrated by Edwards et al. (1992). Their history of the entry of women into the industrial labor market recognizes that insofar as there was segmentation of women toward employers in the peripheral labor market, its cause was as much the result of patriarchal forces as anything. In the New England factory system, "that the new labor force consisted of single females reflected more than the dynamic of emergent capitalism; it was derived as well from the patriarchal system of production in New England households. . . . There was . . . the tyranny of patriarchal authority within the home, which many women wished to escape. . . . The irony, of course, was that they escaped to the carefully controlled patriarchal world of the employers' dormitories" (pp. 71–72). In the discussion of post–World War II labor market segmentation, Edwards et al. (1992) note that "as the primary segment left the secondary labour segment behind, both in manufacturing and in trade, peripheral employers were more frequently forced to turn to women as potential low-wage employees" (p. 206). The primary segment, however, was almost entirely male and unionized. The question of why women were segregated to the secondary labor segment is left to be answered by the hypothesis that patriarchal imperatives overwhelm economic ones, even among trades and industrial unionists.

In the present context perhaps the gravest weakness of a labor market segmentation theory is that it cannot distinguish between segmentation and vertical segregation of women. With the primary labor market, Edwards et al. (1992) drew a further distinction between an "independent primary" and a "subordinate primary" segment: "The independent primary sector includes many professional, managerial and technical jobs. . . . The subordinate primary sector includes any semi-skilled, primary sector blue collar jobs and many semi-skilled white-collar jobs" (p. 202). Unsurprisingly, between-segment earnings differences are greater than within-segment differences for these two groups, thus reinforcing the divergent interests of these segments and weakening labor solidarity. This sort of account, however, cannot explain the horizontal segregation that typically minimizes representation of women in the independent primary segment. This and the vertical segregation they do assimilate to labor segmentation need to be explained and the nuance of a labor market segmentation amendment to Marxian theory cannot provide the answer.

The concept of class turns out to have limited relevance to the explanation of women's subordination despite its central importance in the explanation of other sorts of social and economic inequalities. Traditionally social class theorists simply assimilated women to the social class of their husbands. Even assuming all women have husbands, were this so, the within-class inequalities between men and women would be inexplicable by appeal to class. Since women are in fact employed in the economy, and often in socioeconomic grades different from their husbands, it often turns out that male members of a "lower" social class than their wives exercise subordination over wives who must be classed higher than they, thus robbing class hierarchy of its explanatory power in respect of inequalities. It is possible to reconfigure traditional class analysis so that class status becomes a function of biological and/or social and economic position within the family, and some Marxian and other theorists have adopted this view (Delphy, 1984; Firestone, 1970) in order to hold that class inequalities explain gender inequalities. However, this substitution is a covert return to a pure patriarchy theory in which the word "class" takes on all the meaning of the concept of gender. Nothing is more obvious than that inequalities in the treatment of men and women are ubiquitous across all economic classes from the capitalist class to the lumpen-proletariat. Indeed, many would argue that within classes of the sort Marxist theory identifies, the relevant male/female inequalities are greater than the inequalities between these economic classes. Consider, for example, the data on how trade unions in the United Kingdom worked to restrict access to jobs in blue-

collar industries for women (Hartmann, 1979; and Ellis, 1988). The inef-
fectiveness of theories of class to explain the mechanism of horizontal
segregation at the level of management in the modern corporation is particularly clear. By and large women and men at this level share economic
class and its correlates: social class, race, education, and other socioeconomic characteristics. Labor market inequalities cannot be explained by
class similarities.

There are, of course, reasons why Marxist social scientists should attempt
to preempt accounts of exploitation that do not accord pride of place to
capitalism as the culprit. And more than other social scientists, Marxist
scholars have devoted themselves to the joint tasks of identifying the
sources of exploitation and arguing for the emancipation of societies from
these sources. This interest in the nature and causes of inequalities has made
Marxian social theory a potentially rich source of analogy and theoretical
inspiration, even when feminist theorists recognize its inadequacy as an
explanation of women's subordination.

Thus, criticisms of Marxian theories do not undercut the work of feminist theorists who have exploited Marxian explorations of the details and
intricacies of class subordination without adopting the details of Marxist
economic theory. The mechanisms Marxians have uncovered whereby a
society socializes its members to their class roles may well be the same as
those it employs to organize gender differences as well. One need not buy
into the full Marxian social theory in order to adapt its insights about class
to gender. This fact continues to make Marxian approaches congenial to
feminist scholars. Marxian answers to the question of how capitalism cul-
turally reproduces itself may provide insight into how the patriarchy ensures its own self-perpetuation. Combining class analysis and ethnographic
approaches, which produce thick descriptions and qualitative analyses of
case studies, Marxian anthropologists have, for example, sought to show
how the beliefs, norms, and attitudes of individuals enable capitalism to
reproduce labor power.

Wills (1977) provides an example of this sort of Marxian research that
might be so adapted. His objective was to understand how working class
youths "let themselves" be tracked into "the inferior rewards, undesirable
social definition, and increasingly intrinsic meaninglessness of manual work
at the bottom of a class society" (Wills, 1977, p. 1). The ethnography of
a dozen inner-London working-class boys led Wills to argue that it is their
own (sub)culture that condemns lower-class workers to their workforce
subordination. "This self-damnation is experienced paradoxically as true
learning, affirmation, appropriation and as a form of resistance" (p. 3).
According to Wills, these subjective feelings have an objective basis in the
real insight—or "penetration" of the capitalist system that these youths
acquired through school and guidance agencies (p. 120). Wills' ethnography and theory suggest a novel alternative to the traditional Marxian ac-

count of the role of deception, self-deception, and mystification in the perpetuation of class.

The mechanisms that research like Wills' uncovers may help feminist theorists identify the ways in which society inculcates and enforces horizontal and vertical discrimination. We may ask similar questions about the degree to which women condemn themselves to the gender roles required by the persistence of patriarchal social institutions. Among women the mechanisms that assign them to subordinate roles inside the public and the private sphere may be the same sense of "freedom, election, and transcendence" Wills uncovers in his working-class "lads." Unlike Wills' cases, however, the ones reported in this book represent subjects who attempted to break the ideological mold that consigns women (including working-class women) to a preordained role in the economy and will consider how these women escaped across the sex/gender boundary that socialization constructs. The ethnography in the testing and development of Marxian social class theory may thus serve as a model for ethnography that enriches and confirms patriarchy theory.

Marxian scholars have also uncovered the ways in which inequalities in social power are used to maintain the interests of dominant economic classes. Here too feminist non-Marxists have adapted these approaches to explain how men defend their gender interests. Brownmiller's (1976) focus on violence does not exhaust the sources of power in a society. The threat of violence is itself a consequence of inequalities in access to resources, whether in the military-industrial complex, the home, or the workplace. By substituting "men" for the "capitalist class" at the apex of governments and corporations, feminist theory can take over Marxian analyses of how asymmetries in the exercise of power preserve the status quo. Social control rarely requires the use of force. Social power's hegemony operates through ideology, by defining events and constraining the terms in which they are discussed and by establishing values and expectations. "If authority is defined as legitimate power, then we can say that the main axis of the power structure of gender is the general connection of authority with masculinity . . . or more generally the construction of hierarchies of authority and centrality within major gender categories" (Connell, 1987, p. 109). Connell has substituted masculinity for property and gender for class. In detail, Connell traces some examples of how, like class, gender "imposes order in and through culture" both upon men and women. The cases to be considered in this book reflect clearly the way in which the masculinization of authority operates on and is internalized by women who find themselves at the interface between those who exercise hegemony and those upon whom it is exercised. In fact, like Wills' (1977) working-class "lads" who both internalize the capitalist ideology and see through it, these women managers both internalized the masculine ethic and felt that they had to do so to survive. The difference is that what Wills calls "penetration" consigned his subjects to their working-class roles, while it may in fact have deprived the women in this book of their management careers. The crucial questions about men's power to preserve their domination of women are not why they have disproportionate power, but how it came to be unequally concentrated, why it is not diffused across gender lines, and how it is exercised to ensure its continued asymmetrical distribution.

Aside from their own weaknesses as an account of the organization of the economy, in the hands of feminist scholars Marxian approaches have not fared well. Although individual Marxian social scientists have shed light on the role of women in the workplace and Marxian approaches to class and power have been taken over in analyses of gender and power, by and large patriarchy has survived its objections and at the same time taken over much of the Marxian analytical and explanatory machinery. Gender inequalities cannot be illuminated as a species of class inequalities, though the machinery of inequality Marxian social scientists have hypothesized may turn out to be those that operate to preserve the subordination of women.

The result of the assimilation of Marxian and patriarchal approaches came to be called dual systems theory, the attempt to explain gender inequality as a reflection of two independent structural forces: capitalism and patriarchy. In "Capitalism, Patriarchy and Job Segregation by Sex," Hartmann (1979) argued that long before the emergence of capitalism, men had acquired techniques of hierarchical control over the labor of women in the family. "With the advent of public-private separations such as those created by the emergence of state apparatus and economic systems based on a wider exchange and larger production units, the problem for men became one of maintaining their control over the labour power of women" (p. 207). The problem is solved in part by continuing to exploit the traditional division of labor. But the emergence of capitalism threatens patriarchal control through the creation of a "free" market in labor. The continued position of inferiority of women in this market, indeed its job segregation, is largely the result of the role male workers play in maintaining the sexual division of labor that emerged in the household. Job segregation enforces low wages, makes women dependent on males, encourages marriage and withdrawal from the public labor market, and by reducing labor supply enhances men's wages. "Thus, the hierarchial domestic division of labour is perpetuated by the labour market, and vice versa. This process is the present outcome of the continuing interaction of two interlocking systems, capitalism and patriarchy . . . which has created a vicious circle for women" (Hartmann, 1979, p. 208).

According to Hartmann, job segregation is not the result of capitalist forces, but of more long-standing social relations enforced by male workers. A historical study of the organization of labor from the beginnings of capitalist accumulation shows that job segregation was present from the outset, first in exclusion of women from the guilds or subordination in their husband's guilds, then in the removal of women from their position in early textile factories and exclusion from trades in the postguild period by emerging craft unions. The source of men's ability to exclude women is to be found in the patriarchal social relations of the nuclear family combined with the fact that capitalist modes of production had their origin in the household. As work was removed from the home, this advantage cemented men's economic domination (Hartmann, 1979, p. 216). Indeed, production became less dependent on women and women more dependent on men. The expansion of the wage labor system altered but did not abrogate the dominance of men. Job segregation persisted through trade unions and through legislation restricting factory hours for women but not for men. According to Hartmann, British history strongly suggests that sexual segregation is patriarchal in origin, long standing, and almost ineradicable. It is men's labor unions, which may have their origin in greater awareness of the techniques of hierarchical organization, that Hartmann cites as the source of men's ability to maintain job segregation and the domestic division of labor (p. 223). Hartmann concludes that the contemporary status of women in the labor market and sexual segregation of labor are the result of a lengthy process of interaction of patriarchy with capitalism.

Like Hartmann, Sylvia Walby (1986) holds that men's control over women's labor has little to do with the nature of capitalist exploitation; both women and men are subject to capitalist exploitation. It is through men's control of women's opportunities to participate in the labor market that men subordinate women. Walby recognizes that "many of the grand theories of patriarchy do have problems in dealing with historical and cultural variation, "due largely to employment of a single explanatory strategy—the base-superstructure model characteristic of Marxian theory" (1986, p. 16). This problem, she suggests, can be solved by operating with a number of different "bases," including patriarchal modes of production, patriarchal relations in paid work, patriarchal relations in the state, male violence, patriarchal relations in sexuality, and patriarchal relations in cultural institutions. Walby identifies patriarchal practices from which these relations emerge.

Of special importance is Walby's approach to patriarchal relations in paid work. A fully adequate theory of patriarchy must account for why women earn less than men, are less fully employed than men, and why they experience job segregation, both horizontal and vertical. Walby (1986) argues that history sometimes reveals conflict between capitalism and patriarchy. Since women's labor supply is finite there will be a struggle between the capitalist labor market and the patriarchy's domestic needs. Changes in the character of women's subordination reflect the way in which this conflict has been resolved at various periods of economic development. Significant examples of these compromises are the Factory Acts, in which the patriarchy reduced capital's access to female labor, and the elimination of women from engineering works in Britain after each of the world wars. The predominance of women in clerical trades reflects a victory of employers over the patriarchy.

Following Witz (1988), Walby (1990) identifies two distinct strategies in patriarchal discrimination: a segregational one and an exclusionary strategy. These strategies produce what others call vertical segregation and horizontal segregation. Walby (1990) traces the exclusionary strategy of vertical segregation in the 19th and 20th century history of employment in engineering, where unions succeeded in preventing women from engaging in skilled work except during periods of national emergency. Even then women were restricted to certain areas of engineering and excluded from the men's part of the Amalgamated Engineering Union. The exclusionary strategy is a characteristic device of craft unions, in contrast to industrial or general unions, which have organized less-skilled workers and have employed a segregational tactic. Segregating women into the lower levels of various occupations is a patriarchal response to the failure to exclude them altogether, a failure often traceable to conflicts with capitalist modes of production. Walby cites the attempts of the National Union of Clerks to enforce such segregation in the emerging office bureaucracy (1990, pp. 53–54).

Horizontal segregation is enforced through several different historically and spatially specific subtypes (Walby, 1990, p. 54). In Britain the most effective means of labor market segmentation has been the relegation of women to part-time work, with consequent lower pay and less job security. Part-time work has, however, led to a great increase of women in the labor force.

Where the relations of production can be expected to lead to the labor market's characteristic horizontal segregation they do not operate alone. Rather, the result is brought about by the interaction of capitalism and patriarchy. A comparative analysis of statistical data on part-time working advanced by Brewster and Rees (1995) suggests that "where women are segregated into professions and working patterns that are characterized by low pay, we have examples of capitalism and patriarchy working hand in hand. Where there is a combination of skill shortage, high women's unemployment and increasing numbers of qualified and educated women on the market, patriarchy is holding sway" (p. 20). The Brewster and Rees data include statistics on part-time employment and pay rates, the differential provision of child care in European Union nations, the legal protections accorded such work, and comparisons of rates of unemployment between men and women over the recent past. Much of this data leads to the conclusion that there is a consistent pattern of horizontal segregation in the labor market that cannot be explained without taking gender into account. Labor statistics make it clear that despite growth in employment rates in European countries throughout the 1980s, and in spite of increased skill shortages, female unemployment has fallen less rapidly than men's unemployment. While male unemployment fell by three million in the period 1985–90, women's unemployment fell by less than a quarter of that figure. Moreover, as Hakim's study (1979) reveals, over the course of the whole of the 20th century, horizontal segregation has in some respects increased. The prospect that a man will work in an occupation in which men predominate has actually increased over this period. By 1970, 50% of men were employed in occupations where the male to female ratio was 4 to 1 or higher. If there has been a weakening of horizontal segregation it has been through the penetration of men into hitherto predominantly female occupations (Journung, 1984).

Dual system theory's treatment of the maintenance of vertical segregation is of special importance. This book's subjects are women who unsuccessfully attempted to enter an almost entirely male-dominated procession—management. Walby endorses Witz's account (1988) of "demarcational closure" as of great importance in the explanation of women's subordination (Walby, 1990, pp. 54–55). Witz (1992) provides sustained examples of both exclusionary and segregational strategies, tracing the means by which men have used gender and class to impose boundaries around these professions and especially to exclude middle-class women from participating in them. Witz focuses on medical professions (nurses, midwives, doctors, and radiographers) to illustrate male and female exclusionary tactics in the late 19th and early 20th centuries. The exclusionary closure strategy was employed initially to exclude women from medical schools, and then when they were admitted to medical practice to exclude them from certain high-status specialties, as well as from certain technologically demanding auxiliary professions. For example, radiographic technicians campaigned unsuccessfully for the exclusion of women.

Sylvia Walby (1990) draws three main conclusions from her study of capitalism and patriarchy in the economy:

1. The labor market is more important and the family less important as the determinant of women's labor force participation than is conventionally assumed. Family expectations may play a preponderant role in individual decisions, but they do not explain differential access to better jobs and family position cannot explain women's lower skills. Also, women, in fact, do not function as a reserve army absorbable by domestic production. More important is the segregated structure of the labor market, concentrating women in the lower-paid portions of the service sector. "The causal link between the labour market and family goes largely . . . in the reverse direction from that conventionally assumed; it goes from the labour market to family, not vice versa, when we ask questions about causation at a structural level" (Walby, 1990 p. 57). In contrast to Marxian approaches to explaining women's subordination in the labor market, this claim is the key idea of dual systems theory. Men control and exclude women from the labor market in order to maintain material power over them.

2. Women's lesser participation in paid work is a result of material constraints rather than a matter of "choice" or of cultural values. Women as a class leave the workforce because of agreements between employers and male-dominated unions or because marriage bars continuation in paid work. Individual decisions that appear to reflect deliberation obscure the "deeper question" of "what creates the structures that lead to these beliefs" (Walby, 1990, p. 58).

3. Politics and the state are much more important in the structuring of the sexual division of labor than is often recognized (Walby, 1990, p. 56). The state enforces practices within employment, both directly and indirectly, by limiting women's political power and regulating their work opportunities (Walby, 1990, pp. 50–51). The state can legislate rules on divorce and marriage, abortion, contraception, wage discrimination, rights of lesbians and gays, violence against women, and housing policies for single mothers, to name only a few examples.

All three of these observations are reflected in the case studies examined in this book. Family responsibilities did not impede the women's careers and terminations, women certainly did not choose to leave work, and the internal corporate politics and the governmental climate played a powerful role in their fates.

Walby (1990) notes that the most fundamental shift in patriarchal dominance over the last century has been from the private to the public sphere. The private sphere of patriarchy is that of the family, reproduction, domestic labor, and work in the family-based economy characteristic of agriculture and preindustrial society. Patriarchal structures allow for significant differences in the status of women within the family as a function of social class, confining middle-class women to the home and forcing lower-class women into public labor. Public patriarchy includes the labor market, the state, cultural institutions, and sexual control. These two spheres are also distinguished in two other ways: the predominance of exclusionary strategies in the private sphere and segregationalist ones in the public, and the shift of women from individual exploitation in the private sphere to collective in the public. Private patriarchy excludes women from the public sphere either wholly or partially. Public patriarchy offers access but only on terms of subordination. Private expropriation extracts labor from women individually in their domestic roles. Public expropriation operates through inequalities written into law or practice that exploit women as a class. The emergence of capitalism had a major impact in accelerating the shift in Western societies from private to the public patriarchy. The social distinction, however, predates the emergence of capitalist modes of production (Walby, 1990).

Sylvia Walby recognizes that patriarchies, both public and private, operate to varying degrees in differing societies and time periods. She traces the shift from private to public patriarchy across the six dimensions she identifies as crucial to an understanding of the subject. In wage labor there is a shift from exclusionary to segregational strategies, from the exclusion of women from paid employment to acceptance of women's presence subject to their confinement to segregated jobs at lower grades than those of men. In the 20th century the confinement of women to the domestic sphere lessened over just one lifetime and there was a shift in the main locus of control over reproduction. Major cultural institutions began to accept women, although they continued to subordinate them. The sexual control of a woman shifted from the husband to the public arena. Women were no longer excluded completely from sexual relations but continued to be subordinated within them. The state's exclusion of women was replaced by their subordination within it.

Women have entered the public sphere, but not on equal terms. They are now present in the paid workplace, the state and public cultural institutions. But they are subordinated within them. Further, their subordination, in the domestic division of labor, sexual practices, and as receivers of male violence, continues. (Walby, 1990, pp. 179–180)

Walby draws a further distinction within public patriarchy, between one founded on the labor market and one on the state as ways of bringing women into the public sphere. In the United States, Walby holds, the labor market is the predominant mechanism of socialization to the public patriarchy. In collectivized countries of Eastern Europe it was the state. Western European nations such as Britain fall between these extremes.

PATRIARCHY THEORY RECONSIDERED

Walby (1986, 1990) has certainly improved on classical patriarchy theory, developing its details and showing how the actual working out of patriarchal controls can explain many facts about workplace segregation characteristic of the modern economy. One problem with dual systems theory, however, is that despite its improvements in detail on the programmatic character of Millett's theory (1970) of patriarchy, and despite the specificity of its focus on the role of women in the modern economy, in the hands of Walby, at any rate, the theory remains too general and abstract. It is still too reliant on a Marxian account of capitalist control over women's wages as a separate but equal source of women's subordination. This is something that the analysis of particular sectors of the modern economy and distinctive levels of the modern corporate hierarchy may make manifest. One illustration of how such research has tested the claims of dual systems theory is to be found in Adkins' study (1995) of the U.K. tourism and leisure industry.

Adkins argues that dual systems theory's emphasis on economic control of women by men as the "material basis of patriarchy" prevents it from revealing the connection between work and income on the one hand and other forms of women's subordination on the other. "In particular neither Hartmann nor Walby consider the relations of sexuality to have a bearing upon the formation of the gender division of labour within the labour market itself" (Adkins, 1995, p. 27). As Adkins' analysis of the labor market in the tourism and leisure industries reveals, control of sexuality independent of wage and job access plays a direct role in the labor market. The idea that capitalism produces jobs and that patriarchy controls access to them turns out to be far too simple an account of the matter. Just to be workers, in the leisure industry, Adkins shows, women need to have an attractive appearance and to provide various levels of "sexual servicing," regardless of their occupations (Adkins, 1995, p. 147). This gendering of production "means that men occupy a structurally more powerful position in all these areas of employment, a position from which they can control and appropriate some of the products of the work of women" (p. 148). The upshot for Adkins is to view the labor market in this industry not as the interaction of capitalism and patriarchy, but as largely constituted by patriarchal forces (p. 150).

Adkins' case study is reflected in other broader criticisms of dual systems theory for failing to accord patriarchal forces the lion's share of responsibility for the subordination of women. Critics of dual systems theory have argued that the labor market is not in fact a capitalist construct, as Marxists have held and dual systems theorists have conceded. Rather both capitalism and its labor market are substantially shaped by patriarchal forces (Acker, 1990). Women cannot freely exchange labor for a wage in the way that men can, and the control of women's access to wages does not exhaust men's control of it. Besides determining who will be slotted into the employment hierarchy, patriarchy is also responsible for there being a hierarchy in the workplace. As Pateman (1988, p. 132) argues, women cannot be incorporated into the workplace in the same way as men because they are not free workers. Unsupported by a wife or other domestic female, "most women can find paid employment only in a narrow range of low-status, low paid occupations, where they work along side other women and are managed by men."

We might summarize the current state of theory in the treatment of women's subordination as something of a return to its starting place. Having been advanced, developed, criticized, supplanted, and combined with other theories, patriarchy theory has come again to center stage as an explanation. But patriarchy theory remains very much a work in progress. As critics have noted, patriarchy theorists lack an agreed-on source in prehistory for patriarchy and an agreed-on mechanism that ensures its persistence in contemporary society. Candidates for either of these roles have met with criticism for being biologically reductionistic or failing to recognize the variety of domestic arrangements that characterize ancient and modern societies.

A serious criticism of contemporary patriarchy theory focuses on the silence of patriarchy theory about how the norms that accord power to a hierarchy of males actually work to produce women's subordination. Patriarchy theory is unclear about whether patriarchal structures are the recognized, self-conscious strategies of individual men and women or the unnoticed impersonal operation of an autonomous structure (Hyman, 1990). Little of dual systems theory or pure patriarchy theory is the result of participant ethnography or qualitative sociology. Neither takes sides on the question of whether all, some, or none of the norms that structure sexist society are recognized by all, some, or none of its participants. Even studies like Adkins (1995), though industry specific and detailed in the patriarchal mechanisms they uncover, include little qualitative research that might shed light on these matters. So far as pure patriarchy theory is concerned, women's subordination may as well be the result of some combination of every permutation of these possibilities.

But it is just these questions that the theory needs to address if we are to assess the way in which the patriarchy actually operates, the mechanisms it uses, and the sanctions or rewards it uses to perpetuate itself. Only studies that will uncover the ways in which broad patriarchal forces act through individual lives and careers will uncover the degree to which men and women choose to act in accordance with the prescriptions of patriarchy. Pure patriarchy theory's silence on the matter of "agency" is a significant lacuna. There is some effort in the dual systems theory literature, and especially in traditional patriarchy theory, devoted to identifying the norms that give the meaning of gender categories, roles, and expectations in all the dimensions of human culture. But there is remarkably little in the literature about how these roles operate in determining the actions and behavior of individual men and women. To what extent are patriarchal structures the result of "agency"—the conscious choice of individual men and women—with alternatives? To what extent do agents—men and women—believe that their tactical or strategic choices, as opposed to the operation of a monolithic institution, contribute to the success or failure of their careers? To what extent do patriarchal structures operate through perhaps deceived or self-deceived individuals to fulfill some unrecognized social functions? When and how are they internalized in the socialization of men and women? Are they the sort of invisible constraints that can be broken down once they are recognized by agents? Do they cease to constrain or guide behavior once agents become conscious of them and decide no longer to implement them? Do participants in social processes recognize and act on other norms, ones that reflect the role of class—social or economic, race, asymmetries of power—along with those of gender? Only access to individual experience and its interpretation can shed light on these questions.

Failure to explore the ways patriarchal norms operate threatens to disconnect the theory from the actual experiences of men and women, which can provide crucial tests of its claims. Moreover, answers to questions like these are particularly important given the widespread goal of reducing or eliminating sexism in modern life. If both men and women are unconsciously and unwillingly in the grip of an autonomous social structure, with causes beyond the reach of human intervention, then the patriarchy may be immune to human intervention. If women's subordination is, like capitalism, the result of revisable attitudes, conscious constructions and conventions in the expectations of individual men and women, then understanding the operation of patriarchy and of capitalism will make the reduction of gender inequality a more attainable outcome. If, as one might expect, the truth is something between the invisible autonomy of the patriarchy and the transparent exercise of individual choice, we need to identify which of its components are open to deconstruction and which are not.

The case studies examined in this book should shed some light on which of these alternatives are to be found in the fate of successful senior women managers who lose their jobs. The subsequent chapters examine the degree to which these women experienced their work environments as patriarchal and how their responses to it operated together with this environment to affect their ultimate fates. In addition, the following chapters explore the meanings the women assigned to their workplace experiences and what work norms, if any, they identified in the actions of their co-workers and bosses.

Successful women managers who lose their jobs represent a crucial test case at the borderline of horizontal segregation in modern management. It is at the frontier between the almost entirely male hierarchy of management and the predominantly female support staff that men come face to face with women of largely the same class, race, education, and aspirations for leadership, responsibility, and reward. If there is a patriarchy in operation in modern management it is at this juncture that its operation would reveal itself in the experiences of women. When successful women managers lose their toeholds above the glass ceiling, their stories can tell us even more about the ways in which a patriarchy operates and what becomes of women who confront it.

CHAPTER 4

Profiles of the Women

◆◆

The women featured in this book, age 30 to mid-50s, held successively more challenging assignments as they moved up the career ladder. All were either in middle or senior management when they faced termination or resignation and all described their performance in terms such as "above the norm," "solid," "very good." Their work lives had been made intolerant by constant harassment. Several of the women faced bullying and eventual termination from more than one job. In two of the cases, the women were not technically fired or formally made redundant, but both women described themselves as being forced out. Of the ten women, one was Australian, eight were English, and one was an Afro-Caribbean, who was born in Jamaica and immigrated to the United Kingdom as a young girl. When they lost their jobs, nine were working in the United Kingdom; Caroline had held a senior-level position in Boston, Massachusetts, with an American company. Table 1 provides an overview of these women.

KATHERINE—MARKETING MANAGER

Katherine, age 33, described herself as a hard worker—someone who has to prove to herself and others that she is successful.

Katherine grew up in the London area and was encouraged by her parents to do well at school, take as many "A" level subjects as she could handle, and attend university. She excelled at university, graduating with honors in French and management studies. She decided to join the insurance industry because of the variety of career paths it afforded. A large

Table 1
Profiles of the Women

Name	Age	Race	Marital Status	Children	Highest Level of Education/Qualification	Job Title	Industry
Katherine	33	W	S	N	University Degree (B.S.)	Marketing Manager	Insurance
Diane	52	W	D	N	M.B.A., Certified Accountant	Finance Director	Food Manufacturing
Elizabeth	30	B	S	N	M.A.	Consultant/Trainer	Management Consultancy
Madge	54	W	M	N	A Levels	Director of Human Resources	Retail Clothing
Lesley	50	W	M	N	Ph.D.	Head of Engineering	Electronics
Patricia	39	W	M	Y	M.B.A.	Marketing Manager	Graphic Arts
Karen	41	W	S	N	University Degree (B.S.)	Total Quality Manager	Printing
Fiona	41	W	M	Y	M.B.A.	Manager/Management Development	Financial Services
Mary	45	W	S	N	M.B.A.	Director of Training	Manufacturing
Caroline	50	W	M	Y	M.A.	Senior Consultant	Management Consultancy

W, white; B, black
S, single; D, divorced; M, married
N, no; Y, yes

operation could provide opportunities in such areas as sales, operations management, training, administration, finance, and marketing. In addition, she had been offered a fast-track position as a graduate trainee with a large insurance firm that gave her an edge over other entry-level university graduates. She started as a life clerk administrator but quickly moved into sales, where she saw more opportunity for career progression. She was promoted to sales inspector, a position that gave her experience mediating on behalf of her company with barristers and solicitors. She was excited about the opportunity because she had the distinction of being the only female inspector in Britain at the time. Katherine remarked,

Sometimes being female opened doors for me because clearly men weren't used to seeing a girl on the job. I remember doing a garage survey. I'd be walking around trying to distinguish between a compressor and a high-speed drill. I didn't understand any of the technical machinery, but I managed just the same.

Katherine recalls having a novelty status; as a women inspector she wasn't a threat to men because the position was a dead end. Instead, she was a curiosity as men did not expect a woman to mediate claims. She knew that the sales inspector job would go nowhere because it was not on the management track, did not command a large budget, and was considered an administrative function not central to the strategic running of the business. Katherine used her sales inspector position as a springboard into marketing. Her next position within the firm was as a direct marketing manager, leading a project team in life assurance products. Within three months, Katherine was promoted to her boss's job when he left the company. While she felt invigorated by the new challenge of running a small brokerage, handling regulatory bodies, setting up compliance procedures, and hiring staff, she was annoyed that the salary increase she had been promised was not forthcoming.

Katherine's next opportunity came out of the blue. She was contacted by the head of human resources of a new London-based insurance company, a subsidiary of a large American company. The company wanted her to join as their marketing manager. She recalls why she decided to join,

My primary reason for leaving a quite secure position was the chance to work in a company that would expand into Europe. I also looked forward to working directly for John, the senior vice president of sales and marketing, and clearly a rising star.

Initially the culture at this new venture was nonhierarchical, open, and enjoyable. But as the company grew, people began jockeying for position. Katherine noticed that individuals began doing things for their own gain rather than operating in the spirit of team work to enhance the company's aims. A male marketing colleague seemed to have the ear of the senior vice president and soon was promoted to become Katherine's manager. Her relationship with this individual changed dramatically,

When Grant and I were colleagues, he valued my opinion and appreciated my playing the devil's advocate. He said it made him consider other perspectives. Once I began reporting to him, however, it upset him if I disagreed with him. I suppose he felt I was challenging his authority.

The advent of a hierarchy introduced a distancing of the senior management group from Katherine, which she found difficult. Often she went for weeks without seeing her boss and communicated important issues to him via memos. Although she was promised a strategic role in marketing in which she would be planning campaigns and deciding how financial resources would be deployed, Katherine found herself relegated to writing marketing copy, the company newsletter, and product prospectuses.

Throughout her career, Katherine has been conscious of her status as a woman and particularly how women lose out in hierarchical settings. In her sales position where there was very little hierarchy, she found working with men easy. Her novelty status was sometimes an advantage in what traditionally has been a male role. When she began to climb the career ladder in a more formal corporate setting, however, her perception changed. She found it difficult to work with men when the rules for success were not as clear-cut as monthly sales figures and percentage achievement over target. She described it this way,

There is a feeling that you have to work twice as hard as a man. The main issue with women is that we are very bad at marketing ourselves and playing the politics. I find the political issues at work extremely tiresome and can't be bothered with them. The risk of that attitude is that you end up on the outside. You realize that because you are turning your back on the issues, suddenly you aren't part of the inner circle of people who are making things happen. It's very hard because of the buddy-buddy system between men. Women tend just to get on with their work and they naively expect recognition and team work to come their way because of the hard work. If we don't play the politics, suddenly we don't fit in. We don't have contacts when we need them.

Katherine believed that women's misunderstanding of organizational dynamics contributes to their lack of success. Naively, they expect that following the explicitly stated values of an organization, such as cooperation and excellence, will reward them. However, women find that slavishly exhibiting these traits brings them neither recognition nor career advancement. They cannot find a method for breaking into a male system of entitlement. Katherine found the lack of women at senior levels and management positions in the insurance industry a major hindrance to her and other women's development. The absence of female mentors in a male-dominated culture meant that women were not "sponsored" up the organization. She reflected on the industry with the following comment, "Men in the industry found it difficult to relate to women in management, and women trying to succeed often are labeled as too aggressive or assertive."

In the end, Katherine described her redundancy as politically rather than economically motivated. She'd grown out of her job and become an irritant to her manager, who had no idea how to use her skills or declined to use them. The parts of marketing she was good at and had a track record in—the conceptualizing, planning, and organization of marketing—were the areas in which he wouldn't allow her to become involved.

DIANE—FINANCIAL DIRECTOR

Diane comes from what she describes as a traditional Northern England, conservative family. Her father had been a tax accountant and the family had moved around; by the time Diane was 13 she had been to eight schools and learned how to play the game of just doing enough to get by. Now in her early 50s, she reflects on what it was like growing up when daughters weren't expected to do very much.

My mother and father wanted me to have safe employment until I found the right man to marry. There was no encouragement to do law, politics, or medicine. My brothers were encouraged to do something serious with their brains. I was encouraged to learn secretarial skills.

Although her mother wanted her to do a secretarial course, Diane rebelled. More than anything, she wanted to get out of her home town and move to London to become a shop assistant—something she envisioned as a glamorous job.

After several shop floor jobs in retail clothing, the glamour wore off and Diane began looking for something more rewarding. Her cousin, an accountant, suggested that she interview with his firm. She joined as an administrative assistant, but was encouraged by several junior members of the firm to start studying for an accountancy credential.

One of the partners in the firm talked to my uncle and he said, "Don't worry it's only a passing fad. She won't stick with it." I was so angry. I thought, I'll show you. I'm not going to be treated like someone who can't do it. I always attribute getting into accountancy to my uncle. His patronizing, sexist attitude really spurred me on!

At age 20 Diane realized how difficult it was to study for her exams and live in London where there was constant temptation to socialize. Having passed two of the exams, she deliberately moved back to her home town so that she could concentrate on studying and passing her final two exams. After weeks of studying 25 to 30 hours a week, she passed her remaining two exams and began working for a local firm. After spending several months in her home town and shortly after marrying an accountant, she and her husband decided to move back to London in order to improve their job prospects.

Her first job in the London area after she was qualified was with a Richmond-based insurance firm. She recalls that the job was complex because the company was being taken over and the accounts had to be scrupulously prepared for the prospective buyer. Because there was too much work for one accountant, the managing director brought in another man to help. Diane recalls being angry that the managing director, with whom she had daily meetings, had not involved her in choosing her coworker nor had he told her that the accountant was joining the firm.

When he joined we were supposed to be colleagues. He began treating me as a subordinate right away and he fancied me. I didn't respond to his advances and that made him angry. People in the firm came to me first because they knew me and that made him angry too. I didn't like working with this person and at the age of 24 decided I could move on and work elsewhere. I didn't want to face a battle with the M.D. [managing director] or with him.

Diane quickly found another job as an accountant for a wealthy man who owned several businesses. At this time, she also left her husband and moved to Hampstead. Although the new job afforded Diane a sizable income, it was not challenging. After two years, Diane moved on to join a publishing company, part of the Maxwell empire, as its finance director.

The company had just had the DTI report.[1] There was me, six weeks into the job and on one side of the table was me and on the other side the three Coopers Lybrand auditors. I learned a lot about dealing with unions. The company was taken over and several hundred people were going to be laid off. I did all of the final salary payments and personally talked to people as I gave them their checks. I didn't want people with 35 years to just get an envelope and go.

Diane was laid off with everyone else. Her next position, at age 27, was chief accountant for a firm in the laboratory instrument field. It was a new challenge because Diane had never managed anyone and now she had a staff of 40. Diane recalled accepting the job on the condition that she would wear long skirts; she had unwittingly worn a trouser suit to the first interview. In her early days in the job she clashed with the finance director, who wanted her to quickly produce accounts for each department.

I told him the accounts would not be worth the paper they were printed on. I suggested that the department heads had to sort out the underlying numbers first. I worked with the department heads first and then produced the accounts. At first this made my boss angry. Then he began to appreciate that I had been right.

In the four years that Diane was with this company, she eliminated the entire accounts backlog, produced accounts for a business that her company took over, and introduced new computer systems. She began to want a bigger job with a larger company where she could use her computer knowledge.

Diane found a position in a large group as a systems analyst and spent two years learning about computers and programming. She came to understand the significance of controlling information,

I realised that systems are really important in organizations. By controlling systems you control the organization. I soon realized that I had lots of power because I knew where information was. Women are rarely systems analysts and I had this feeling that I had never had before about holding the cards. People had to come to me to understand the system. I could give or withhold the information. I didn't use the power as much as I could have but now I am aware that I had lots of it.

Diane came to realize a phenomenon that has been written about in the literature of patriarchy: technological jobs are gendered—men hold jobs of authority and real power such as systems analyst and programmer while women hold clerical and computer operator positions (Wajcman, 1991; Kirkup, 1992; Banks and Ackerman, 1990; Cockburn, 1983).

For a period of time, Diane did all of the long-range planning for the organization. Then a new finance director, who wanted to decentralize all of the planning, was recruited. The organization would have kept her on in a project capacity without management responsibilities or budget authority, but she felt this was not why she had joined the company. Diane's next position was as a financial controller for a wine manufacturer. Again she had a staff of 40, still more computerization, and a costing function. She analyzed and determined which functions needed more money to perform effectively and which needed less.

I began to realise I had problems in this job because I behaved in a non-female way. The M.D. [managing director] would say "Diane is a very good technical accountant, but . . ." It was as if to say there are problems with me as a person. I am assertive, strident, I want to get somewhere. Those sort of things for a woman are not seen as being a team player.

At the beginning of this job, Diane had been promised that after a proving period she would be promoted to chief accountant. She had done everything that had been asked of her but the promotion never materialized. She was always told to be patient. After several months of delays, she decided either the managing director had never intended to promote her or he felt uncomfortable with her assertive style. At age 38 she moved on to finance director of a large retail group, a publicly held company. She discovered that the board had sacked the former finance director and the accounts were badly organized. In order to sort out the problems, she would require additional staff and a budget. The managing director refused to give her the requested resources. As she examined the accounts she uncovered that three of the directors had been defrauding the accounts; one had been her predecessor and the other two were still employed. Assuming that the managing director would be pleased with her thoroughness, she immediately informed him.

The M.D. didn't like it that I had uncovered the fraud. He either felt like he'd been conned and was embarrassed or perhaps he was guilty of little transgressions himself. The company was being taken over and they found that an excuse to get rid of me.

Diane's next and final job in accountancy was as finance director for a food company in Northern England. She had decided to leave the London area to be nearer her father, who had recently lost her mother. During this time, she tried to advise the directors about acquisitions since, by this time, she had several experiences with the accountancy side of acquisitions. She found herself excluded from decision making and information, and was told to "just stick to the accounts and not intrude into strategic decisions." While working for this company, Diane began taking courses toward an MBA degree.

Diane was fired by the company after 23 months and 2 weeks, just two weeks short of the statutory requirement for employment protection. At this point she left the private sector and joined Hull University as a lecturer in business studies.

The change was a welcome one. She reflected on the differences between her past and the present,

For once, I don't have to be on my best behaviour, not be too assertive or too emotional. I don't have to be grateful to be a Director and I don't have to walk on egg shells to say something that I believe is right. I can just be myself.

Perhaps Diane, more than the other women in the study, encountered the double-bind of being a woman in the senior management ranks. As Powell (1993) suggests, at her level she was supposed to exhibit masculine traits of decision making and risk taking, but as White, Cox, and Cooper (1992) discovered, she would be criticized for being assertive and overly masculine. This phenomenon was pronounced because she was a woman operating in what is traditionally accepted as the male-only domain of accountancy.

ELIZABETH—MANAGEMENT CONSULTANT AND TRAINER

Elizabeth, age 30, was a full-time staff employee of a large consultancy group, which works with companies across the United Kingdom in the areas of equal opportunities, employment law, survey research, and management and staff training. After ending her relationship with the consultancy, she agreed to discuss her career history and her abrupt resignation from the consultancy firm. As a black woman, she felt that race as well as gender had affected her career trajectory. Elizabeth grew up in East London and left school at age 17 to take a secretarial course. Her mother did not expect her to go to university but did insist that she obtain some practical skills. She attended secretarial school for a year and recalls thinking that even then she had not aspired to do secretarial work. She did, however, enjoy the word processing and computer parts of the course. After several temporary jobs in word processing, she wanted to look for something with better career prospects.

Elizabeth's first permanent position was as a clerical assistant for a local authority in the London borough of Newham. Initially she did mundane tasks such as typing bank receipts and processing checks. But soon Elizabeth gained a reputation for having excellent computer skills. She was approached by East Ham College, part of the local authority, to teach classes in word processing and business studies. While she taught, she decided to get a teaching credential in adult education and further education—an endeavor that took her two years in the evenings and on weekends.

Seeking more interesting work, Elizabeth left the college and went to work in housing as a fair rents assistant. When her department manager left, she managed the fair rents department for six months. Although she had trained two people and managed the department, she was not allowed to apply for the vacancy created by the department manager's departure. After she filed a grievance over this issue with her employer, Elizabeth was finally given a job as a fair rents officer with the authority. However, she became victimized in a variety of ways by the director of housing, who, she said, was "going to teach me a lesson for filing the grievance." Not able to withstand the director's systematic harassment, she decided to leave the department. As part of her housing training, she had taken an outdoor leadership course offered by a London-based consultancy group. She had kept in contact with this group and approached them for work. Working first in a women's research and training unit, she was hired as a race coordinator. When this unit disbanded, Elizabeth was moved to a trainee consultant position and finally was promoted to a consultant position responsible for affirmative action, communication skills, and management training for a portion of the London metropolitan area. Despite being the highest fee earner in a team of 20 consultants, she found that her manager bullied her constantly.

I found that as I challenged his judgment or when I asked questions, he found fault with trivial things and gave me unnecessary paperwork to do. He denied me training that others were getting, told me I needed to follow his orders because he was my boss, and ignored the good work I produced with clients. In the end, I filed a grievance against him.

Racial prejudice seemed to combine with gender issues in Elizabeth's case. Her manager openly described her as "a strong black woman who wanted to get her way" and on several occasions told her that because she hadn't come up in the traditional way with a first class degree from a first class university, she'd "better watch [her] step." On one occasion after watching her make a proposal to clients, he remarked that he hadn't expected her to be as good as she was in front of clients. This was surprising to Elizabeth because he knew she was the top income earner in the team and had many clients who were extremely loyal to her.

Although Elizabeth's grievance procedure resulted in a favorable decision for her, there was no punishment for her manager and no monitoring of his behavior. Even though Elizabeth's manager was told to change his behavior and work more constructively with her, nothing changed. A month after the grievance proceedings, Elizabeth felt she had no option but to leave. She now works as an independent consultant in equal opportunities, supervisory, and management training for a variety of companies in the London area.

MADGE—HUMAN RESOURCES DIRECTOR

Although Madge always wanted a university education and a career in law, she was forced into early employment by her father's death. Unable to manage on her own financially, her mother needed Madge's help with the household finances. Her two brothers also contributed a portion of their income to their mother, whom Madge described as "really poor—without any resources of her own." Madge decided to pursue a career in personnel management and in the early days of her career changed jobs every two years to increase her career prospects. After 15 years of experience for large companies, she decided to move to smaller companies where she felt she could make a greater contribution.

I realised what I liked to do most was building and developing things so that I could feel that the organisation had moved forward and begun to do things in an innovative way as far as people were concerned because of me.

The first small company she worked for, an electronics firm, had no personnel systems. She had inherited the personnel function from an elderly man who simply administered the payroll. She introduced several new systems including appraisals, medical, and death-in-service benefits and developed formal communication channels. Seeing an advertisement for a similar job at board level with higher pay, Madge applied. This organization was a family-owned business managed by the mother. Madge recalled how this woman influenced the business:

She recognised people with skills and rewarded them. When I was appointed to the board, I was paid the same as the male directors and accorded the same respect. Her sons had to prove themselves like every other employee.

Although very comfortable in this family business, Madge felt the urge to move on to something better. She applied for another position, again as a personnel director with board-level status in a larger company, a multi-site manufacturing company. Madge instituted many personnel practices such as performance appraisal systems, health and safety training, client service functions, standard recruitment procedures for site staff and for site managers, standards and fair procedures for promotion, and a bonus scheme for high performers. Her dismissal by this employer came when she filed a grievance over equal pay for equivalent work. Madge had been repeatedly threatened for bringing the grievance forward, even though she had waited out a period of two years in which the managing director had promised to improve her pay to an equitable status with her male co-directors. The more she insisted on fair treatment, the more her fellow directors systematically excluded her, bullied her, and demeaned her work. Eventually, with the assistance of a solicitor and the Equal Opportunities Commission, Madge took her case to a tribunal and received a record award. Madge, now in her mid-50s, is engaged in volunteer work for senior citizens.

Throughout the many stressful months working and her legal battle, Madge was encouraged and supported emotionally by her husband. He encouraged her to do what she felt was right.

LESLEY—HEAD OF AN ENGINEERING DIVISION

An Australian, Lesley attended Adelaide University, majoring in physics. After her first degree she decided she enjoyed the sciences and wanted to pursue a PhD in physics experimenting in rocketry. She spent nine years conducting a series of experiments on ten different rockets and also during this time published two scientific papers in addition to her thesis.

At the time in Australia, you literally had to build your own rockets from scratch to be able to conduct your research. If the rockets didn't work the way you expected them to, you had to start all over again.

Lesley married a fellow graduate student who was involved in studying rockets as well. After she and her husband finished their PhDs, they were both recruited by GEC in the airborne early warning aircraft division. She became an expert in systems engineering, dealing with navigation and electronic surveillance. Lesley also learned to manage other engineers. After spending six years at GEC, the engineering project on which she worked was canceled, resulting in redundancy for a division of 1,000 staff. However, she quickly found another position as a systems engineering manager for an electronics company, a U.K. subsidiary of a large U.S. electronics group. In her position as a systems manager she went from managing 2 staff to 11 systems engineers, all male. Lesley described her philosophy of management as profoundly simple,

The best authority you can have is that which other people concede to you without you asking for it. The other type is just not worth worrying about because people can easily get around you. If you impose authority people begin to resent you and do things behind your back.

She found the first big project her team had to undertake very difficult to understand. She became mired in the detail, until finally she decided to forgo her need to have total understanding and instead simply ask people to get on with their assignments. "I suddenly realised I didn't need to get my head around it. I needed to organise it and trust other people to understand their pieces of it."

When Lesley's team came to the end of this project, she was beginning to feel bored. The company's managing director asked her to take charge of a large project engineering group, at a 50% pay increase directing 250 engineers. After accepting the offer, Lesley realized that the group was demoralized because the group's former head had spent all of his time absorbed with subcontractors instead of working with his staff. Lesley spent time getting to know her staff and their skills so that she could get the most out of them.

I feel I have a very female way of management that isn't soft but that lets staff know that I value them, that I want integrity in the function, and that if they aren't pulling their weight I'll let them know straight but in a caring way.

Lesley felt that she created a good team largely because she allowed herself to be convinced to another point of view. "I don't have an ego thing that says I have to be right. I think that earned me respect. I often said I was wrong and we went down a course of action that was not my original plan." She had to teach some of her engineers, particularly those with military backgrounds, not to expect to take orders from her. Rather she insisted that they disagree with her if they felt she was pursuing the wrong course of action. "I hired these people for their critical thinking skills. Not to be yes men. I found my leadership style worked, but that it was atypical of the style of my male colleagues."

During her tenure as the head of engineering, her group was awarded the ISO 9000 quality award[2] and she reduced overhead by 15% and gave her managers total responsibility for costing projects, establishing quality standards, and determining overall project design.

Lesley's redundancy emerged as a result of her repeatedly challenging the vice president of the parent company about how to reengineer her area. Because she knew her people, she knew who should stay to be retrained as software engineers and who the company needed to let go. She did not challenge that a certain number of employees had to be made redundant as a matter of business exigency. However, she believed it inappropriate for the vice president to decide which of her people should go or stay, especially because he knew none of them and worked in another country. Lesley recognized that she was stubborn and outspoken with this individual, whom she hardly knew, "I can remember now that he was frustrated with me and probably I was in transit mode rather than listening mode." In spite of this self-reflection, she said she would have had a difficult time handling the situation differently. "I don't regret it. I would do it again because I created an engineering division that had morale and was doing really great work so I don't regret it at all." Her U.K. managing director would not support her in the face of pressure from his boss, the vice president of the parent company. Lesley felt that he had been supportive up to the point of the company reengineering exercise, but had no choice given the fact that he had a family to support and a mortgage to pay. In the end, she was called into the managing director's office and told that "it wasn't working out."

PATRICIA—MARKETING MANAGER

Patricia, age 39, is married, has two young children, and currently has given up corporate life to help her husband in his business and to spend more time with her family. She was encouraged to study and achieve by her parents. Her father urged her to meet the challenge of bigger jobs should they present themselves. Until her redundancy, Patricia had climbed the career ladder in marketing.

Patricia read modern languages- French and Italian—at the University of Lancaster from 1975–79. Although she loved languages and had a facility for them, Patricia felt that to secure a good job she would need an advanced degree in a business subject. Consequently, she began a postgraduate course in international marketing at the former North Staffordshire Polytechnic. After completing the degree, she joined Unipart, a division of British Leyland, as a graduate trainee in international marketing. In her two years with Unipart, she was treated as a young talent on the fast track and was given interesting assignments, exposing her to many aspects of marketing. From 1982–84, Patricia worked with a pharmaceutical company, learning about traditional U.K. marketing practices and brand management. As group product manager, she managed the marketing budget, designed advertising campaigns, and conducted marketing promotions for the company.

In her third position, Patricia was in the Manchester area with the Co-operative Wholesale Society, again undertaking brand management in the pharmaceutical arena. However, the cooperative structure of the business was too conservative an environment; she found herself unable to make commercial decisions or to compete with the larger rivals such as Sainsbury's. In 1985, Patricia married and moved to Hull. She worked for three years at another pharmaceutical company as a senior products manager, managing all of the company's major product launches. The position was a greater challenge than she had previously had; it included two professional staff and a very large budget. When she fell out with her department head over his hiring a girlfriend for all of their advertising, she decided to leave.

It was in hindsight unwise to object. I did feel it should have been my decision about which supplier to use and I did not believe in this kind of favouritism—she wasn't the best candidate. I also thought it was a misuse of his position.

Patricia considered her next position as the marketing manager for a graphics company a promotion because she was hired to develop the marketing strategy across all four major divisions of the company. She was to work with the four division sales managers, all men, and her four professional staff to execute the marketing strategy. During the three years she spent in this job, she completed an MBA degree at the Open University.

Patricia believes her redundancy was caused by two factors: a charge of sexual harassment that she made against one of the sales directors and her trying to exercise real power in the job when she had been accorded none. For several months, she had argued that the marketing budget should rest with her and not the sales directors. She continued to lock horns with the sales directors. Although Patricia was marketing manager, the directors wanted to make all of the marketing decisions without consulting Patricia: to determine how money was being spent, what marketing literature went out to customers, and how promotional campaigns were structured.

I went to the managing director on several occasions to complain, saying that this company had hired me to run the marketing for the divisions and to set the strategic direction of marketing. He told me I needed to consider the needs of the sales directors. In effect what he was saying is you don't have any say. You need to defer to them.

The official reason given for Patricia's redundancy was that her position was being restructured into a larger one. When asked if she could apply for this role, she was told "no, you're not the right type of person for the role." Ironically, the job was given to one of the sales directors who had no marketing experience.

KAREN—TOTAL QUALITY MANAGER

Karen, age 41, attended Salford College initially to study home economics. After studying this subject for a time, she concluded that home economics could label her a domestic servant for life or at least as someone who was very traditional. She saw herself as an independent thinker; someone who did not take the traditional route. During the home economics course, she was exposed to psychology and decided she preferred the study of human nature to that of domestic science. She quickly opted out of her course to try for a university place in psychology.

Unusual for the time, Karen entered university without exam results by convincing the interviewer that they should take her because she would work hard, loved psychology, and would not disappoint them academically. She was uncomfortable about entering the institution with only two A levels, neither of which were in psychology. Although not a requirement, she decided to take her A level in psychology during her first year at university. Studying in the evenings, she passed it after a year.

During her university years, Karen decided she would enjoy working in personnel. After attending a job fair, she was invited for an interview with British Steel. She felt fortunate because British Steel had decided to positively discriminate in favor of women in their recruitment practices. She and another woman were hired into the industrial engineering department. She recalls what it was like being the minority in a heavily male-dominated industry.

I remember we were the only two women in the department. It was a manufacturing company—all the men in the department had come up through the shop floor. It was a very male environment and very tough for women, especially for educated women. Remember it was 1977. To hold your own in the department you had to be like they were. Shock tactics were about the only thing that worked. The things that happened would be considered sexual harassment these days.

Karen recalls holding her own by telling dirty jokes and acting as if nothing any man might say would bother her. As a university student, Karen was chairperson of the Equal Opportunity Society. At university, there was considerable interest and support for equal opportunities. Once employed in the engineering field, Karen came to realize there was little consciousness of issues and little support for equal opportunities practice. Repeatedly she encountered inappropriate, demeaning, and denigrating treatment on the shop floor and in management. It was ironic that now she was subjected to male culture where redress of gender inequalities was not easy because it was hard to enforce without backing from management.

In particular, Karen felt stifled by her immediate manager who would not let her grow in the job.

I had to go down to the shop floor to do time studies which then involved negotiations with the unions to change something. He would never let me go to the unions to present our case. Even though I knew the research backwards and forwards, he would always present it.

Because Karen joined the company with another woman who had the same job as she did, the woman became a direct comparison on equality-related issues. Her colleague was given more autonomy and had been allowed to present time and motion findings to the unions. Unable to deal with this unequal treatment, Karen decided to complain. Over a period of time, she drew attention to her manager's behavior. Unfortunately, the director was not prepared to transfer Karen out of her section to another one. After 18 months, Karen decided to leave.

The next job Karen applied for, value engineer, seemed to be a golden opportunity to her. Not only would she be able to use the skills that she had developed at British Steel to help reduce costs and improve product performance at a much smaller company, but working for a smaller company and reporting to the managing director would give her the visibility she needed to progress up the career ladder. As a value engineer, however, Karen required further training. The managing director agreed to send her to Cranfield Management School for several weeks. As at British Steel, the new position involved working on the shop floor in an all-male environment, looking for ways to reduce inefficiencies and improve product quality. Karen was very conscious of the way she would be perceived by others. She worried that they might view her as an informant, reporting to the managing director on individuals who were either negligent or inefficient. The focus, however, was on improving the product without punishing people for their mistakes and she felt comforted by the fact that no one would lose his or her job because of her recommendations.

Karen found her work relationships with men intriguing. Although she had a good deal of power to change their work practices, the men did not seem to acknowledge it.

They told me quite damning things, assuming, I suppose, that I wouldn't do anything with the information. They thought I wouldn't be as hard as a man; they thought I wouldn't make any changes or any significant decisions.

The managing director who hired Karen was fired, leaving her vulnerable to the same fate. Several employees who had been closely associated with him or with his ideas began to leave. Seeing the handwriting on the wall, Karen decided to look for another job, but within the same company. Because she had been working in the same office as the production engineers, worked closely with them, and had learned about their role, she approached the production engineering manager about a position. He agreed to transfer her from her former post to the production engineering team, an all-male team. In spite of her enthusiasm, her new colleagues in production engineering did not welcome her with open arms. She was earning more money than any of them without qualifications previously deemed prerequisite for the job. The resulting atmosphere of conflict and animosity soon got the best of her. Karen decided to look elsewhere for a job. She sought to change her environment from the cutthroat business world to what she hoped would be a more cooperative, educational environment so she applied to a university business studies department. She thought that sharing what she had learned with students and immersing herself in a subject she liked would be refreshing changes from the shop floor. The illusions Karen harbored about the idyllic environment were shattered in her first week on the job. Once again she found herself the only woman in the department. Instead of a harmonious unit, the department was rife with politics. As the most junior person in the department, Karen found herself relegated to the most unpopular courses.

After five years of working for the college and many hundreds of hours of teaching undesirable courses, Karen felt she was due a promotion. In this environment, however, promotion was not possible unless someone died, retired, or moved to a better job. Therefore, she began applying for jobs at other academic institutions. Karen found that consistently she was reaching only the second interview. Eventually one prospective employer told her why. Her department head had been giving her an unfavorable reference because of her role in the territorial army. He had written, "Karen attended camp for the territorial army in the *pertinent* [emphasis added] term of the year." Karen believed that the comment was damning since it suggested that she had shirked her responsibilities during a crucial term. When she spoke to the department head, he agreed to change the reference and this appeared to solve the problem; she was hired for a post in South Devon as a lecturer on business studies (human relations and management) to catering students.

In the late 1980s, Karen decided she wanted to return to industry. She began looking for personnel management positions, but found it impossible to break into the field. Without specific personnel experience, she couldn't compete with people who had experience and formal qualifications like a diploma from the Institute of Personnel Management. Total quality management was coming into vogue. Instead of personnel management, Karen applied for a job as a total quality manager with a medium-size printing firm employing about 400 people. After interviews with the personnel director and the operations manager she was hired. Once integrated into the company, Karen realized that again she was the only woman in the senior management ranks in a company that predominantly employed men. She wondered if the personnel director had deliberately tried to bring women into the organization to try to look progressive.

As Karen began to make more demands on the organization for the change and quality improvements that she was hired to design, her relationship with her manager began to deteriorate. She was asked to consider taking another job within the organization; she and her manager agreed on the job content and approximate salary. When eventually he attempted to renegotiate the terms with her for a lesser role and salary than they had agreed, she expressed dissatisfaction with the position and rejected it. After a few weeks, she was called in to his office and told that the company no longer needed her.

FIONA—MANAGER, SALES MANAGEMENT DEVELOPMENT

Fiona, age 41, has two children (Alicia, 8 years old, and Matthew, 5). Her house has all of the signs of children's active lives: scout notices on the refrigerator, toys in the living room, and school notices posted on bulletin boards. Fiona grew up in South London and was educated at independent schools during her secondary years. She recalled influences she felt in her teenage years and early 20s,

I am the youngest of three. My older sister became a G.P. [general practitioner] and my brother is a solicitor. My father is retired now but he was a surgeon. My mother, although she is bright and capable, didn't work while we were growing up. There was also the expectation of achievement in our family although no one ever talked about it. I remember choosing economics because it was a nontraditional subject for women and I was good at maths. At the time, I thought a degree in economics would give me more opportunity than a teaching or nursing qualification.

After graduating from the London School of Economics and Political Science, Fiona took a job as a graduate trainee with one of the large banks. She did a variety of jobs during her trainee experience including stints in the marketing, client services, and accounts departments. Fiona settled in the accounts department as a supervisor of six accounts clerks. Finding the job repetitive and lacking challenge, she began looking around the bank for other positions for which she could apply. At the time the bank was not expanding and there were no positions available in the management grades. She decided to leave the bank to pursue an MBA degree at Warwick University.

The M.B.A. would probably take me two years. I thought I'd be better positioned to come into an organisation at a higher level and I thought the degree would be interesting. I was bored at the bank and needed some intellectual stimulation.

After completing her MBA, Fiona began applying to financial institutions—investment houses, banks, and insurance companies. Taking a job in a financial institution, she was hired as a regional manager of a small team charged with training field managers on new products. She reported to a manager to whom four regional managers reported. During this period, she married Steve whom she met at Warwick. Alicia, Fiona's first child, was born a year later and Fiona took four months off to care for her daughter. She liked her job because of the interaction she had with people, the variety it afforded, and because of her opportunity to travel.

After four years as a regional manager an opportunity arose to apply for her manager's position when he decided to leave the organization for a better position. All of Fiona's regional manager colleagues also applied for the job, but Fiona was selected.

The job was interesting at first because I had to plan all of the product training for the whole country. I worked closely with the marketing director and other senior managers and I had to manage managers who were bright and sometimes demanding. The disappointing part was I began to lose face to face contact with the field managers since I had to work through my team.

During her time in this position, Fiona became pregnant again. After the baby was born, she took three months off. She came back to work with the same company in a different job. She needed a less demanding role in terms of hours but still wanted stimulating work. Taking a new position reporting to the head of human resources as manager of employee communications and head office development, she was able to negotiate a part-time commitment, three days a week, at a manager grade without staff responsibilities. "I had to build programmes from scratch—compensation and bonus schemes, the company newsletter, quality improvement programmes and training for head office staff."

At first the job was satisfactory because Fiona had two days a week with her children. Gradually, however, the amount of work she was being asked to do increased to the point where the job had become in effect full-time.

For several months I worked 45 hours a week, although some of that time was at home. I realised I was being exploited—getting paid for three days when really working five days. I went to my boss and said that really this wasn't working out. If all the work had to be done I was not prepared to get paid on a three-day contract. He said it all had to get done. I asked about job sharing and he said he really needed the consistency of one person and thought I was doing excellent work. In the end, I asked to be put on full-time. At least, I thought, I'd be paid for what I was actually doing.

During this time, Fiona made a conscious decision to work very hard. The organization was expanding via acquisitions of smaller banks. She frequently talked to her manager about job opportunities and what she might do to further her career. She wanted to be in a position where she would be viewed as someone who could take additional responsibilities. She had been thinking about what the organization needed and decided to approach her manager and the sales director about an idea she had to create a formal assessment process for promoting sales managers. In her view, these managers were wrongly promoted on the basis of their sales ability rather than their management skills. The company had had some recent failures in promotional decisions made on this basis and because it was expanding dramatically the right people needed to be placed in sales management jobs.

By the end of the discussion, Fiona was asked to put her ideas in writing to both her manager and the sales director. She highlighted the structure of a management development process for field managers and then described an assessment and selection process to ensure that the right sales managers were promoted into sales management positions. At the time, the head of training provided a minimal program for sales management that sales managers took after they were promoted to management. Fiona was asked to take on a new position as manager of sales management development and began designing and implementing her programs. The move was a lateral one, but Fiona felt it was an opportunity to prove herself by creating new programs. She was once again managing people as she hired two assistants to help her deliver the assessment and training programs. Her new manager was the head of training who reported to the sales director. The resulting position rapidly grew in responsibility and influence; for example, Fiona was soon managing five professional staff plus a secretary and her budget had increased significantly.

Fiona's redundancy came as a result of pushing for a fairer job evaluation to a higher level. She appealed a decision made by the job evaluation committee, a group of senior male managers. To prevent her from moving up, her manager claimed that he had been far more involved in decision making for her role and in overall supervision of her than he actually had been.

In the end I made things difficult for them and for my boss whom I expected to support my appeal as he knew the work I had been doing. I met with him once a week to simply keep him informed about the work I had been doing. He had no involvement in designing or developing the systems I had put into place. They clearly didn't expect an appeal and didn't want to promote me to the level that I should have been at given their criteria. In the end, they said the position was no longer required and that my boss could manage the programmes that I had put in place. They ended up hiring someone more junior to manage the two staff I had and to maintain the programmes that I started. The one thing I learned from the whole experience is that organisations are not meritocracies. I had worked very hard and received excellent performance reviews but in the end they did not want to make me a department head where I would be dealing at the senior manager level and sharing in the big financial rewards.

Like Lesley's boss, Fiona's manager had been supportive up to the point of her difficulties with senior management. Fiona felt that before the job evaluation process she and her manager had enjoyed a good working relationship. Similar to Lesley's boss, Fiona's manager had decided to back senior management rather than perhaps putting his own career at risk.

Fiona has left the financial services industry to set up her own business in providing training and development opportunities for managers of small- and medium-size organizations. Ironically, she said,

I now seem to be able to influence in the same kind of organisations that I used to work in. Senior managers can't place me within the hierarchy. On the outside, I can't threaten the hierarchy.

MARY—DIRECTOR OF TRAINING

Mary, age 45, attended university from 1970–74, gaining a Bachelor's degree in social science and history and a teaching credential. She taught secondary school in the London area for one year after graduating but, deciding the disciplinary issues were overwhelming and interfering with her teaching the subjects she loved, she left. For the next two years, she pursued an MBA degree in the United States at a large university in the Midwest.

I thought I could do anything. I did very well in school and was encouraged by my lecturers and my parents to go for the best jobs I could. I also had role models in my older brothers, one was an accountant and the other a solicitor.

Operations management and human resource issues captured her attention more than anything else so she decided to specialize in them. After receiving her MBA, she returned to England to look for employment. She was hired as a manufacturing supervisor, a job which she did for two years. Then she was promoted to an operations manager, supervising 20 staff. In 1982, she interviewed and was hired with a multinational company with a large U.K. operation as their manager of client operations. The position was exciting because the parent company was investing a great deal of attention in managing clients by giving them better service and Mary was given a great deal of scope to make long-needed changes.

I hired people in all of the sales offices that could assist sales staff in resolving client complaints. This way the clients got immediate attention whether or not the salesmen (they were all men) were out on a call or not. I also revamped the computer systems and the databases which weren't giving us flexibility in dealing with client records. I started conducting client focus groups as a routine and we brought down client complaints dramatically which in the end improved sales.

After being in the client operations job for seven years and not moving up the career ladder, she decided to seek another position. "I remember thinking that I needed to make a move before I turned forty or no one would look at me despite experience or qualifications."

The next position for which Mary applied was the head of training with another large manufacturing company based in Birmingham. The position carried substantial responsibility: all the health and safety training, sales training, technical training, and management training. Mary had seven direct subordinates and a department of 50 people working in various sites across the United Kingdom.

The job was exciting at first. I was told I was hired because I had made improvements in other jobs I had held. Soon things became difficult, though. I was never given equal status with my male colleagues. When I tried to get things done I had to go through a million people for approval which was uncalled for as a head of function, and I was systematically squeezed out of decisions that affected my area. Many times there wasn't even dialogue, I was told to do something that affected my people.

Mary objected to the treatment she received and found that the more she voiced her opinion the more hostile the environment became. In the end, her job was given to another woman who assumed the role without any training and development experience. Mary was told she could remain at the same salary but she would have to report to this individual who had taken her job and would now serve as a member of the team she had managed for more than five years. Because she had above-average performance reviews for several years running and had received an ex-gratia bonus payment for outstanding performance only a few months before the organization displaced her, she felt more than justified in filing a grievance. Not only was she told by the personnel manager, to whom her new manager reported, that she could not apply for this position, he also said she "should just get on with [her] new role and not make a scene." Mary insisted on having the grievance heard by someone other than the personnel director or her new manager. Within a month and before the grievance was heard, the personnel director asked her to take redundancy, saying, "I'm afraid this isn't working out. We haven't been happy with your performance of late and would advise you to take redundancy rather than go through a disciplinary procedure."

Up until the day she left, Mary endured bullying from the personnel director, unfair work assignments from her new manager, and routine intimidation. She hired a solicitor, secured union support, and eventually settled her case out of court. At present, Mary is unemployed and seeking a position as head of training for another company.

CAROLINE—MANAGEMENT CONSULTANT

Caroline, age 50, grew up in the town of Halifax in Yorkshire, England. Because her mother left her father when Caroline was only ten years old, she learned to be independent at a very early age. She remembers that she had to take care of herself emotionally and she had to take care of her father by doing many of the chores that her mother would have done. Feeling that education was important and not knowing exactly how to raise a daughter by himself, Caroline's father eventually sent her to a convent school. Caroline grew up with the idea that one had to overcome adversity because one never knew what cards one would be dealt in life. She also learned how to make the best of opportunities and as such was never afraid to move on to try something different. Married in her early 20s, Caroline had two children. Both are now grown, one with his own family.

After completing a Bachelor of Science degree in management and psychology, Caroline accepted a job developing and conducting training for about 1,300 government employees. These employees required training in operations management, budgeting, employment law, forecasting techniques, and basic management. After two years, Caroline was promoted to regional operations manager for another division of government. During this period, she completed a diploma in adult education and divorced her husband, raising her two children alone.

After six years as regional operations manager, she wanted a change from the bureaucracy of government. She was chosen for a job in sales and marketing with the University of Southwest England in Plymouth. While developing the university's marketing strategy and organizing public relations events, she pursued a Master of Arts degree in industrial relations at Keele University in Staffordshire. The degree gave her greater confidence and the motivation to seek a still more challenging job, as lecturer and then principal lecturer at Luton University. For the next six years, she taught management development courses to undergraduates and graduate students, supervised student research, and worked as a consultant through the university's management center. Moreover, she became the account manager for a management development program with General Motors, a highly competitive contract that she won for the university.

Although her position with the university was challenging and afforded Caroline a degree of status, it lacked adequate financial rewards. She decided to transfer her management skills to the private sector and began looking for an appropriate corporate position. Caroline accepted a position with a London-based insurance company as a management consultant. She worked with all of the company's managers, providing them with training in financial management, change management, and sales management. During this time, she met and married Anthony, a mature student at Oxford's Ruskin College. Shortly after their marriage and while Caroline was working for the insurance company, Anthony was admitted to a PhD program at a university in the Eastern United States.

The strain of trying to maintain a long-distance relationship and working 65 hours a week led Caroline to seek a position in the United States. After six months of scouring the papers and meeting with recruiters, she was offered a job with a small human resource consultancy group called Systems, Inc., in Boston, Massachusetts. The firm was an American one, owned and run by Jim, the president, and three male partners. The job offer as a senior consultant was extremely attractive; Caroline's starting salary was $100,000 and she would achieve partner status within two years. She recalls negotiating hardest for the partner status because it meant that, along with three other men, she would own an equal share in the company and as such would have decision-making power, financial rewards, and voting rights equal to that of her male colleagues.

After about a year with the organization, the owner and his three partners announced that they would be selling the company to a larger consultancy group. Caroline discovered that the decision to sell the company was made before she had joined the organization and this information had been deliberately withheld from her. Moreover, her male colleagues all knew she had a comparable job offer from a large consultancy but declined because of the opportunity to achieve partner status quickly. She made it clear to her male colleagues that she expected to join the new company under the same terms that she had enjoyed at Systems, Inc. She did not see this as a problem because they were all going into the negotiations as if they were partners. They had said from the start that she would be a partner in a very short time and they continued to stress how valuable her skills and experience were to the company. She told Peter, Systems Inc.'s negotiator with the new company, that he should negotiate with the new group as if Caroline were already a partner. As the negotiations proceeded, Caroline found herself cut off from conversations, updates, and important meetings, in which all the other consultants were included. As she demanded to be included in these meetings, she found herself bullied by the others.

Every time I brought up the subject of partner I could quite visibly feel them closing ranks. The subject seemed to be taboo even though it was clearly part of why I agreed to take the position.

The clients that she had worked hard to secure were taken away from her; this unethical activity ironically gave her colleagues the moral high ground. After scouring her client database and contacting her clients, against her knowledge, to suggest they work with them instead of Caroline, her male colleagues told her that she did not warrant partner status because she did not have enough clients to justify this preferential status. Caroline recalled her discussions with her male colleagues as she tried to negotiate better terms for herself,

I asked that I be treated as a principal in the discussions with the new company, so I would have the same status as the other consultants. They said this was not possible because the new company was making them offers based on their ability to bring in clients to the business and since the clients were being distributed based on the principals, it was a "catch-22." I asked if I could at least retain the clients I had been working with, but these were reassigned to the principals and I was asked to continue the work in the interim and would be paid by the principals directly until the new company decided if they wanted to take me on as a consultant.

Caroline was eventually told by Peter that she had better negotiate the terms of her contract with the new company by herself. In the end, all of the male senior consultants joined the new company with the title and status of partner in the firm while Caroline was excluded from partner status.

Furthermore, when Caroline approached the new owners she discovered, to her utter disbelief, that Peter had negotiated a position for her at less than half the salary ($48,000) she had been making with Systems Inc. She found herself in a cubbyhole with the new employees, mainly young graduates, while her former colleagues all had their own offices. Although she felt demoralized, Caroline decided to see if she could negotiate better terms once things had settled down in the office. Because she was supporting her husband as a graduate student in one of the most expensive cities in the United States, she could not afford the luxury of resignation. In the first week, Caroline was asked to rescue one graduate who could not handle a large-scale project for an important client. Reaching the point of exasperation and after rescuing the company from an ill-fated project, Caroline tried in vain to renegotiate her terms. "I was told by the new CEO [chief executive officer] that because the others [Caroline's male colleagues at Systems, Inc.] were so expensive to maintain that he couldn't raise my salary." She resigned after three weeks.

I could not take the abuse. I had no computer and no office and was not officially on the payroll. My colleagues from Systems, Inc. had taken my best clients and they were not about to share any new business. They treated me like an "admin."

person, but when they needed help were only too ready to use me. On the one hand, my former boss told me I was the best organizational development consultant he had ever seen and on the other hand I was treated like I didn't exist.

Although Caroline is searching for full-time work with a company, she is now working as an independent consultant, living near Boston, Massachusetts.

NOTES

1. The Department of Trade and Industry is a government department and one of its many duties is to scrutinize organizations for fraudulent and corrupt business practices.

2. The ISO 9000 quality award is an international standard. Companies are only given the award if they meet criteria that is assessed by an external examiner.

CHAPTER 5

Becoming "Difficult": Women Managers Encounter Subordination

◆◆

All the women interviewed for this book experienced being marginalized and were eventually pushed out of their organizations for questioning policy, openly debating sensitive issues, disagreeing with the male hierarchy, or objecting to unfair or sexist treatment. In short, they came to be labeled "difficult" women. This chapter explains how each woman encountered the patriarchy as she began to try to exercise power and influence in the organization. Chapter 6 explores each woman's termination in detail and demonstrates how equal opportunity initiatives and legal recourse do not sufficiently threaten the patriarchy to change its underlying character. Chapter 7 explores other contributing features of personality that had a role in these women's terminations. Although male domination featured predominantly in these cases, the women, through self-admission, were not "political" as they moved up the career ladder. They were direct, confrontational, and unwilling to compromise what they called "their principles" and what they perceived to be "right." Had they been more cautious and not challenged the hierarchy directly, perhaps like Lesley's and Fiona's manager, they may not have been made redundant. These men, unlike the women studied here, seemed to instinctively know how far they could push the hierarchy without risking their own positions.

Eight themes emerged from the experiences of these women as they moved up the career ladder and began experiencing the patriarchy face to face. The more strategic and important the role they held, the more these women felt they were marginalized and made to feel that their contributions were undervalued and even rendered insignificant.

The eight themes, which will be explored in greater detail, are introduced here:

1. Communication Patterns: The communication patterns of men in meetings and in one-to-one situations effectively minimized the contribution of women or degraded their status. Many of the women received a verbal dressing down for something that was either unsubstantiated or trivial.

2. Withholding Information: Information (memos, decisions, important meetings, reports) were withheld from women to diminish their role in decision making and to make them less effective in the function for which they were hired.

3. Denying Status: Material items designating status (cars, telephones, offices) were denied to these women even though their grade in the organization warranted them, while men at their level received them as a matter of course. Denial of these standard items was meant to demean the women and remind them that they did not have equal status with their male colleagues. Furthermore, when they complained about the lack of these perks, they were treated as if they were being petty.

4. Denying Resources: Some of the women indicated that they had been denied resources that would have made their jobs infinitely easier if they had them. These resources most often were adequate staff and budget. They were often told to perform their function "on a shoestring" or without the necessary staff to deliver programs. Denying the necessary resources is one way of intentionally making it difficult for women to succeed in high profile positions.

5. Lack of Mentoring and Networks: These women were not mentored and were not afforded the same networks as men. They were systematically excluded from informal gatherings, showing them that they were not in the important circle constituted by men.

6. Tests Designed to Intimidate: The women described being tested in a variety of unreasonable ways to deliberately cause them stress or to demonstrate a failing. This type of treatment became worse as they tried to assert themselves in the roles for which they were appointed.

7. The Double-Bind in Seeking Justice: When these women complained about unfair treatment they faced a double-bind. On the one hand, they could ignore the unfair treatment and secure no improvement in terms of equitable status; on the other hand, they could complain and be accused of not being team players.

8. Closing Ranks: When women threatened to take action to remedy unfair treatment, the male hierarchy closed ranks. Those men who may have been supportive at another time or privately, sided in public with their male colleagues.

COMMUNICATION

Many of the women experienced a variety of communication patterns in which men degraded them or minimized their contribution. These verbal encounters may have happened in one-to-one situations, in small group meetings or in large group settings. But they always had the effect of decreasing the impact these women should have had in the public arena.

The women reported that men often attributed their ideas to another man in the group; some felt this was done intentionally and some felt it was done unconsciously because the men in question could not envisage women authoring original ideas or suggestions to resolve problems. Fiona recalled an incident that left her feeling powerless,

I was in an important meeting to discuss the strategy we should use to promote new managers. I went through a lengthy explanation of how we could do it and about five minutes later a colleague said, "Andrew, that's a brilliant plan for promoting new managers." He went on to heartily support this approach. I couldn't believe what I was hearing. No one called him on his mistake and I felt I would look petty if I had said, "Steady on, that was my idea." It made me very angry.

Karen reflected on a similar incident with her manager and the production engineers in a quality circle,

I had prepared a brief paper on some ideas I had to improve the print production process. We were in the meeting and my boss gave credit to Steve, one of the engineers, for the ideas in the paper. I pointed out that the ideas were actually mine. My boss then said, "Well, it doesn't really matter. Ideas are usually the contribution of many and not one." Instead of feeling vindicated I felt he made me look small for bringing it up.

Mary noticed a similar pattern in a large group meeting of her peers and more senior-level managers than herself,

I was in a half day meeting with field and head office people to review the effects of a culture change programme. One of the women in the group was bright, enthusiastic and well educated and she made several suggestions that one man in the room credited to another man. With this same individual, I made a suggestion which he later credited to his boss, a male. After the meeting, I asked my female colleague if she had noticed. She said, "He does it all the time. I think he doesn't think any of us [the women] are capable of coming up with a thought."

A similar verbal pattern described by many women in the study occurred when men paraphrased women's ideas and gave themselves credit for coming up with them. Patricia described this well,

After I had explained a marketing campaign in great detail, my boss would chime in with "I think we should do this and that and it would be a good idea to try this"—a complete regurgitation of what I had said 10 minutes before.

This happened to Diane on many occasions and she did try to correct the misattribution,

In board meetings the men liked to stroke each other. If I had had a good idea it originated with Peter or Ian. I would stand up for myself and remind them that I had thought of it. Usually there was a brief pause but no acknowledgment or apology for the error. We just moved quickly on to the next agenda item.

Caroline, who worked in Boston, Massachusetts, for an American consultancy group, described her male colleagues taking credit for her ideas in meetings. She was not afraid to call them on their behavior, but when she did one of her male colleagues told her that they all had difficulty understanding her British accent and perhaps this was why they had not given her due credit. It was simply a misunderstanding caused by their inability to decipher what she was trying to say.

The women reflected on the meaning of these incidents in which men took credit for their ideas. All agreed that one's image before one's peer group is vital for success in an organization. Mary put it this way,

Careers are made and destroyed in meetings because they are the places where intelligence and originality are displayed. Being dismissed or ignored in a meeting contributes to your perception as a weak player. That is why men assuming credit for women's ideas is a serious thing. It's a great psychological ploy, too, which gets you off balance and angry. When you are off balance and angry and can't figure out how to get back, it makes you seem ineffective.

For more than 20 years, Deborah Tannen (1990, 1995) has been studying the linguistic styles of men and women. She suggests that in business settings women often do not get the credit they deserve because of the differing linguistic styles of men and women. Women often describe their contributions with "we" instead of "I," ask questions that downplay their certainty and may be interpreted by men as displaying ignorance, and speak in ways to include others. Men, on the other hand, often describe their contributions with "I" statements, are likely to minimize their doubts with assertions, and speak in ways to demonstrate their superiority over others (Tannen, 1990, 1995).

Men tend to be sensitive to the power dynamics of interaction, speaking in ways that position themselves as one up and resisting being put in a one-down position by others. Women tend to react more strongly to the rapport dynamic, speaking in ways that save face for others and buffering statements that could be seen as putting others in a one-down position (Tannen, 1990, p. 141).

Although Tannen concentrates primarily on describing the linguistic styles of men and women, these styles point to more fundamental attitudes that men have toward women. Ignoring women's contributions in meetings or taking credit for their contributions is a way of placing them in an inferior category. Other research points to the differences between men's and women's communication styles. Men typically respond to a question with a solution whereas women will ask more questions to try to gain insight into a problem (Marchetti, 1996). The effect of this difference may be damaging to women in the workplace. Men may appear to be more assertive and more confident than women, when in fact women are simply trying to gain the relevant facts before making a decision.

In a social services report, women described their contributions in meetings as being ignored or trivialized by men. One individual described making a serious point in a meeting while she was partly obscured by a pillar in the room. "The Chair's response [to her] was, 'that's not the tea lady, it's . . . ,' whereupon laughter followed and the point was lost" (Allan, Bhavnani, and French, 1992, p. 40).

Caroline experienced her male colleagues simply ignoring her suggestions. In her work arena, it was typical for the senior consultants and partners to discuss upcoming ideas for client interventions. Each individual would give his or her ideas in a round-robin format; every time the consultants and partners met, Caroline's ideas were demeaned with a silent reception while the others' suggestions were followed by animated discussion.

Some of the women reported that these same verbal patterns were repeated with written reports or written project work. Several had given men copies of their working notes or finished reports about something only to find their material reproduced, sometimes without changes or with only slight alterations, with the man's name as the author and no mention of contribution or acknowledgment of help from them. Karen remembered one such incident,

I had prepared a report about union involvement in our industry, which I gave to my boss. He took the cover page off and replaced it with a new one with his name on it and then sent it up to the board. I called him on it and he said something like we all need to be a team here and that he represented our group and it was appropriate for him to be the spokesperson for the document.

Fiona had a similar issue with her boss,

I had prepared a document about how the board members could go through a group process event so that they could work better as a team. It contained some current research on teams in large organizations and interventions that work. My boss presented it to the board with his name on it. I didn't even get a thank you.

Mary met with the sales director's personal assistant, a young man eager to prove himself to the organization. He had heard that she had done a project for a multinational company in another job and wanted to interview her about it because he had to do a similar project for his manager.

I sat down with him and discussed the project. I told him what I had done in the past and he asked to borrow a document that I had created. Stupidly I gave it to him. In two weeks I saw the ideas from my work appear in a document he produced for the board. No mention was made of me. He eventually returned my original document but never said or wrote thanks.

On another occasion, Mary had discussed with the sales director a series of courses her department would run for his salespeople. They had agreed-on dates and general thematic areas for the courses. A few days later, she was out in one of the field offices and was asked by a sales manager about the sales director's memo. She asked to see the memo.

He had written to the entire sales management force about the programme that I would be running for him. Neither I nor my staff was copied in on the memo. I was livid; I suggested to him that the memo should have come from me as it was my area and routinely I communicated with the field about programmes. I said, "I would never send something out about your area under my name." He then said, "You're being too sensitive. It was just an oversight. I meant nothing personal by it."

Mary recorded many similar incidents in her diary entries where she registered frustration about not getting credit for her ideas and programs.

Mary felt this misappropriation was deliberately done to decrease her area of influence and increase the sales director's; sales figures had been down for three years running and the sales director seemed to be doing everything in his power to look like he was managing Mary's department and doing something productive. Mary also felt that his treatment of her had been sexist, "I am sure that he wouldn't have dared to do the same thing to a man in my position." This situation would be repeated in another guise. Mary was asked by the sales director to produce a report highlighting the evaluations from a training program for which her team had been responsible and send it to the board. She wrote the report and sent it to the board with a copy to the sales director. The sales director called her and reprimanded her for sending it out in her name.

He said the report should have gone out in his name. I said I disagreed as I had written it and he was kept informed. I said the organization was making efforts to empower people and this would be against this ethic. He didn't respond to my justifications but repeated that I had acted "inappropriately."

Elizabeth, a woman in middle management, suggested that not being given credit for written work or verbal contributions in meetings affects whether or not one is viewed as a candidate for higher-level jobs.

If you remain invisible because you aren't getting credit, you won't be in the frame for promotion. Men, in a sense, narrow the competition by ignoring women's contributions. Doing good work and working long hours isn't enough, you need the recognition that should go with it.

As Kahneman, Slovic, and Tversky (1982) noted, women suffer in job promotion and recruitment because of framing effects. When a male manager is scanning his mind or his personal network for available candidates, women are often excluded because either they do not exhibit the male characteristics that are associated with successful candidacy or they simply are not remembered. Tannen (1995) also recognized framing effects. People in powerful positions, predominantly men, tend to reward their own linguistic style. Women are often assessed as not having the self-confidence necessary for promotion when in fact they do possess it. At an early age, women develop speech patterns that are less assertive than men's speech patterns. These patterns are carried over into adulthood and into the world of work.

The rhetoric of being a team player was used to make these women feel small when they objected to being ignored in meetings or if they complained about their written work being misappropriated. If they tried to assert themselves and correct an error that had been made at their expense, they were accused of caring too much about their own reputations and individuality rather than making team goals their priority. These accusations are interesting in light of Rosener's research (1990) reporting that women are described by others as being inclined toward participation, motivated by including others in decision making, and as having a desire to improve the work climate whereas men are described as basing their management styles on power and contractual exchanges. Similarly, Rigg and Sparrow (1994) in their study of district housing managers reported that both women and men described women as emphasizing team management and being other-centered rather than self-centered. The relatively recent practice of team working in corporations may disadvantage women (Tannen, 1995). In mixed team working groups, men are more likely to take credit for the team's contributions. Women are more likely to consider "taking credit" as boasting and consequently will not risk taking credit for their contributions.

Being made the object of a verbal dressing-down for something inconsequential or unsubstantiated was another technique for diminishing the power and influence of women. Hammer (1990) suggests that women are used to being held responsible, while men are not used to being held responsible for anything negative. A social services report indicated that women in management posts feel visible and vulnerable. One senior manager reported that she felt "there were fingers ready to point if she slipped up" (Allan et al., 1992, p. 40). Some of the women profiled for this book experienced being held individually responsible for company inadequacies or mistakes. For example, Diane was held responsible for problems with her company's acquisition policy even though she advised her company not to go forward with it. On one occasion, Madge's managing director suggested that it was her fault that the company was losing some key staff, even though these staff were not in her area. The personnel director suggested that it was Mary's fault that some equipment had been stolen from a hotel even though it had been securely locked away in a storage cupboard.

Many of the women endured verbal dressing-downs. This happened on several occasions to Elizabeth, who had been identified by her manager as "a strong black woman."

Norman (my boss) had large team meetings. Forty or so people would be there. I asked a question at one of his meetings, something like, "I don't understand your point. Could you explain it?" He would come back with, "Well you wouldn't. That's just typical of you. I'd expect that of you." I felt so humiliated.

In her diary, Elizabeth labeled the incident as an example of her manager's patronizing behavior toward her.

Madge was dressed down on several occasions and this became worse as she tried to assert herself as the director of personnel.

I had seventeen years experience recruiting staff and a good track record of picking reliable people who would stay. Of course, no one has a 100% retention. My managing director, in front of my staff, gave me a dressing down about one woman who joined and then left on maternity leave and then proceeded to tell me how to select sales staff. He railed "Couldn't I select staff who would stay? Couldn't I get it right?"

Diane experienced a dressing-down from her managing director after writing a discussion document for BS5750, the national quality award.

The M.D. [managing director] called me in and said people had been offended by my being critical in the document. I said I hadn't been critical of anyone personally but I wanted people to know what the problems and risks are of trying to get the award before we are ready. He said it read like I was preaching to people. I said the title indicated that it was only a draft document for discussion and to stimulate people's thinking.

Diane felt the document was a routine paper; men at her level often distributed similar documents outlining their point of view. At this brief meeting, the managing director also told her that she shouldn't feel that she had to use her MBA knowledge because it made others feel uncomfortable. In her diary entries, Diane reiterated how her managing director criticized her for wanting to use her MBA knowledge to help the company,

> Decision Diary, February:
> I asked [the managing director] what we should do. After all the company was paying for my [MBA] course. I thought I should be helping the company get its money's worth out of it. What should we do—keep our ideas to ourselves? I was just trying to help. He [the managing director] said, "Maybe people don't want help."

On another occasion Diane was reprimanded over a letter that the managing director wanted her to send out as from him. Rather than send the letter out immediately, Diane kept the letter for a few hours so that he could put an insert in along with it if he chose to do so.

I was yelled at for not getting the letter out. I said I had checked with his secretary who said she thought he might want to put something else in. It was a matter of three hours difference. He said his secretary was useless and I should have known better to get it out. It was not urgent correspondence anyway and his response was totally out of proportion.

This incident was also documented in Diane's diaries, written several months before the author's interview with Diane. The description of the event in her diary closely corresponds to the event she described during the interview.

On other occasions, Diane had been dressed down by the managing director, sometimes in the presence of other male directors and sometimes alone. These incidents increased after Diane had uncovered some fraudulent activity by three of her co-directors.

They would suddenly call me to meetings and give me a dressing down. The M.D. would say let's have lunch together in the board room and then he would tell me everything he thought I'd done wrong. He would have a long list of minor incursions.

A week before Patricia's manager was promoted to managing director of one of the divisions, he launched into a vehement attack on her in front of her staff,

He said the managing directors of other divisions had complained about me and the service I was providing them. I felt dressed down and humiliated in front of my team. There was no warning and no mention of dissatisfaction with my work before this happened. I didn't feel I was under performing. He said my attitude was wrong.

As can be seen in these women's cases, verbal patterns in the workplace have a subordinating effect on women. Misappropriating women's ideas and contributions, taking credit for women's work, and public and private verbal humiliation are all exclusionary tactics that have three effects: (1) they severely limit women's opportunity for advancement, (2) they diminish women's power in organizations, and (3) these patterns erode women's self-confidence.

WITHHOLDING INFORMATION

Many of the women experienced the deliberate withholding of valuable information. This information would have helped them have an informed opinion, make the right decision, or respond intelligently in meetings.

If information is power then withholding it will make the person without information less powerful and less effective than he or she would have been with it. Mann (1995) describes two behaviors that are used in organizations to keep information away from women managers. First, meetings may be scheduled at inaccessible hours, conflicting with women's domestic responsibilities. The 7:30 A.M. breakfast meeting or the after-work board meeting presents problems for many women managers who must prepare children for school in the morning or pick children up from day care in the early evening. Second, informal male networks are used for sources of information. Women are excluded from these networks; therefore, men control what women ultimately receive. Moreover, lack of information contributes to an impression that the individual is weak. Why is she not in possession of important information? Isn't she on top of her job? Did she lose the information? Is she so disorganized in her work that she didn't have time to read the information? Why doesn't she have an opinion about something that is so important? Unless the individual forming these opinions understands that the woman is systematically bypassed in the information network, he or she may form negative reasons for her not being informed.

The importance of being briefed before a business meeting has a long tradition. Typically in business meetings, several agenda items are covered and people must be given background information before the meeting so that decisions can be reached with efficacy. Jane Drabble, assistant managing director at BBC Network Television, suggests that when you reach the top of an organization the hierarchy imposes lack of consultation and secrecy. Decisions are made before and after, rather than during, meetings. And men are used to working with other men and not women (Figes, 1994). Mary recalled how not having relevant information disadvantaged her.

I went into strategy meetings with information I'd been given. I always found out that one of the directors had neglected to copy me in on an important memo or report that all of my male colleagues had received. I'd have to read over someone's shoulder or ask for a copy. It made me look stupid.

Madge, a board-level personnel director, constantly had to ask for information that should have been sent to her as a matter of course. Because she recruited all staff, she wanted to know what the sales figures were in various branches so that she could provide development to the branch managers and better analyze staffing requirements. This information, however, routinely given to the other male directors, was withheld from her.

Another thing I asked for from time to time was information. I was told that I was being political. I asked for some quite valid information like sales figures and they didn't allow me to have it until I'd passed all of their tests.

The tests Madge spoke of were what she referred to as "earn your stripes tests" designed for her to prove that she was competent in and committed to various aspects of her job.

Patricia had budget information withheld from her so that she couldn't make decisions about her own area.

Budget information about marketing was given first to the sales directors and eventually, after lots of asking, to me. Many times decisions had been made before I even had a chance to see the budget. Even though I was marketing manager I think they honestly believed the budget should be of no consequence to me. They saw me as the implementor of their decisions not someone involved in the decision.

One of Katherine's peers had recently been promoted to become her manager. Formerly, she had enjoyed working on marketing strategy with him and he felt that she had contributed greatly to the department's approach; however, now that he had become the head of marketing he withheld information from her.

I used to get market trend information as a matter of course and we'd discuss it. Now he kept all of that stuff to himself I suppose because he saw me as a competitor. He wanted to clearly differentiate himself from me and one way was to keep this information from me and have me do more menial tasks.

Fiona described a pattern by which her manager went directly to her clients instead of giving her relevant information so she could consult with them and make decisions with these clients about their development. She felt this pattern made her look like she was incapable of making these decisions herself and reinforced the notion that she was an implementor of her manager's vision rather than someone who could come up with it on her own.

Many times the really important information that I should have had from him skipped me entirely. He liked to interact with the sales managers himself, decide what I would do and then tell me. Usually weeks later he would give me the relevant piece of paper saying he'd already taken care of it and that he'd like me to follow-up. This caused real problems because I had usually been working with them on something that was related to what he'd asked me to do or on a different strategy entirely. I'd remind him that we were confusing the client. They wanted to know who was running my department—me or him.

Caroline was excluded from important meetings dealing with the sale of the company to another consultancy group. Since she was told she would be made a partner and the core employees in the company was very small (four consultants), she felt that she should have been involved in these meetings. Caroline recalled,

Suddenly the four of them would be together with the door shut. When I asked whether I could be part of their discussions they said, "This doesn't involve you." They would meet for breakfast and then claim that it hadn't been planned.

Diane found herself pitted against her male directors in board meetings because they had information that had been withheld from her.

I was expected to stay in my little accountancy box. I thought and demanded that as a director of the company I should be involved in general strategic decisions. I once asked the managing director why he hadn't given me a report and he said, "We hired you to do the accounts not to get involved in running other depart-ments." I had ideas about the business, whether acquisitions were smart and so on. I was kept out of these discussions and information wasn't circulated to me.

As with verbal communication patterns in the workplace, the scant in-formation women receive makes them as a class unable to participate as equals alongside men. Diane and Madge discovered that their male direc-tors often held pre-board meetings in their absence to hide information from them or to effectively make decisions covertly. Diane recalled that,

Meetings would be organised without me being advised. I wasn't told what was going on. You'd suddenly find out that they had had meetings before and would bring things in as a fait accompli.

Madge commented,

Board meetings were stitched up before you got there. I knew my colleagues had met before without me or at least conferred on what they were going to do. You weren't in the decision making process. That was for the men.

Ironically, even women at board level, like Diane and Madge, lacked basic information to make decisions about their functional areas of accounting and personnel, respectively.

DENYING STATUS

As one moves up the career ladder in the business world, material items that denote status are important symbols of success. Whether they be a car, a mobile telephone, the corner office, shares in the company, or secretarial support, symbols of status position one within the hierarchy. Perhaps the women profiled in this book did not place enough importance on these status symbols and initially underestimated their importance. Withholding status symbols from women is a way of saying, "You aren't really part of the inner circle, we don't value you the same way we value our male colleagues, and we don't take you seriously." Denying material perks to a female director or manager is also a way of impressing to the rest of the organization that this woman, even though she has achieved a certain level in the organization, is of lesser significance than male managers and directors.

Millett (1970) identified different rituals for men and women in patriarchal societies that accorded more status to males. For example, women were thought to be unclean during their menstrual periods and were isolated, they were required to eat apart from men, and when the sexes did dine together men were expected to eat first and to eat better food.

In contemporary society, denying women their rightful status was noted in a social services report where one black woman said her colleagues, social workers, and probation officers ignored her status as a manager and professional, preferring to deal with her deputy, a white male (Allan et al., 1992).

When women take issue with not receiving the same perks as their male colleagues they are made to feel petty for asking for them. When Madge complained about not receiving the same perks as her male directors, she was told by the managing director that she shouldn't concern herself with those things, saying, "After all I made you a director, didn't I?"

I was supposed to keep quiet about not getting the perks. My boss said something to the effect of "be happy, be pleased, you've got the status of being a director, now be quiet."

Madge was denied several things that her male counterparts received as a matter of course, including relocation expenses, a comparable car for her grade level, secretarial support, and a mobile telephone.

I travelled extensively with my job visiting our many sites. I didn't get a car phone until I had been there five years. I was expected to pull off the motorway and find a public telephone box. My staff complained to the M.D. [managing director] because they couldn't reach me in emergencies. Finally he relented.

Patricia had similar problems when she became the marketing manager of a graphics company.

I arrived at the company. I didn't have an office or a telephone. How did they view me and the job I asked myself. The rest of the male managers had offices. I asked for an office and was told, "We are reorganising and don't have offices right now." My immediate boss didn't do anything. I had an opportunity to talk to the M.D. about the office situation and he said, "Well, I think this is your first test. I'd like to see how a woman can use her wiles to get an office."

In the end and after much frustration, Patricia waited eight months to secure an office. Fiona declined an office at first because she felt it was not very important and she was out in the field working with her internal clients most of the time anyway. When she did ask for one, it was for her staff to use as well as herself.

I was given what had been a broom closet converted into an office. It was miles away from everything and I felt isolated. There was no natural light and no place to store my files and materials. I had to have those out in the hallway. What irritated me most was that it was so clearly different from my boss's other direct report. During this time, he was at the same level as I was and his office was large and comfortable and right next to my boss's office. I felt the organization could have found me something better if they had tried.

When Fiona complained to her manager that the office was inadequate, he said that he thought these things weren't really important to her because she had always been so much her own person and had not paid any attention to things like offices and cars.

Because Madge's position required extensive travel throughout the United Kingdom, she was concerned about having a safe car. When she was made a director, she was promised that her car would be upgraded. But months went by and she was still driving a "supermini" car. Again, she reminded her managing director that she wanted a more stable car on the motorway and one that had new tires (her car's tires were nearly bald). After a further delay she finally got her new car. Then the managing director and the other directors began chiding her about it.

They ribbed me about it being a goldy colour. It was a deliberate way of making me look petty. Making me look like I cared about the colour when I could have cared less. I just wanted a safe car.

Diane described a similar situation that occurred after she was made a finance director.

My predecessor, the finance director, had had a similar salary to mine. When he left they gave me his company car, an Audi, and they let me drive it for a brief time. They replaced it with a Mini Metro. This was their way of putting me in my place. A new production manager, not even a director, came on board and they gave him the Audi. All of the directors had parking spots in the front of the rank except for me. I was made to feel petty if I complained about these things. They would say, "We aren't into cars here" in spite of the fact they all had Range Rovers.

When the head of Caroline's company made an important announcement, Caroline noticed that even though she was a senior consultant, she was informed with the administrative staff, instead of with everyone else at her level. She felt that this was a way of indirectly saying that she was not really in the same category as her peers. Another situation indicated to Caroline that she was supposed to view herself as inferior to her male peers. After Caroline joined the company to which the former consultancy she had worked for was sold, she found that instead of an office, which the other male consultants had, she had been given a "cubbyhole among the new graduates" and had not been put on the payroll like the other consultants, but was to be paid out of cash funds. This meant that she did not receive benefits, such as medical insurance, which her male counterparts had received as a matter of course.

In *Sexual Politics*, Kate Millett (1970) suggests that the patriarchy has historically accepted the use of force against women. In contemporary times, violence against women has been considered a result of individual deviance and not as a tool of control. Hostility and intimidation toward women, however, may be the contemporary equivalent of what was formerly institutionally accepted violence. Withholding of material goods (cars, telephones, shares, offices) is one way for the patriarchy to continue to exert its force over women. This force becomes more overt hostility and intimidation as women begin to compete with men in the business hierarchy. The obvious lack of items denoting status is one way for the patriarchy to remind the woman of her inferior status in the eyes of her male colleagues.

DENYING RESOURCES

One way of designing failure is to deny an individual the tools to adequately perform her role. Some of the women in this study commented on what they described as the intentional denial of resources that would help them succeed. Often the denial of resources occurs as part of an overall strategy to marginalize a woman's role. If she sees that others are being provided resources, it is also a message to the woman of her powerless.

Mary's e-mail correspondence documents her struggle to obtain additional staff. She approached a senior management group in the first instance and finally the chairman.

> February 7, 1996
> . . . The team's morale is down and I keep trying to bolster them up. I've asked for additional resource but was turned down. I went to the senior management meeting with a plan to get additional resource by seconding two extra people in. They don't see the need. Sweat shop mentality!

> April 16, 1996
> I told him [the chairman] in my 10 plus years of training and management experience, I had never had to cancel an event because I had no time to prepare it and no staff to run it. . . . I told him that although the job had doubled in size (nearly twice as many people to train) the headcount in my department had stayed flat. . . . He said to put my ideas in writing and give them to my manager. It felt like I was totally written off. I've done all this before.

After Madge filed a grievance against the board of directors for equal pay, she was denied the resource of a secretary. Her secretary had taken maternity leave and the board decided she could conduct her function without hiring a replacement. Madge described how difficult it was to run her function without this resource. She was accountable for all of the health and safety in the retail outlets as well as all of the human resource policies and practices. Madge felt that the board used this as a warning to suggest how powerful they were and how weak she was in opposition to them.

LACK OF MENTORING/LACK OF NETWORKS

The theory of patriarchy suggests that men will discourage and even prevent women from forming their own networks for the advancement of their careers and obstruct mentoring relationships that could help them move up the career ladder. Sophie Anderson, a consultant anesthetist, found that when she joined an informal group of women anesthetists for support, she was viewed with suspicion by her male colleagues (Figes, 1994). In a U.S. study of executive women, an engineer recognized that informal networking leads to male privilege. In her organization, some women attempted to combat exclusionary male groups by forming their own networks outside of work. These women damaged or ended their careers because they were viewed as troublemakers (Bierema, 1996).

Indeed, none of the women profiled in this book felt that they had been mentored by men on their way up, and none had women role models because there were no women available to be role models at the top of their organizations. The importance of mentoring cannot be underestimated. Witz (1992) explains how exclusionary strategies have the effect of subordinating women, reducing their power to secure, maintain, or enhance their access to rewards and opportunities within an occupational group. When men mentor each other within an organization, they are in effect narrowing the chances of women to secure promotions or better, more visible job assignments that might lead to promotion. Witz suggests that exclusionary strategies place women in a class of "ineligibles" by excluding them from routes of access to resources such as skills, knowledge, and entry credentials into occupations. Morrison et al. (1987) and Morrison (1992), like Witz, identified mentoring as a critical success factor for women in management. Sponsorship by superiors and support and encouragement were among the factors reported in Morrison et al.'s work that had a significant impact on women's achievement. Similarly, a U.S. study of women executives suggested that having a male mentor throughout one's career was essential to surviving within the corporate culture (Bierema, 1996).

In a study of health care workers, women earned significantly more if they had male mentors, if they had a spouse willing to relocate for their career, if they had worked for an employer with policies that accommodated women, and if the women themselves socialized informally with health care executives, the majority of whom were male (Weil and Kimball, 1996). Mann (1995) suggests that mentoring is used by workers to fill gaps in formal communications, to do one another favors, to enhance one another's morale, and to advance careers because the majority of jobs come through personal networks.

Despite the fact that women need mentoring to succeed, it seems to be in short supply. Ragins (1989) found that women are mentored less frequently than men. The Opportunity 2000 report (Court, 1995) suggests that networks for women are ineffective unless the underlying culture values and rewards women. Equal opportunity initiatives, like mentoring for women, will not change the concentration of power accorded to males unless the organizational culture fundamentally changes to let women share equally in the control of resources, technology, and information (Still, 1994). A recent study of the mentoring of certified public accountants (CPAs) demonstrated that mentoring had little positive effect on the earnings of women (Brown-Johnson and Scandura, 1994). From a 20-item mentorship questionnaire given randomly to 571 men and 293 women CPAs, only the coaching variable was significantly and positively correlated with earnings for women. Gender-role style, whether a man or woman had a stereotypically "masculine" or stereotypically "feminine" style, influenced earnings more than mentoring. Significantly higher earnings were accorded masculine men, but not masculine women. Furthermore, feminine women had significantly lower earnings, whereas men's adoption of a feminine style did not effect their earnings.

Many of the women described in this book worked in male-dominated industries such as financial services, printing, aerospace, and management consultancy. The opportunities for finding women mentors at the top were nonexistent and men did not readily volunteer to become their mentors. Being mentored by a male can in some environments be interpreted negatively. Moreover, mentoring can damage a woman if not provided out of a genuine interest in helping to promote the woman within the organization. A comment from Katherine typified what happens in these types of environment.

You were just supposed to be good at your job and understand the rules. It would have been taken as a sign of weakness to go to someone for help and going to someone for advice puts you on an uneven footing with them because it isn't reciprocated. In a subtle way, if you share confidences and men don't share them back you're in a vulnerable position.

Fiona described going to her manager for advice on a few occasions. She thought that later he used this against her in a job evaluation situation.

He said that I wasn't making decisions without his supervision and therefore, was rated down. This was total nonsense as I had only asked his advice twice and made most decisions without consulting him. I wondered if this would have happened if the relationship had been more equitable from the start. If he had come to me more often in confidence.

Male to male mentoring is informal, disguised, and unacknowledged within the organization whereas male to female or female to female mentoring, as the previous examples reveal, calls attention to the special needs of women and stigmatizes them as needing greater support than males.

Informal networking, like mentoring, is essential for success in organizations. Both men and women agree that networking across an organization is critical for advancement in the organization. After a certain level, technical competence in a functional specialty is no longer as important in job progression as networking. Technical competence will have been proven during assignments one had in lower-level jobs. The ability to network, however, is indispensable to middle- or senior-level managers because they need to gather support for their ideas, budget, strategy, and programs. In Marshall's account (1995) of women managers, Dorothy deliberately built alliances with men whom she felt held similar values to herself as a way of facilitating change. Fiona recalled how networks operated in her organization,

I think there is a long tradition of you scratch my back and I'll scratch yours that men do very naturally. This kind of networking perpetuates the favouritism accorded men over women. I saw this often. For example, my boss would often say things like "he owes me a favour" or "don't worry I'll talk to him and get him on our side." I knew two women at my level in the organization but I never felt comfortable doing that. I don't think women know how to ask for favours or they feel it is a little unprofessional.

Kottis (1993) discusses the bartering nature of networking; women, because of their subordinate position in organizations, have nothing of substance to exchange with men. Their lack of access to information and technology and their inability to pull strings does not provide the inducement for men to invite them into networks. Barbara Mills, the first female director of public prosecutions, felt excluded because of her sex. Although she is a graduate of Oxford University and an honorary fellow of a college, she was not a full member of the Oxford and Cambridge Club simply because she is female (Figes, 1994). While men engage in tit-for-tat cooperation, women cannot because they have not built up a network or do not have the power to return favors. In her study of 16 women, Judi Marshall (1995) uncovered women's reluctance to network based on their feelings of isolation from men, men's territorial attitude in the workplace, and their sense that they were too unlike their male colleagues to build relationships with them.

Fiona talked about how a large part of networking was knowing people well enough to ask them for favors. She thought men were socialized early in their careers to know how to do this, probably because it had been modeled for them. Men often need only imply that a favor was owed to them to secure it, while women feel awkward asking for favors and don't have the vocabulary or experience to openly ask for them. Mary described a situation where networking and relationships among men at senior levels allowed or encouraged men to violate promotion and recruitment procedures.

I was very annoyed at the personnel director who on the one hand set up the rules for applying for internal jobs and on the other hand allowed the sales director to by-pass them completely. The job was supposed to be evaluated and advertised internally. Instead the personnel director allowed him to simply place one of his buddies in it at a higher salary than it warranted. I complained to the personnel director and was told that "sometimes there are organizational circumstances that warrant not following the procedures."

At the top, networking often occurs during social events: golf, barbeques, fishing outings, and drinking in the pub. Mann (1995) identifies discussing football as one means of excluding women. Women are made to feel unwelcome in discussions about sports. Corcoran-Nantes and Roberts (1995) suggest that men are uncomfortable with women because their very presence suppresses normal conversation and swearing. These discussions often take place down at the pub and are interspersed with "male talk" and sexual innuendo. Women managers are generally excluded from these activities on three counts. First, they haven't the experience to participate on equal footing with men in sports, such as golf or football, that have been traditionally male dominated. Second, they are unwelcome by men even when qualified (by experience or formal invitation) to participate. Third, if spouses are invited, the male organizers assume that their wives will be uncomfortable with entertaining the lone male spouse.

A housing association report identified that women may not be able to or may not want to join in informal activities that revolve around sports or drinking (Office for Public Management, 1994). Similarly, in a social services study highlighting interviews with 48 women managers, respondents reported the prevalence of male networks and clubs that offer men information sharing and decision making outside the formal organizational structure. Exclusion from these male networks makes women feel their effectiveness is being undermined (Allan et al., 1992). Fiona recalls several events that demonstrated these points.

For years I went to weekend sales conferences. The men were always invited up one day before the proceedings started so that they could get a round of golf in and the spouses joined later. Usually activities like shopping excursions were organized for the wives while the business proceedings took place.

Spousal involvement reinforces the patriarchy in a subtle way; as wives become acquainted with each other the relationships between their husbands deepen, and men find it more demanding to make difficult decisions that involve one of their peers or male subordinates when they have established a friendship outside of work. Moreover, firing someone or denying him promotion will weigh more heavily on the conscience if there is a friendship between wives.

Diane recalls many social events that kept her from networking with her fellow male directors.

I wouldn't be invited to things that other directors went to. They put it down to the fact that I wasn't a major shareholder. They all lived in the same area and they socialised together. Their wives got to know one another.

Elizabeth's male colleagues networked with one another down at the pub on a Friday afternoon after work and they made many business decisions that were presented as *faits accompli* in meetings the subsequent week. Because she didn't drink and did not like the smoke-filled atmosphere, Elizabeth declined to attend these pub evenings. Although she suggested to her manager that a smoke-free environment would be more productive, he continued to invite his direct reports down to the pub. Mary recalled many social events at which networking took place where she was conspicuously absent. "I wasn't invited to the go-karting event or the golf weekend. I was the only female direct report and the only one not invited."

As marketing manager, Patricia was always invited to sales meetings, but she was routinely excluded from the informal cocktail parties that took place in one of the director's hotel suites before the formal dinner.

These cocktail parties were important because they signalled that you were in the in group and that the directors liked you. I always felt left out because the men often carried over their discussions from these informal gatherings to the dinner table discussions.

Caroline experienced her male colleagues sharing what she referred to as "war stories" about work. She said,

The meaning of these war stories was that these men shared a history. Because you didn't participate in these stories and they didn't ask you if you had any war stories of your own, it was as if you didn't have a history of your own. I've worked for more years than they have and it was as if I had no work past.

Katherine discussed how her male colleague networked with her manager, a factor she believes ushered him up the organization.

He always seemed to be having lunch with our boss, a senior vice president. I felt that his getting to know him [the V.P.] played a role in his being promoted rather than me. I had more experience in marketing and was doing a good job. I suggested meeting over lunch many times, but my boss was always too busy for that.

A logical result of men networking with other men is the extension of privilege. This privilege may come in the form of better job assignments, more developmental opportunities, and more attention because of more visible support from male colleagues. One study of 308 male and female managers found that men indeed had more developmental challenges than women, tasks with higher levels of visibility, and more assignments with cross-functional responsibility. Women managers, however, reported receiving less personal support from peers and felt greater demands for influencing people over whom they had no authority (Ohlott, Ruderman, and McCauley, 1994).

In addition to the different developmental opportunities that men and women experience, many women find that they are unable to network with one another. Diane talked about the double-bind of being a woman in a male-dominated organization, "By virtue of my status—the fact that there were no women at my level—I had no women to network with. The men simply wouldn't let me into their little circle." This isolation of women who have reached senior levels is one very effective strategy of the patriarchy for reducing women's overall influence in the organization.

Women organizing themselves is often criticized by men as women being "divisive." It is discouraged in organizations and women who try to organize or who identify themselves with women's causes or networks are often labeled as "anti-men," "lesbians," or from the "looney left" (Cockburn, 1990, p. 85). A housing association report suggested that women have difficulty forming networks because men label women's networks as "hostile or unhelpful" (Office for Public Management, 1994, p. 50). This labeling of women who have sympathy with other women is a divide and conquer strategy employed by the patriarchy and as such is very effective in keeping women isolated and powerless.

TESTS DESIGNED TO INTIMIDATE

As the women became more assertive in their roles and more outspoken about receiving equitable treatment, men in dominant roles put them in situations or "tests" designed to intimidate women. Many of the women reported stress as a result of trying to meet these situations. If they objected to these tests in any way, unreasonable assignments or untenable demands were placed upon them.

As Diane began trying to exercise her role on the board as a general decision maker in addition to an accountant, she found her managing director and fellow male board members used a variety of intimidation tactics to remind her of her place in the organization.

They used to have me write up the minutes in the board meetings. At the next meeting, they would challenge what had been written in the minutes and I would have to look up the activity in the minutes and of course, find out that I had documented it correctly. This might happen two or three times in the meeting, always with the same result.

On another occasion, Diane's managing director brought in external accountants to check on her work without telling her. After the accountants told the managing director that she was "thorough and professional," he called her in and said, "If the accountants hadn't given me a good report I would have sacked you." Diane adapted to the threat of constant criticism by producing the accounts at the last moment so that her fellow directors did not have time to object to them. She recalled that this delay tactic was not good for the organization, but recognized that it was necessary for her survival. On other occasions, the managing director gave Diane many little projects that had no significance to the organization but that were very time consuming. When she challenged the managing director about the importance of these projects, he chided her saying, "You'll have to manage your time better so that you can get them done."

After Elizabeth filed a complaint, she learned that her head of department had been looking through her desk drawers after hours to try to find some area in which to criticize her work. In addition to going through her desk, Elizabeth's manager intimidated her by constantly asking her for paperwork that she did not understand how to complete.

It was a game with my manager. I had asked him to explain how he wanted a piece of paperwork completed but he could never find the time to help me. Then he would call me in unexpectedly and read me the riot act for not completing it. This happened at least three times and I kept explaining to him that he had promised to find time to show me what he wanted.

Elizabeth's diaries reveal an incident providing further evidence of tests designed to intimidate. In preparation for completing a large contract for a client, Elizabeth requested additional administrative support. She indicated to her manager that this support would be paid for by the client, rather than paid for out of her manager's budget. At the last moment, her manager supplied her with a temporary worker without the requisite skills to do the work. Not only did Elizabeth's manager put her in a difficult situation with the temporary worker, he also set her up for failure with the client.

Similarly, after Karen found out that her manager was setting up a business on the side, he began to punish her merely for having this information. He called her in to ask her to do menial and unimportant work and withdrew his support for her total quality programs with other managers at his level.

On one occasion, the head of the consultancy for which Caroline worked asked her if she would be willing to take on a difficult client. She designed and conducted a development program for this client that was met with favorable reviews. When she discussed the program with the head of the consultancy, he said that three other consultants from their organization had tried to design something for the client, but the client has very unhappy with the product. She wondered why he hadn't discussed this with her at the beginning of the project and showed her the work that had already been done.

It was as if Jim [the head of the consultancy] wanted me to have trouble with the assignment. A logical thing would have been to give me as much information about the situation as possible so that I wouldn't repeat mistakes others had made.

In another situation, Caroline had been asked to do some development work for a client, again by Jim. He would not give her information on what had already been done, which would have saved her considerable time and effort.

It was as if I was being tested on how original I could be. When I would bring in an idea, he would say, "This won't work, we've tried that before." I'd say, "Why didn't you tell me?" He'd say, "Oh well, we didn't realise."

As Madge tried to exert influence in her role as personnel director, she found herself routinely confronted with tests designed to intimidate, humiliate, and demean her.

The [work] sites were always closed on Good Fridays, but I was expected to work. I worked all Good Fridays and bank holidays but the men [her fellow directors] did not. On one Good Friday my managing director knew I had driven in eighty miles to one of our offices in spite of the fact that my husband was very ill and might be hospitalised. He called me on Saturday to insist that I take him some papers that were at the office. At this point I explained that I was again waiting for the doctor with the expectation that my husband would be hospitalised. He really pressured me and I found myself justifying the situation. Eventually I agreed to pick up the papers and again drove at breakneck speed there and back.

On several occasions Madge and a fellow female director were reproached for putting miscellaneous items on their personal expenses.

We were not supposed to put drinks or newspapers on our hotel bill even though we were never told this wasn't allowed. A colleague [a female director] did and was hauled over the coals, even when she pointed out that at the bottom of the bill it was clear she had paid for her drink with her own cash. They [the male directors] however charged all of their expenses.

Being the brunt of men's jokes is a form of humiliation and hostility. Madge found herself deliberately placed in compromising situations so that her male directors could laugh, not with her but at her. She and her male colleagues were attending a meeting in an office located above one of the retail outlets.

I was sent down to the store and our office was above one of the stores and there was a security camera focussed on it. On this occasion there was a very large aggressive customer possibly shoplifting. I was asked to deal with him. I did so calmly. When I returned I learnt that the men [the directors] had all been watching this on the TV monitoring and laughing at me.

On another occasion, Madge's brakes failed on her company car while she was driving down the highway. She took the car in to be repaired and found that her male colleagues had been laughing behind her back. Madge recalled their derision, "It was 'Ha, ha, ha, ha—woman can't drive kind of thing.' I was made to feel like I was a car hypochondriac."

Mary was training an all-male audience in the insurance sector. At the beginning of the session, she asked them what they expected to get out of the course. A group of them came back with, "We expect you to strip." Obviously, they did not expect her to take her clothes off, but they found a way to demean her and demonstrate their superiority. During a sales conference, Patricia also bore the brunt of male humor. The punch line of a dinner-table joke told by one of the sales managers involved reaching over and grabbing Patricia's breasts. Graf and Hemmasi (1995) suggest that risqué humor in the workplace is yet another way of subordinating women; making women the brunt of jokes places them in an inferior position to men.

Collinson and Collinson (1996) reported several incidents of sexual harassment and taunting of women managers working in the insurance industry. In these cases, management excused the behavior of men and placed the onus of responsible action on women. The organizations suggested that women would have to adapt to the male environment by not taking the incidents seriously and by excusing the natural, biological urges of their male colleagues.

Millett (1970) discusses how humor often demeans women, "Hostility is expressed in a number of ways. One is laughter. Misogynist literature, the primary vehicle of masculine hostility, is both hortatory and comic genre" (p. 45). For Mary, Patricia, and Madge the misogyny was not in literature but in real life. They were the subjects of "the jokes" and as such were made objects by the men making fun of them. Humor at their expense was yet another way of reminding them of their inequality and warning them to stay in line. Derisive humor has been noted elsewhere as a form of harassment. Sophie Anderson, a consultant anesthetist, remarked that she was teased by her male colleagues,

I don't hide the fact that I am a mother, so they tease me. "Ah, so you're here today," they say, as if I wasn't there on all of the other days, when they haven't seen me simply because we weren't working the same shifts. If they don't see me they think that I'm not working. Whatever I do I'm noticed more as a personality, and what I do gets commented on. (cited in Figes, 1994, p. 64)

In a local government report, teasing women managers was identified as one means to establish a pecking order and to make women appear inferior (Young and Spencer, 1991).

In addition to inappropriate humor, other "tests" were designed to intimidate women. When Mary protested to senior male managers about her team's work schedules (they were expected to travel steadily for nine months without a break or any time at home to be with their families), she found tests put before her that were intended to intimidate her.

When I asked for reasonable schedules for my staff during the culture change training project, I found myself cut out of the decision making even though the decisions would affect me and my team the most. When I created staff schedules for my team, I would find them redone for no good reason. Just to undermine me.

Mary, as well as one of her staff, had received very good feedback about the culture change training that they had designed and delivered within their organization. She and her team had independently managed large culture change projects in other large companies. In spite of their experience and Mary's protestations, external consultants were hired to displace Mary and her department. She even attended one board meeting in which she outlined her team's experience managing other culture change programs; the team's experience was with two multinational companies, in which hundreds of staff were trained and fundamental systems changed over several months.

The directors clearly weren't interested. No one asked any questions about the projects I or my staff had formerly been involved in even though they had been much larger and more ambitious than what the directors intended to do. I had the feeling that as I stood up for myself and wanted to be more involved in decision making that affected me or my team specific types of intimidation were used as a warning for me to just get on with the work.

Intimidation is a very powerful tool, especially if it is done over ostensible performance issues. Many of the women described being treated unjustly but were afraid to call attention to the treatment because it might further highlight their alleged shortcomings, instead of punishing their intimidators. If they did not do as they were told, they could be accused of inappropriately discharging their responsibilities, managing their time poorly, or having an attitude problem. In one study, female managers noted that they experienced men sabotaging their efforts. This sabotage occurred in two ways. First, women were given less responsibility after returning from maternity leave and, second, male superiors often scrutinized women's work looking to find fault with it (Swiss, 1995, cited in Rheem, 1996). The study also suggested that women do not litigate for victimization because of the expense of litigation and its personal consequences; if they bring a claim forward, women fear that they will be labeled as troublemakers.

THE DOUBLE-BIND IN SEEKING JUSTICE

The women profiled in this book faced a double-bind: if they complained about their treatment, they were labeled as either petty, aggressive, or un-committed to organizational goals; if they did nothing, their situation did not improve. Because these women were ambitious and wanted to advance in their careers, they challenged unfair treatment and intimidation. When Mary asked for reasonable work schedules for her staff, her commitment to the change management program was questioned.

I remember them [the sales director and the project leader—both men] saying that I needed to understand the importance of the programme and the commitment it required from all of us. I felt angry. I had been working months on it and spent many nights away from home or working very late. I *was* committed. I didn't see that making people work until they were too exhausted to work made any sense.

Madge was made to feel that if she did not work holidays, was ill, or needed to take time off for domestic emergencies she would be shirking her responsibilities.

My mother had Alzheimer's and she stopped eating and drinking. I needed to get her into psychiatric care. I had to go and interview a few places to see if they were suitable and I took two hours off. I was told to keep my mobile phone on and made to feel that I was abandoning my duties. And yet the individual who told me would regularly go have his hair cut at 10 o'clock and not return until 1.

When Elizabeth objected to doing senseless paperwork she was made to feel that she was not a team player.

My boss kept coming back to the issue of me not being a team player because I didn't do the paperwork. This was crazy. I had trained many members of the team and showed them how I wrote client proposals for business. I got on with them and helped them when I could.

Fiona had two days booked as holiday the week before Christmas. For two years running, she had been unable to use her holiday entitlement due to work commitments. On this occasion, she wrote to her manager several months before, as was the customary procedure, requesting the holidays. He approved them. But thereafter, he scheduled a department luncheon that he wanted her to attend. When she explained that she had already made her holiday arrangements, he expressed his frustration that she "was going to set a bad example to the team." Moreover, after team meetings in which Fiona disagreed with her manager he called her into his office and expressed the view that she needed to be "more co-operative and build on other people's ideas instead of debate things." Fiona described the double-bind of trying to assert herself, but being labeled as aggressive and un-cooperative.

I always considered debate to be healthy. When I agreed with someone, I said so, but when I didn't I wanted to put across an alternative view without being labelled aggressive.

Caroline often challenged Jim, the head of the consultancy. At one point when she was frustrated by how Jim and the other consultants were treating her, she asked Jim, "Why did you appoint me? If you didn't want my opinions and my expertise, why didn't you just appoint a young graduate?" Caroline found that sharing her frustrations was met with silence and indifference. No action was ever taken to change things.

Mary reflected on this double-bind dilemma in one of her e-mails to a friend.

> April 6, 1996
> . . . Anyway I feel like the only way you can get anywhere is to challenge and get in their faces on a regular basis. I feel though when I do this that I am labelled as non-feminine and pushy but I can't see any other way. I am not doing it for just me. I am doing it for the sanity of my team. If I don't push, they suffer. Any suggestions?

These women's experiences of the double-bind of seeking justice when unfair treatment takes place and being labeled unfavorably is closely related to the literature on gender stereotypes and their effects. In their work on whether women succeed or are derailed from their careers, Morrison et al. (1987) uncovered several conditions for success, including taking career risks, being tough, having the desire to succeed, and having an impressive presence. In the case of the women profiled in this book, taking risks and being tough were seen by their male colleagues and superiors as too aggressive. As in Morrison et al.'s study, "They [women] had to avoid being feminine and avoid being macho" (1987, p. 145). Research suggests that no matter what women do or how they behave, males will be stereotyped as better leaders. Schein (1973, 1975) found that the successful middle manager was labeled as masculine by both men and women. Virginia Schein (1990) repeated her earlier studies to see if anything had changed. In her study of managers, 420 men and 173 women within nine U.S. firms, men perceived managers as possessing characteristics they ascribed to men rather than women, whereas women associated successful management characteristics with both men and women. Neither age nor tenure in the job moderate these perceptions. Fifteen years had elapsed between reports yet little progress appears to have been made in changing male attitudes toward women. Brenner, Tomkiewicz, and Schein (1989) reported that male managers felt that management qualities were associated with men and not with women. Finally, Heilman et al. (1989) found that male managers described women as generally more deficient than men in those attributes deemed necessary for successful management.

More recently, Baack, Carr-Ruffino, and Pelletier (1993) noted that both male and female managers perceived women as more emotional and less committed than men, although women are viewed as more attuned to customer relations. The Trent Regional Health Authority (Hay, 1993) examined male and female perceptions of leadership. Male subordinates managed by women thought that their women managers used a pacesetting style of leadership more than other styles of leadership. The report also indicated that when women use a pacesetting style, they are perceived to have a more negative impact on the organizational climate than when men employ a pacesetting style. The report concludes that the style used by female managers is not perceived to be authoritative enough by their male subordinates. Women did not subscribe to the "male model" of leadership and this seemed to affect their managerial reputations (Baack et al., 1993 p. 14). Jago and Vroom (1982) conducted research on men's and women's decision-making methods. In spite of the fact that women used more effective decision-making methods than males, those in the women's peer group evaluated the women's styles as less effective than men's styles.

Johnson and Powell (1994) argue that much of the research on the quality of decisions and gender distinctions, showing that women are more risk averse and less confident than men, is misleading. Most studies have been conducted with total-population samples rather than managerial populations. Their work compared a total-population sample with a sample of management students. They found women more likely than men to be risk averse in the non-managerial sample, but no significant differences between men and women in their managerial sample on three decision-making variables: risk propensity, locus of control, and quality of decision.

A U.S. study of women managers found that women outperformed men on 28 of the 31 skill areas surveyed, including critical management attributes such as meeting deadlines, being highly productive, and generating new ideas. Yet, in spite of women's accomplishments, in the United States they are still underrepresented at senior levels. An American government-financed Glass Ceiling Commission estimated that in 1995, only 5% of senior executive positions were held by women (Through a glass, darkly, 1996). All this research points to one conclusion: in spite of women's accomplishments, at the management level they are likely to be judged as less successful than their male counterparts and possibly unsuitable for future influential roles within their organizations—no matter what style of interaction they adopt.

CLOSING RANKS

As the women profiled in this book began to assert themselves and particularly when they had openly filed a grievance for unfair treatment, the men around them closed ranks against them. Managers who had formerly been supporters disappeared. The patriarchal character of their organizations overwhelmed even those individual members who might have wanted to publicly support these women but felt they could not. When men close ranks their actions are subtle and not openly discussed. Their actions, however, carry explicit meaning: do not threaten our way of doing things. In a recent study of women managers, some respondents "felt that men had banded together, bypassed them in communication, publicly blocked initiatives to which they had agreed in private and protected each other" (Marshall, 1995, p. 302).

Similarly, a study of local government identified closing ranks as one means of placing obstacles in the way of women managers. One man in a discussion forum said,

We took on a girl who became quite ill with M.S. [multiple sclerosis] which is notorious for symptoms which don't appear as symptoms. People (men) decided she was swinging the lead . . . and the group closed ranks on her and were very, very cold, which made her illness worse. (Young and Spencer, 1991, p. 53)

Collinson and Collinson (1989) discuss Chris, a supervisor in the fire and accident department of the social services department who was caught defrauding the flex-time system so that he could spend more time with his mistress, one of his direct subordinates. After being reported by his team, he was only minimally punished by his male colleagues. He received a warning and was transferred to another location but was not demoted to a lower grade or removed. After he accepted these terms his boss said,

I am delighted to hear this. I will now go on record to say if you perform as I know you can, I would seriously consider you for promotion to a supervisor's position even within twelve months warning period. (Collinson and Collinson, 1989, p. 106)

Even when men are found to be guilty of harassment or fraud, their colleagues seem to be sending a message of "we will stand by you."

The women profiled in this book described themselves as suddenly "feeling on the outside of the inner circle" or as finding themselves not invited to important events or meetings. Madge described board meetings in which she felt men had closed ranks to support each other.

There was always the inner circle. In fact they themselves called it the inner sanctum. Two employees had left the company. The M.D. [managing director] absolutely attacked me for these people leaving. Someone from another director's area had left and she had raised a hue and cry about how she had been treated but the M.D. said nothing about this. The chairman asked me why this person had left but the M.D. stopped me from answering.

When Madge filed a grievance for equal pay, the male directors began to close ranks around the issue. The company's chairman, although he did not bother investigating her claim, called her in to his office to say that she was never promised equal pay by the managing director. She suggested that he investigate the claim by asking the other female director who would verify that the promise had indeed been made; this suggestion was also written in her grievance letter to him and the board. After she had filed the grievance, the managing director told her that "relationships will be difficult." The other directors stopped speaking to her and she was no longer invited to any directors' meetings.

Madge's situation was similar to a female trade union official in Collinson and Collinson's study (1989) who was elected to a previously all-male executive committee. The male executive members closed ranks around the woman in a campaign of harassment and intimidation. False allegations about her sleeping with other executives were made. When she objected to the allegations and insisted on an apology, she was told she had to take it, or get out of the trade union movement. She was warned that if she took the union to court, she would risk losing her job. She received anonymous threatening letters asking for her resignation before the annual general meeting (Collinson and Collinson, 1989).

After Fiona objected to an unfair job evaluation, her manager, who had initially been supportive, would not support her appeal. She wanted to attend her own appeal hearing of the job evaluation committee to hear what was said and to present her case, but the all-male evaluation committee meeting was closed to her. During the appeal process, her manager cancelled all of their one-to-one meetings, saying he was too busy to meet with her.

When Elizabeth filed a grievance against her manager, she found that the personnel manager and her manager had met behind closed doors for two hours before the grievance was formally heard. She felt that the management ranks had closed against her in favor of her manager before she could even state her case. Elizabeth discovered that her manager had had two previous grievances filed against him by women who had complained about his behavior toward them. In spite of his evident unfair treatment of women, his superiors seemed to put little effort into investigating Elizabeth's claims.

One of Mary's e-mails to a friend revealed how an assistant sales director closed ranks with his male colleagues after Mary had been displaced by a new manager. The assistant sales director was unwilling to support Mary as this would have meant "pulling rank" on his peer, the personnel director.

> May 28, 1996
> Dear [friend],
> Today was tough. Lots of emotion. After people heard the news, managers called from the field offering their astonishment and their support. I met with [the assistant sales director] as I new [sic] he had a job advertised. It left me feeling very angry. I've worked designing programmes for this guy for five years. I asked him if he could help me, whether he could see options for me. I think he knows the personnel director wants me out. He told me he had offered the job to [XX], a buddy of his who has been fired from two senior jobs in less than six months! The job wasn't even advertised although this is a requirement. He even said he wasn't sure the company would let him hire [XX] because of his bad references. Although the guy is completely incompetent, he is apparently willing to take him over me.

When Karen's manager spoke to her about a change in job assignment, Karen asked for a salary increase. The manager indicated to her that he would support her request for an increase in salary. However, after attending an all-male board meeting at which the matter was discussed, he was unwilling to support the increase and insisted that she take the position with no change in salary.

I think that he must have promised the board that he would persuade me to do it at the same salary and of course then he had to go back to the board and say that I wouldn't do it. He could have negotiated for me but he didn't. We could have worked on a strategy for getting it through but he wouldn't even discuss it.

Patricia found that her manager, who in private had supported her point of view that she should manage the marketing budget, publicly went along with the sales directors' view that they should control it.

My immediate manager sympathised with my point of view that the budget should be controlled centrally by marketing, not by the divisions. He didn't help me fight the fight, however. He was promoted—to an M.D. of one of the divisions. Now he was peers with the people I thought we were jointly fighting for control over the budget.

Patricia's situation may be similar to a phenomenon reported by senior-level women in Britain's National Health Service (NHS). Some women in the NHS had been asked to lead change projects, which were potentially problematic, without formal authority to lead them. Their male bosses, who had formerly been supportive of them taking on the additional responsibility, withdrew their support and distanced themselves when the women encountered resistance in their positions. "If resistance to change becomes powerful he [the male boss] may qualify his support and the career prospects of the women may be damaged" (Proctor and Jackson, 1994, pp. 202–203). When times become tough and men risk exposing themselves to controversy if they support a woman, they often abandon her and pull together rather than risk aligning themselves with someone who seems to be supporting an unpopular cause.

Caroline recalled how her once supportive fellow consultant, Ron, who had been her mentor and friend, began to distance himself from her during the negotiations that took place between the consultancy they both worked for and another consultancy that hoped to buy them. Instead of encouraging the acquiring company to include Caroline in the acquisition at her current salary, Caroline said,

Ron totally absented himself. He sent me an e-mail which said he didn't think supporting me would do me any good at all. He assured me that I would be OK. He said he didn't feel it would serve my cause to support me.

As the negotiations proceeded, Caroline was cut completely out of the discussions with her peers. At one point, she was told by the former owner of the consultancy that she would have to negotiate her terms of employment by herself with the new owner. All the other male consultants had the support of the former owner and he had been negotiating with the new owner on their behalf.

As Katherine complained to her manager about being given menial work in the marketing area, her associations with others in the marketing area became distant. Moreover, she felt that her manager and the personnel director had closed ranks.

My boss went to the human resources director to find a way to ease me out. It was interesting that she [the human resources director] supported him without question. No one ever came to me to get my point of view. All I wanted was interesting work to do. They could have resolved it easily.

Closing ranks is a phenomenon that men have learned since time immemorial (Remy, 1990). Andocracy, rule by men, has its origins in patriarchal societies where men exert dominance in a variety of ways. The men's hut encouraged secrecy of its male members. Moreover, men took an oath of loyalty to one another and excluded women in all of their dealings. The men's hut is not far removed from today's male organizations. For example, the Freemasons, which originally constituted a class of skilled itinerant masons has become a fraternal business organization that keeps its rituals secret, excludes women, and because of loyalty "contracts" provides its members favors.

In these examples, the unyielding patriarchal character of organizations is further evinced by the fact that when pressed, women closed ranks with men against other women. If they openly support another woman, the threatening character of men in their organizations may be turned on them, making them vulnerable to the same sanctions the victimized woman has been given. Or, at least, this was widely perceived. "They [women] would be tarred with the same brush if they didn't go along with it [the unfair treatment of a woman]," said Madge. Mary remembered asking a female colleague to support her,

I asked her to say something to the personnel director about my performance— that it had been good. I got the distinct impression that she would not stick her neck out for me. That she felt vulnerable herself and that supporting me would make her even more vulnerable.

After Madge filed the grievance for equal pay that led to her managing director's warning that "relationships would be very difficult" between her and her colleagues, Madge did indeed find that even her female colleague, also a director, distanced herself from Madge. She recalled,

She said, "I know you are going to understand but I think we should not discuss the matter [her industrial tribunal case] any further." She did say that if she was asked to speak at the tribunal she would tell the truth, but that she couldn't become anymore involved at work.

CONCLUSION

The women profiled in this book experienced eight differing mechanisms of control and subordination exercised by the patriarchy in corporate management. In the process, they increasingly were identified by the system as "difficult," because they disagreed with the hierarchy, challenged policy, debated issues others sought to avoid, and refused to remain silent about unfair treatment. The degree of patriarchal resistance these women faced increased as they approached the higher levels of management. As Symons (1992) suggests, female managers contaminate the office with the notion of gender but secretaries do not. Secretaries fit into the hierarchy, while managerial women expose the gendered substructure to critique. As long as managerial women are able to construct their daily work experience with no reference whatsoever to gender, they are left alone. Once, however, they begin to object to treatment that is gender based, they are labeled as "difficult" women.

In addition, as the roles of these women became strategic, their valued contributions were arrogated to men, and they became increasingly isolated. Oral and written communication patterns minimized the contribution of these women or degraded their status, and information was withheld to diminish the women's effectiveness in decision making. Similarly, status and resources were denied to reinforce the signal that women do not have status equal to their male colleagues. The absence of networks and mentors prevents women from penetrating the important inner circle constituted by men. When women become "difficult," they are frequently tested by the male hierarchy to produce stress or to demonstrate a failing. Women face a double-bind if they complain about unfair treatment. If they ignore the unfair treatment they will secure no improvement in their situation, but if they complain they will be further victimized and will be the subject of accusations. Finally, and relatedly, men close ranks to prevent women from taking action to seek redress.

CHAPTER 6

Finally Forced Out

◆◆

When the women profiled in this book took exception to their work situations or raised objections to unfair treatment, they were eventually informed that they would have to leave their organizations. The patriarchy was provoked by these women's challenge of it, until such a point where it responded by removing them.

Usually the terminations were explained to them by their managing directors or managers in euphemistic language: "It just isn't working out," "We've decided that there is no longer a role for you," or "We need to restructure your position." To prevent legal action and the ugliness that occurs with straightforward dismissals, most of the women were told that their positions were redundant. In many cases, the women were told that their performance was below par, despite the fact that they had received above-average performance reviews and special bonuses. Several themes emerged in these women's experiences as they began to break through the glass ceiling. Each of these themes reflects a different but related response of the patriarchy to the threat of their breaking through the glass ceiling. These themes are analyzed in the following categories.

1. Promises Unfulfilled: Two of the women had been made promises about their careers by senior-level managers or by the managing director that were not kept. In one case, the individual decided to join a company on the condition of a promise of comparable pay with her fellow directors that was made to her by the managing director. "Ceiling breaking" promises are sometimes made by sexist men, as in this case, who never intend to keep them. At other times, they

are made by nonsexist men who are prevented from keeping them by the response of the patriarchy. These nonsexist men fear they will jeopardize their own positions if they do not follow the dominant group.

2. Responsibilities Denied: Many of the women expected to be given a degree of autonomy and responsibility usual for their positions as middle or senior managers within their organizations. Instead, they found that once in their positions authority was never provided, was undermined, or was usurped. Several of the women were still held responsible for outcomes but were often not given enough authority to influence them.

3. Unexpected Allegations of Poor Performance: Some of the women found themselves defending themselves against allegations of poor performance, although prior to discussions of dismissal they were given no indication of performance problems. In fact, the women's performance as indicated by company performance appraisals was above average and even exemplary on occasion. Because the women had already been marginalized by their organizations and isolated from their colleagues, they found defending themselves against these charges difficult. Patricia Yancey Martin (1996) noted in her case study research of men and women that men often openly criticized women publicly while women refrained from publicly criticizing men. Her data showed multiple instances where men acted in concert with one another to criticize or depreciate women.

4. Isolation and Stigmatization: Isolation is the patriarchy's reaction to women who threaten to penetrate or change the nature of the hierarchy. Once these women begin to take exception to their treatment by filing a grievance or by formally complaining to someone of higher rank, they find themselves further isolated from their colleagues and from senior-level managers and stigmatized as "untouchable." Cutting one off from work colleagues makes the individual powerless and serves as a lesson to other women who might be tempted to follow her path. The patriarchy is sending a signal both to the woman who tries to assert herself in her position and to other women to "toe the line."

5. Further Victimization and Sexual Harassment: When these women resisted the patriarchy, they were systematically victimized or harassed. Victimization occurs when a woman is singled out and intimidated, threatened, or bullied. Sexual harassment occurs either when a woman is the object of sexual advances or sexual humor or innuendo, or when a woman feels her workplace presents a hostile environment because of sexual overtones. Women with pending promotion or equal pay cases reported treatment ranging from finding themselves ignored to orchestrated campaigns of victimization (Leonard, 1987). It is likely that harassment is used as an indication of male power. Carothers and Crull (1984) argue that male workers are overtly hostile to women who challenge or compete with them for jobs. This hostility is translated into harassment at work. The effects of harassment are serious for anyone, especially senior women trying to achieve equality with men in the board room. Being the object of sexual harassment or bullying behavior is one way of trivializing the contribution of a woman. When people see sexual behavior in the workplace, they attribute it solely to individual wishes and actions and ignore the influence of the hierarchy, work roles, or organizational norms (Gutek, 1989). Sexist attitudes about

women and sexual behavior at work often go unnoticed because they are institutionalized. When the dominant group controls major institutions, it manipulates behavioral norms on the macro level. Women, however, are less powerful and are forced to deal with issues on the micro level. Their efforts to control their environment are noticed and soon women are asked to justify their actions. A woman's psyche becomes scrutinized in how she deals with a sexualized environment, rather than the workplace environment being scrutinized for how it treats her (Lipman-Blumen, 1984).

6. The Grievance Procedure—Tool of the Patriarchy: In these women's cases, the grievance procedure was captive to the patriarchy. Instead of being the neutral processes they purport to be, grievance procedures were often staged, mock attempts to investigate the women's claims. In many cases, the personnel function was co-opted by the patriarchy to swiftly adjudicate against the woman. This occurred in several ways. For example, in some cases personnel managers had collusionary meetings with management to orchestrate the outcome. In other cases, personnel managers did not divulge the grievance procedure completely, purposely leaving the women "in the dark" and unaware of their rights. Some of the women found the grievance or appeals procedure a "closed shop" where they were denied access, even though their adversaries had access. In none of these cases was the grievance procedure undertaken by an independent agency with an arm's length relationship to patriarchal management. Collinson, Knights, and Collinson (1990) substantiate the view that personnel managers and junior personnel officers are co-opted by the patriarchy. Their study of recruitment and selection procedures reports that junior and senior personnel managers resist challenging the sex discrimination practices of line managers for fear of being labeled "feminist or troublemaker" (p. 197). Moreover, their research suggests that in all five of the business sectors studied, the balance of power in organizations is held by line managers who claim to be the producers of wealth and profit, while personnel is viewed as an unproductive welfare function (p. 208).

7. Sacking Out of the Blue: In most cases, the women profiled in this book could not have prepared for their loss of employment because their redundancies took them completely by surprise. Many of the women expected a normal day's activity on the day their employment was terminated, but found they were called into an unscheduled meeting or into a meeting with a different agenda than the one expected. Their surprise terminations left them unable to defend themselves against the charges of inadequate performance or conduct, or against the claim that company restructuring dictated their redundancy. In addition, their employers put immediate pressure on them to agree to an uncontested separation.

8. Buying Off Women: When many of these women were offered redundancy, their organizations were assured of no adverse publicity or a further fight from them because of the settlements offered. Many of the women said they wanted to take their employers to court or an industrial tribunal for unfair dismissal, victimization, or sexual harassment but were aware that they would risk losing more. In short, they simply could not afford to take the risk. Their reputations would be at stake. Even if they won their cases, their financial settlements would likely be reduced from what their employers had offered in redundancy, and they

feared they would find re-employment more difficult if they continued to fight. Their employers bought them off to ensure that the patriarchy could continue its dominance. In some cases, the victims were required to sign a legally binding agreement absolving their employers of any wrongdoing and abandoning any further legal action. Many were forced to sign "gag" clauses in their settlement agreements, preventing them from talking about their cases to the press.

9. The "Reserve Army" of Compliant Replacements: Three of the women found themselves replaced by more compliant women who accepted the terms of patriarchal subordination. These replacement women were paid far less than their predecessors and allowed their position and function to be controlled by the hierarchy. The women profiled in this book said that their female replacements were more stereotypically feminine than themselves and often resorted to flirtatious behavior to signal their nonthreatening personalities. Their replacements were order takers, while the women in this book performed their roles as assertively as their male counterparts and wanted to partake in decision making. Because they witnessed the recent terminations of their predecessors, these replacement women knew what behaviors to avoid. Cockburn (1990) noted a divide and rule strategy that men use against women to maintain the male hierarchy. If women view each other as competition or if men isolate women from one another, women will not be able to organize themselves to assert their rights. In this case, the compliant replacements were often pitted against their predecessors.

PROMISES UNFULFILLED

In four of the cases discussed in this book, the women had been promised a level of status and remuneration commensurate with their abilities and with the job they were already performing. Fiona, Caroline, and Madge had put in energy and demonstrated commitment with the assurance that they would be financially rewarded for their efforts. Similarly, Mary was promised a cash bonus after delivering a strategic project and reorganizing her department.

Prior to Madge's accepting appointment to the board of directors as personnel director of a large retail group she secured a promise from the managing director that her salary would be raised to that of a director. The first year of her appointment went by and the organization had done nothing to rectify the inequality of her salary compared to the other directors. In fact, during the second year of her appointment, the managing director approved a pay increase for one of her male colleagues, who frequently threatened to leave the organization. This raise in salary was paid even though the directors voted as a group not to take increases because the business results had been poor. In addition to failing to correct the pay disparity between Madge and her male directors, the managing director had taken on a male manager, significantly below Madge's status, at only £2 thousand less than Madge's salary. Subsequently, the managing director informed Madge that the male director who had just received a salary increase after threatening to leave would receive a further enhancement, taking his salary to double that of Madge's.

Madge's experience is similar to that of other senior women managers in the retail industry. A survey of senior-level women in retail indicated that salary increases for women were held back on the grounds that they didn't need the money and that, "she's only here for the pin money" (Brockbank and Traves, 1996, p. 89).

When Caroline joined the small consultancy group in Boston, Massachusetts, she was told that because of her level of expertise and experience as a consultant she would be made a principal (part owner of the business) in two years. Since she had been offered a job with another company and had turned it down, she felt that this promise was a critical part of her financial package. She later discovered that the owner of the business had the business for sale when she applied for the job; clearly, this promise, given the circumstances of an imminent sale, could not be guaranteed.

Fiona's experiences were parallel to Madge's. Over several months, Fiona's new position as manager of sales management development had grown in influence and overall responsibility for programs and staff. She asked her manager to request a job evaluation to have the position reevaluated at a higher grade level. Her manager's other direct subordinate, a man, had been reclassified as a director several months before. Fiona's position was at least equal, if not greater, in scope than his: they both had budget and staff responsibilities; his position involved delivering standard, generic sales training programs on a routine basis whereas her job was less routine and more complex. She had responsibility for more programs; although they managed the same number of staff, she managed more senior-level staff than he did; and she delivered programs to senior and middle managers whereas he delivered programs to sales staff.

The change in grade level she had requested was important to Fiona for several reasons: she had made sacrifices at home in terms of time away from her husband and young children; it would mean a jump in salary of about £7 thousand and a potential bonus of 30% of salary rather than 15%; and, finally, she felt the organization should formally recognize that she was performing a director-level job. After hearing her arguments for reclassifying her position, Fiona's manager agreed to take her case to the job evaluation committee, a group of senior managers. He expressed confidence to her about being able to make a strong case for her promotion and told her not to worry about what he saw as a mere formality. Together they worked on a lengthy written argument for reclassifying her position. But when he met resistance from his male colleagues during the job evaluation meetings, he withdrew his support of Fiona. Fiona said,

It was as if our former discussions had not taken place. He had changed his tune completely and was saying that the committee had said he had been heavily supervising me and making decisions for my function, which of course, he hadn't.

Fiona's job evaluation situation not only points to promises unfulfilled but also to the problem of men evaluating women. In her case study research, Yancey Martin (1996) identified three gender-based evaluation frames that men used against women. First, men defined their potential as generally greater than women's although they had no evidence to support this and in many cases had evidence that the woman they were evaluating against a man had greater potential in terms of experience and qualifications. Second, men assumed to have a right to a position, often stating that they needed a higher rank than a woman for their own career progression. Third, in evaluation situations, men's successes tended to be amplified while their weaknesses were minimized or ignored.

Like Fiona, Madge, and Caroline, Mary was promised financial remuneration that was never delivered. Mary's e-mail correspondence records a conversation with the personnel director regarding a bonus that was promised to her. She also suggested that it was unfair that the company would deny her a bonus that she was assured would be given and yet give underperforming sales managers (all of whom were men) large additional bonuses. The personnel director advised her not to push the matter further or meet with the chairman to discuss it. He also suggested he was "unwilling to make comparisons with [Mary] and the underperforming sales managers."

These cases suggest that even talented women have difficulty progressing up the corporate career ladder. According to one study of 461 female executives from *Fortune 1000* companies, 52% said that male stereotyping was the greatest barrier to their career development. In the study, 325 chief executive officers (CEOs) were surveyed; 82% said that women's lack of career progression was due to lack of significant general management experience (Davis, 1996). If women like Madge, Caroline, and Fiona are not given the status, recognition, and opportunity for more senior-level positions, it will always be easy for their organizations to deny them access to these positions by insisting that they do not have sufficient general management experience.

RESPONSIBILITIES DENIED

Many of the women profiled had reached a level where they expected a degree of autonomy and responsibility equal to that of their male counterparts. They were continually frustrated by being denied responsibility that should have been accorded.

As marketing manager for a financial services company, Katherine had been pushing her manager for some time to give her more challenging work. She reflected, "I could have done many of the exciting projects that he took for himself. I sometimes think he didn't delegate anything important to me for fear I'd do too good a job."

Over a one-year period, Katherine felt that her relationship with her manager had deteriorated, but at the time she couldn't put her finger on the reason why. In hindsight, she believes it was due to her wanting to be recognized as his equal, not so much in terms of her position in the hierarchy but rather in terms of her ideas. Katherine and her manager had formerly been colleagues at the same grade level and they both had had a history of moving up the promotional ladder until he was chosen to manage Katherine.

After I requested that we together work on a development plan to help me progress in the organisation, I recognised that something was wrong. He hadn't put any thinking into the plan and in fact had cancelled our meetings to talk about it.

As she made more demands for her own development, Katherine felt she became uncomfortable to her manager. He knew that she had left her former organization for a greenfield opportunity, yet he was not giving her work that would hold her interest. On several occasions, he had intervened to give her assistant challenging work. "I had the sense that he was developing my young assistant instead of me. She was brand new to marketing, in her early 20s and certainly not a threat to him," Katherine recalled.

Katherine began to feel that her manager was putting distance between her and the organization. Although she had previously handled projects alone, now he was asking other people to assist her.

I had always done the newsletter for the organisation before when suddenly he [Katherine's manager] asked another manager to co-write it with me. This was a simple newsletter and didn't require two people to write it.

As marketing manager for a graphics firm, Patricia assumed that she had authority over her budget and that she was responsible for the marketing strategy. Looking back, Patricia recalls several signs that suggested she was not fitting into the male-dominated culture and that men in the organization could not tolerate women in positions of authority. Patricia remembered, "There was one point where my boss said to me, 'Perhaps we shouldn't have chosen a woman for such a senior-level job.' "

As Patricia tried to assert herself in the marketing function, she found the organization took more and more of her authority away. When the division sales managers began taking over her budget, her objections fell on deaf ears. She recalls trying to adjust her behavior in various ways to win the sales managers' support.

I consciously tried different behavioural styles to see if I could get through to them. First I tried going along with the macho culture. With the sales force I tried to be approachable and informal. Next, I tried to be super business like. I unfortunately got labelled as Margaret Thatcher or the battleaxe.

In her diary entries, Diane recalled how she was constantly denied authority in her role as finance director. When she suggested that she could use information learned from her MBA program to help the senior management group, she was told that the senior management group did not want her help. In one instance, the managing director intervened on a trivial matter with one of her staff. He ordered Pippa (her staff member) to drive to Swindon on her holiday to pick up some company samples. When Diane suggested that the company could have them delivered by courier, the managing director suggested that Diane was trying to overrule his authority.

As head of engineering for an electronics firm, Lesley had been charged with and willingly agreed to re-engineer her department. However, she believed that determining how to re-engineer her department of 250 engineers should be her decision. After all, she knew her people, their backgrounds and personalities, and their strengths and weaknesses. Lesley conducted a presentation for the vice president of the parent company about how she planned to re-engineer the department. The vice president was not himself an engineer. She presented a detailed plan about hiring new engineers with software experience and making redundant those who would either be incapable of learning new skills or who would resist the changes that needed to come. As an engineer and manager, she believed that she knew the complexities of the engineering projects for which her group would be accountable and challenged the authority of the vice president, a non-engineer. At the end of her presentation, she suggested that the vice president allow her to make the decision about how to restructure her group,

I told him straight out that I wanted to make the decision about how to re-engineer the department. This frustrated him and really got him upset. In the end, I don't think he thought I was going fast enough, although he was not well enough informed about engineering to know whether going faster would be wise or even possible given our obligations to clients.

Sexism in the engineering environment, similar to the kind Lesley experienced, has been noted by other researchers. Smith-Keller (1992) reports the difficulties of women scientists and engineers in dealing with tokenism, unequal treatment, and discriminatory practices.

Mary's position as head of training had been exhausting; she and her team were launching a culture change program and had been training nonstop for nine months. Mary was particularly frustrated because she was allowed little input into the decision-making process in the months leading up to and during the culture change program. For example, when she wrote up a long involved schedule for her team members showing dates of training, locations, and with whom they would be training, she found the sales director altering her schedule without consulting her.

I was furious. I was head of training and he felt he could manage my function for me. He made trivial changes—rearranging names of people and where they would train. It was simply a power manoeuvre.

Mary's diaries reflect several instances of being denied authority and responsibility commensurate with a well-seasoned senior manager. She recalled how senior management arranged consultants to manage the change program instead of allowing her and her staff to manage it. Moreover, her diaries explain how the organization put her through endless loops of approval before she could take actions that involved her staff or function.

As Caroline's company progressed in its negotiations with another consultancy, her colleagues began taking her clients from her. If Caroline's clients called, the other consultants intervened. Soon, the owner began to give business that should have been Caroline's to the other male consultants. This was an obvious ploy to make them more attractive, and her less attractive, to the new owner in the negotiation process. Caroline reflected, "It was easy for them to justify a lesser deal for me if I appeared to bring fewer clients to the table. It didn't matter if they took them from me."

These women experienced what Wajcman (1991) discusses as patriarchal control by the definition of male and female work contributions. Men position themselves as planners, strategists, and designers as a way of elevating their status while women are classed as implementors and doers. In Fiona's case, her manager suggested that he made decisions for her even though she reports having made decisions and defined the strategy for her area herself. Although capable of defining strategy for their departments, Patricia and Katherine were not allowed input into the marketing strategy of their organizations. Similarly, Lesley was not allowed to determine the strategy for re-engineering her department.

UNEXPECTED ALLEGATIONS OF POOR PERFORMANCE

When some of the women pushed for more influence in their organizations or fair treatment from their male colleagues, their performance was questioned. After Patricia complained about sexual harassment and her lack of real influence as a marketing manager, her manager complained of the service she was providing the sales directors (one of whom had been her harasser). Her manager was unable to provide her with any specific examples of her behavior, just that "others had complained about her lack of service."

At the grievance meeting, Elizabeth's manager raised the issue of her not following procedures for filling in paperwork. This, he said, constituted poor performance. Elizabeth countered his charges by pointing out that others on the team had not filled in the paperwork and they had not been accused of poor performance. She also indicated that she was the highest fee-earning consultant in their group. This, she suggested, was more important to the organization than filling in forms. When Mary was called into a meeting with her new manager and the personnel director, she was told that her performance was not adequate, in spite of the fact that she had above-average performance reviews since joining the company and had received special bonuses. She was not given any specific examples of her lack of performance and, like Patricia, was told that a senior sales director had complained about her. Since leaving the company, Mary has been in touch with this senior sales manager, who invited her to lunch after hearing that she was leaving.

He expressed amazement when I told him he was used to discredit my performance. He told me he never said anything of the kind. He said he was asked by the personnel director about how I might feel about my new role and he said I probably wouldn't be happy not managing the function any longer but he insisted that he had not complained about my performance.

Mary's diary entries describe how the personnel director made allegations of underperformance and how Mary reminded him that she had recently been given an ex-gratia payment for outstanding performance. She had also been told by an external consultant who had worked for the company that she was highly regarded by her field clients and when word got out about her leaving several called her to express their shock and regret.

Mary, Fiona, and Katherine retained copies of the performance review documentation from the employers who had terminated them. In each case, their performance was rated well above average. This is further evidence of the patriarchy's attempts to rid itself of successful women who do not conform.

Mary's organization's performance appraisal system consisted of one general rating of job performance from a five-point scale: 1 = Far Exceeds Requirements, 2 = Exceeds Requirements, 3 = Good Performance, 4 = Development Needed, 5 = Not Able to Assess, Too New to the Job. Mary received a "2" rating with the following comment from her line manager, "Mary has worked well at integrating what had formerly been two teams. She brings a much needed business oriented approach to the team. This ties in particularly well with the needs that are now being expressed by senior management. Mary has demonstrated strengths in terms of designing and developing programmes."

During the job evaluation proceedings, Fiona was told that her decision-making skills and leadership abilities were underdeveloped due to her manager's interventions to supervise her in these areas. Her performance reviews suggested a different picture of performance: above-average performance in nearly all of the areas rated.

Fiona's employer used a performance evaluation process that measured goal achievement on the following six-point scale: 1 = outstanding performance, 2 = excellent performance, 3 = high standard of performance, 4 = acceptable performance, 5 = below acceptable performance, 6 = unsatisfactory performance. Only 20% of employees perform at the "1" and "2" levels, while the majority perform at the "3" and "4" levels. On two goals, Fiona received a "1" rating and on four other goals she received a "2" rating. Fiona's employer also rated employees on their management skills. The management skills portion of the performance appraisal consisted of a four-point scale with the following values: highly developed, developed, developing and making progress, and not begun to develop. On seven of the management dimensions, Fiona received a "highly developed" rating and on three dimensions she received a "developed" score. On the leadership dimension, she received a "developing and making progress" mark. Fiona's line manager concluded that, "Fiona juggles priorities and produces excellent work without fail. She uses good judgement and continually receives praise from her client groups. Her leadership skills are sound and her instincts in this area are good, she simply needs more years experience in this area."

Katherine was told by her organization that her position was redundant and that "she didn't seem busy enough" even though the company had hired an assistant to help her with the volume of work. Her performance review listed several major projects that she had completed. In fact, the human resources director told Katherine that she had attained the second highest bonus of anyone in the company for achievement of annual objectives. Her manager, however, rated her as "satisfactory" under the rating guidelines. She thought this was his way of justifying getting rid of her and this was his subjective evaluation of her merit. As Katherine said, "He could hardly have dismissed someone whom he had rated as superior." Katherine's annual bonus was more objective; it measured whether and to what degree an employee achieved the many objectives set out at the beginning of the year.

ISOLATION AND STIGMATIZATION

Both before and after they were asked to leave, the women were isolated from others in the organization and as such were stigmatized as either failures or troublemakers. It was as if others who might associate with them would be guilty of the same transgressions simply by association. In some cases, this stigmatization went beyond their immediate workplace and cost them their reputations outside of their organizations.

Madge recalled how her female co-director told her one afternoon that she regretted that under the circumstances she could not be seen with Madge. She feared that her own livelihood was at stake and she could not take the risk of being fired along with Madge. Although Madge continued to work for the company after she filed a grievance and before her case was heard by the industrial tribunal, she was systematically excluded from board meetings and tarred as a "disloyal member of the board."

After Mary had filed a grievance about being displaced from her management position, she was isolated from the rest of her team.

All of the other team members were working together on project work. It was obvious to me that my new boss wanted to separate me from the group. Perhaps to show me that I was no longer fitting in. I also noticed that the team seemed to suddenly keep their distance from me. The chain of command had changed and they had to demonstrate their immediate allegiance to it. One of my team members said to me, "I plan to keep my head down. I need my job."

After she began to have trouble with the managing director, Diane, like Mary, found herself isolated from her staff. The managing director used another director to put distance between Diane and one of her female staff members.

They [the managing director and one other board member] would call her [Diane's female staff member] into private meetings to suggest that I did not value her work or her opinion. It couldn't have been farther from the truth because she was very talented. They just wanted to drive a wedge between us.

In addition, Diane found a divide and conquer mentality on the board of directors. When she demonstrated to her fellow board members that she wanted to be more fully involved in decision making about the acquisition of a new company, she found that she was isolated from her colleagues. When she pointed out the problems with the acquisition and the financial risks, she was told the acquisition had nothing to do with her and that she should stick to the accounts.

After Fiona made it clear to her manager that she would appeal the job evaluation decision, she found that he systematically avoided her, canceling their routine one-to-one meetings. Fiona prepared a lengthy written response to the job evaluation committee citing examples of her decision-making skills, which had been questioned. When she asked her manager if she could present her own case or at least be present at the job evaluation meeting, he told her that this was not allowed; her manager had to present her case on her behalf. Fiona was physically and psychologically isolated. Not only was she physically kept away from all meetings about her situation, she was also psychologically isolated by not having any information about what or why her opponents had denied her promotion. She was required to submit written briefs defending her position, but the job evaluation committee provided her only anecdotal comments through her own manager.

When Elizabeth filed a grievance with the director of housing over not being allowed to apply for the fair rents officer position, she pointed out that the chosen candidate did not have the credentials that were directly relevant to the job, nor did he have managerial or housing experience. Elizabeth had trained two individuals within her department and had been managing the department since the former manager moved on to another position. After filing the grievance, she became stigmatized by the organization and marked as a troublemaker who should not be allowed to rise within the housing profession.

After I took the grievance up it became very uncomfortable. I wanted to get out of the department so I started to apply for other housing officer jobs. I applied for eight different positions and wasn't even getting an interview. Finally, a director in the local authority and a friend, told me, "Elizabeth, forget it. What you did to the director of housing in terms of filing a grievance made the other directors mark you as untouchable. The director of housing is saying, 'I don't want that cow working for me. If she thinks she is going to work here and do that to me, she's got another think coming.' "

Elizabeth's female director friend was present at the hiring discussions and discussed their contents with Elizabeth. "She told me that I came out excellent on everything but there was this problem with me as a person and I shouldn't be hired because of it. They [the directors] never mentioned the grievance but it was implied that I could make trouble," Elizabeth said. Elizabeth realized that the director of housing had also negatively influenced her chances of finding a position outside the authority. Potential employers were phoning him for a reference and he was cautioning them not to hire her. Elizabeth recalled, "The interviews were always very short. I hardly had a chance to talk about my background. I'm sure that the director said, 'Don't touch this woman.' "

In all of these cases, the isolation and stigmatization served as punishment before the accused was tried. This type of punishment is difficult to address because it is not conducted openly. In many cases, the women did not realize they were being isolated and stigmatized until well after the events, when at some future point they reflected on what had happened to them. Isolation and stigmatization act as mechanisms to try to stop these women from carrying their grievances forward. Along with victimization and harassment, these mechanisms are powerful psychological ammunition that the patriarchy uses against women it cannot seem to control.

VICTIMIZATION AND HARASSMENT

Victimization and harassment are two sides of the same coin. Although women are substantially similar to men in terms of characteristics germane to employment, men still treat them unequally at work and label them as different, inferior, or unable (Abrams, 1994). This initial attitude about women becomes a breeding ground for serious types of discrimination such as victimization and sexual harassment. Schein (1994) argues that sexual harassment occurs when the sociocultural power model of male dominance operates within organizations. In these situations sexual harassment is often tolerated rather than reported because women fear retaliation.

A plethora of harassment examples exists, spanning the professions and organizational levels. In accounting, starting a family, the inability to penetrate the glass ceiling, the corporate culture, and sexual harassment were reasons given for women leaving the profession (Ferrers, 1995). In another accounting study, a survey of 514 internal auditors reported that 24% had been sexually harassed. The male supervisor was most often cited to be the harasser. Of the 121 internal auditors who had been victimized, 78% were women; however, 36% of the respondents answered "no" when asked if they had informed anyone about the harassment (Serepca, 1995). Women experience gender problems in their attempts to reach partner level in the accounting profession; less than 5% of partners in the United States are women. Attitudes toward women and harassment are two contributing problems. In a U.S. study, 51% of respondents said that they knew women who had been sexually harassed in public accounting (Stanko and Warner, 1995). In the legal profession in the United Kingdom, according to the first large-scale survey of women junior members of the bar, over three fourths of women barristers had encountered sex discrimination and two fifths had experienced sexual harassment (Junior barristers face sex discrimination, 1995). In a professional U.K. services firm, data were collected from 829 women and 766 men. Women reported significantly more sexual harassment than did men. For women, harassment produced lower job satisfaction, a greater intention to quit, and greater cynicism about the firm's commitment to fair treatment (Burke, 1995).

Victimization and harassment are two mechanisms used by the patriarchy to denigrate women, to suggest to them their powerlessness and to intimidate them so that they would give up fighting. Victimization is sometimes subtle. For example, any treatment that was deliberately orchestrated to further disadvantage women can be labeled as victimization. Some women discover that their superiors deliberately put them into unreasonably tough situations, setting them up for imminent failure. Others find that in spite of excellent performance, their work is meticulously scrutinized for the purpose of finding some trivial fault. Like isolationist and stigmatizing tactics, victimization and harassment effectively set a woman apart, making her an example to others and warning her not to take her complaints of unfair treatment further.

Caroline felt victimized as she tried to assert herself in the negotiation process during the time in which the company for which she worked was negotiating its sale to another consultancy. She described how Peter, a consultant and the chief negotiator with the company for which Caroline worked, would invite her into his office to discuss the issues she raised. Caroline wanted the company to negotiate for her as if she were a principal consultant, the title that she had been promised, and not as a senior consultant, a position with less remuneration.

He would invite me in and then ask me to sit down. He would then come around where I was sitting and stand over me and jingle coins in his pocket. It looked as if he was playing with himself. When I asked why he would not negotiate for me as if I were a principal consultant, he would say, "I have no commitment to you. I can drop you out of the deal in a heart beat."

Madge encountered victimization as she brought her claim of unequal pay to the attention of the Equal Opportunities Commission and finally to an industrial tribunal. Between the time Madge submitted her claim and the time it was heard, she continued to work for the company. She was accused by the other directors of sullying the managing director's reputation by questioning his honesty over his promise of equal pay. She was completely ignored in board meetings and told by the managing director that she would have to "rebuild relationships as everyone on the board had lost confidence in her." She continued to run a large personnel function, but without the help of a secretary. Her secretary had left on maternity leave and the directors refused to hire a replacement for her.

Patricia, a marketing manager in a sales organization, found that as she tried to assert herself in her role and with her fellow sales managers she was sexually harassed. The harassment occurred at a time when she was trying to regain the marketing budget the sales managers had taken over from her. At a sales force conference where two senior sales managers sat across from Patricia at the dinner table, one told a joke whose punch line involved reaching over and grabbing her breasts. Patricia recalled how she felt, "I saw red. I shot up from my chair and shouted 'you pig' and then I sat down. I was embarrassed. I felt so degraded and humiliated." Patricia told her manager about the harassment and was taken seriously only because she insisted that if nothing were done she would take the episode up with a tribunal. Her manager discussed the incident with the male personnel director who, in turn, spoke to the sales manager involved. Patricia received an apology from the manager but no further investigation of this man's behavior occurred and he was not punished. What happened to Patricia has happened in countless other organizations. The way in which

Patricia's organization dealt with the harassment suggests that the prevailing attitude was, as Collinson and Collinson (1989) report in other cases, men cannot control their natural biological urges and women, as objects of sexuality, precipitate men's natural urges.

Other instances of victimization occurred as Patricia tried to regain power as a marketing professional. Her manager had recently been promoted to managing director of one of the sales divisions. As her manager was brought into the sales directors' fold he would not support her. In fact, even before his promotion he took several opportunities to humiliate her publicly and privately.

A week before his promotion he called a meeting for all marketing personnel. He launched into a vehement attack of me saying the M.D.s [managing directors] of other divisions had complained about me and the service I was providing them. I felt dressed down and humiliated in front of my team. There was no warning and no mention of dissatisfaction with my work. I didn't feel I was underperforming.

On another occasion, Patricia held her ground in a disagreement with him about a marketing decision she expected to make.

This frustrated him to such a point that he swore at me—"you bastard" and insulted me. I had a word with the managing director. My former boss was forced to come to me and apologise. I accepted but said I could tell that he wasn't sincere, that he'd been asked to say it. After that incident my relationship with the marketing director for the entire company became distant.

Lesley encountered victimization by being singled out and treated different from her male engineering colleagues. Lesley felt that her managing director had succumbed to pressure from the vice president who was not happy with the way she intended to conduct the re-engineering of her department. She noted that her male colleagues had been allowed to determine how to downsize and reorganize their departments.

Differential treatment of women versus men in the engineering profession has been documented by the National Science Foundation in the United States. A study of over two thousand doctoral students (Wolff, 1996) in science and engineering concluded the following:

1. Men are more likely to be taken seriously and respected by faculty.
2. Women are more likely than men to feel pressure to produce research results.
3. Women report more difficulty in collaborating with male graduate students and male faculty members on research.
4. Men are more likely to receive help from male advisors on research design, grant writing, publications, and organizing people.
5. Women are more apt to view their relationships with male colleagues as "student and faculty," while men view their relationship as "mentee and mentor."

It is reasonable to suggest that Lesley encountered similar differential treatment at work. Engineering firms employ people who have been through the university system and received engineering degrees. Preferential treatment for men is likely to be reproduced in the business environment. As Lesley commented, "In engineering and science environments the execs usually, at the very least, listen and want to understand the arguments of the scientists and engineers. In this case, the vice president couldn't be bothered with my view."

Ironically, Lesley subsequently discovered that after she had been made redundant the managing director had been forced to follow her initial plan for the re-engineering project in order to meet client demands. "In the end, the company needed software engineers and had to hire them as I had suggested. They waited too long to take my recommendation and found themselves panicking to meet a project deadline."

After Elizabeth had won her long battle with the director of housing to become a fair rents officer, she found her position markedly changed. The director of housing arranged for Elizabeth to manage a notorious problem area rife with drug addicts and criminal activity. "I realized that their strategy was to give me the greatest problem area, set targets that would be impossible to achieve so that they could sack me. What happened instead was I turned the area around and I became a very good housing officer."

In spite of her success, Elizabeth was still harassed by the director of housing, who by now was rummaging through her desk drawers after hours in search of evidence of some minor infraction. "He would call me in and yell at me about some minor issue or write caustic remarks in the margins of my paperwork like, 'This isn't exactly right. Do it again.' "

In the end, Elizabeth felt exhausted and unable to pursue yet another grievance against him. She simply wanted out of the organization so she resigned.

Elizabeth's next employment situation as a management consultant has several parallels with her fair rents officer position. As a black woman, she was in the minority and she felt continually bullied by her manager, in spite of excellent performance.

I was working very hard. I didn't have holidays for two years and couldn't resource the work I was selling. My boss wanted me in the office three days a month to do paperwork. It wasn't feasible because of the business targets I'd been set. He just got angry. I wasn't toeing the line. I tried to talk to him about the catch-22 I was in. I was expected to sell more than everyone else because targets were based on historical performance but I was also expected to attend meetings and do paperwork that I couldn't fit in and hit my business target. I asked him to try to work out a solution with me. He said I was lying about the amount of business I was producing. I brought in invoices and letters from clients to prove to him that I couldn't do more. I told him that I would try to rectify the situation but needed to know specific areas to work on. He wouldn't give me any.

During a period of several months, Elizabeth's manager intimidated her in various ways. She suspected that part of her manager's treatment of her was the result of her applying to a senior consultancy position within the firm. On several occasions he would request a one-to-one meeting with her and then not be in the office. He would then reschedule the meeting when Elizabeth had an important client meeting and chastise her for not attending the meeting, in spite of the fact that she provided him with her monthly diary listing all her appointments. He continued to insist that she fill in needless paperwork and then criticized her for "not being a team player" when she did not complete it. At the last minute, he would renege on permission for her to attend a conference, saying that she must attend a meeting with him at the office. He then would not be at the office. At a particular one-to-one meeting he began berating Elizabeth,

He said, "I don't understand why you won't do the paperwork." I said, "I don't know what you want me to do. I don't understand it." He then went mad. He said, "Who the hell do you think you are? What have I got to do to make you do what I want? I'm the boss around here." He was screaming and pounding his fists on the table.

At this point Elizabeth asked that they recess. Her manager was clearly out of control. After 40 minutes they tried to reconvene, but again Elizabeth's manager lost his temper. When she went home that evening, she reflected on what was actually occurring between her and her manager. "I was bringing in more fee income than any other consultant in his team. I was working—training other consultants and doing strategy work for the organisation, yet he [Elizabeth's manager] wouldn't support my application to senior consultant."

Elizabeth cataloged incidents of victimization in her diary entries. Specifically, she mentions her manager's unyielding attitude over trivial paperwork; his canceling her performance review as a form of punishment; his withholding his nomination for her to post for a senior consultancy despite the fact that, by his own admission, she met all the criteria; and his refusal to let her attend development activities even though he had previously agreed to let her attend them.

Elizabeth decided she would file a grievance against her manager on two counts: first, for his bullying behavior and, second, because he wouldn't support her application for a senior consultant position even though she met all the criteria. One of her manager's female colleagues told Elizabeth to "watch her back" as her manager was talking to the other directors about the problems he was having with her and clearly fishing for criticism of her from others in the organization. Elizabeth thought about the underlying reasons why he wanted her out of his organization,

I didn't fit any of his stereotypes of what a consultant should be. He was annoyed by my success. The younger consultants were from top universities and I hadn't come up through those channels. He referred to them as "golden nuggets." I was from East London, a poor background, and a minority. I also didn't fit the feminine stereotype. I don't wear short skirts or lots of make-up. I don't flirt with men or tell them how wonderful they are unless I think they really are.

Elizabeth's experiences as a management consultant are also documented elsewhere. In western Europe, women in the management consultancy arena faced three barriers to achievement of career success: the hiring process often discriminates against them from the start, the internal career development systems does not recognize their accomplishments, and their clients may not accept advice from women (Berry, 1996).

Diane was the finance director of a food wholesaler when she was made redundant. Before her redundancy, her managing director tried many tactics to intimidate her and to catch her off guard. The managing director used a pattern of victimization designed to constantly belittle her and berate her skills in front of her peers. In board meetings he would inappropriately expect Diane to take the minutes rather than have his secretary join the meeting and take the minutes. The directors repeatedly challenged her financial accounts even though time and time again they were proven to be accurate. In addition, when Diane began taking courses toward her MBA degree her fellow directors teased her, implying that the skills she was acquiring were not "real world skills."

I was getting more skills from my M.B.A. and wanting to use them and in fact they wanted me to use less skills. I was becoming knowledgeable about strategy, marketing and operations and honestly thought I could contribute my opinions. The production director told me I wasn't supposed to know about those things.

Diane's managing director brought in outside consultants to evaluate her accounts. Because he did this without informing her, Diane felt an atmosphere of distrust was developing. The external assessors told her managing director that she was a good accountant and that there were no problems with her work.

I think the fact that the accountants told him that I was good annoyed him. This was going to be his excuse for getting rid of me. The directors didn't like me challenging things, asking questions or being involved in the business.

Incidents of intimidation were also described in Diane's diary entries. Mary, head of training, was intimidated and harassed on several occasions after she tried to assert herself in her role. The sales director had asked her to compile a thorough evaluation report on training and send it to the board. After she sent the report off, she received a telephone call from the sales director criticizing her for sending the report out in her name.

Although only a small occurrence, this incident reveals how intimidation works in practice. A woman does as she is instructed and then is criticized unjustly. She cannot win because, in cases of intimidation and harassment, she will be set up for failure or criticized no matter what type of behavior she exhibits.

After Mary filed a grievance for being displaced by a woman without any experience in training, she was subjected to harassment and bullying from the personnel director.

This was his way of warning me not to take this matter any further. He would call me into the office early at 7:30, and make me wait for him for three hours. Then he would ask to see the work I'd been doing and rip it to shreds. He spent two hours going through a piece of work when I suggested that at his level perhaps this was a misuse of his time. He would send me back with new marching orders and tell me that he needed a report in the morning for a board meeting. I phoned my secretary to ask her to find out if there was really a board meeting. There was no meeting scheduled.

Mary suggested that, because she had agreed to redundancy, perhaps the company would let her begin searching for a new job rather than report into the office. The personnel director, she believed, continued to harass her as a way of intimidating her during the negotiation period up to signing the redundancy agreement. Only a few days before her official redundancy was to go into force,

He asked me to put together an induction process for my new manager's team. I suggested that perhaps I was the wrong person to do this as I would not be part of the team. He said, "do it anyway." He'd give me project work, but incomplete information [to accomplish it] and then criticise me for not having included the relevant statistics that he instantly produced. When I worked from home, he would telephone me three or four times a day just to see if I was there. Oh yes, we had had some equipment stolen from a hotel—it was in a locked cupboard, but was stolen by hotel staff. I had filed insurance claims and gotten the hotel to accept all liability. He told me that I was incompetent for having let the equipment out of my sight.

The personnel director's campaign of intimidation and bullying behavior is well cataloged in Mary's diary entries. The diary entries focus on the period of time after Mary refused to rescind her grievance against the company and before she accepted redundancy terms.

After Karen, a total quality manager, had uncovered her manager's affair with one of her colleagues, Karen was victimized. Her manager began publicly criticizing her work and stopped supporting her programs. On one occasion, during a termination discussion, Karen's manager physically threatened her by pushing his finger into her chest.

All these examples point to several features of the patriarchy. When the patriarchy feels threatened by women, it pushes back to put them in their place. Putting a woman in her place very often occurs through the mechanism of harassment or victimization. A study of 360 workers in three different companies concluded that women in the traditionally male work environment of manufacturing may make equal pay to men; however, they report more harassment than women who work in non-male environments. "By entering the male job market women place themselves in competition with men, who then attempt, if they have the power, to secure their dominant role by emphasising the 'womanness' of their female co-workers and subordinates" (DiTomaso, 1989, p. 88). By virtue of their senior-level positions, the women profiled in this book worked in all-male environments. Their male colleagues often tried to point out their femaleness as a means of suggesting they were different and, therefore, inferior. Millett (1970) also noted that patriarchal societies focused on the alien features of women as a way of placing them in a lower order from men. Once placed in a different and lower order, they could be treated as an inferior class.

The strategies for dealing with victimization and harassment in organizations that do not value women are ineffective. If women formally complain about harassment they are not taken seriously, as in Patricia's case, or the harassment becomes more frequent and more serious, as in Mary's case. A study of 34 women and 16 men in managerial and professional organizations in Canada (Sheppard, 1989) suggested that women used three strategies when confronted with gender issues at work. First, they attempted to desexualize themselves by wearing masculine clothing and by talking like men. Second, they tried to blend in by being feminine enough but also business-like enough. Third, they attempted a "rightful place strategy," where they would not accommodate men to make them feel more comfortable with them as women. None of these strategies worked well. "Women's sexuality is available to be used as a method of control through humiliation and discomfort" (Sheppard, 1989, p. 154). Being the object of harassment and bullying puts the woman on trial; the focus of attention becomes how the woman handled the situation. Did she react too aggressively? Did she show a sense of humor about the incident? Did she provoke the incident? Harassment and victimization are often used as ways of denigrating a woman and calling into question her work performance.

GRIEVANCE PROCEDURE AND REDUNDANCY PROCESS: TOOLS OF THE PATRIARCHY

When the profiled women in this book decided formally to file a grievance they discovered that the grievance procedure, far from being an unbiased process, was dictated by the patriarchy. The women found themselves defending themselves in hearings in which the human resources department had colluded with management. Even when perpetrators of harassment had been found guilty, they were told only to apologize. No serious punishment was meted out and the human resource department, usually in charge of managing grievances, did nothing to monitor the behavior of the offender. Similarly, when individuals were forced to take redundancy, the cards were stacked against them. Often they were told they were underperforming, although evidence for underperformance was lacking. In fact, many had evidence to the contrary, suggesting that their performance had been significantly above average. One of the women was awarded an ex-gratia payment in May of £2 thousand for outstanding performance. She was forced to take redundancy in September of the same year. Redundancy discussions proceeded as *faits accompli*. Often women were surprised by the discussions and outnumbered in them by several senior managers or human resource professionals.

Madge, a human resource director, filed a grievance on the grounds of not receiving equal pay. When she told her managing director that she intended to file a grievance, he suggested that her situation would improve in time if she could just be patient. She reminded him that she had waited for two years for the pay disparity to be rectified. He then suggested that perhaps her life "on the homefront" was making her act so aggressively. The company grievance procedure required that Madge would have to write to the managing director and to the internal board, which included the individuals against whom she was taking the grievance. She told her managing director that this was an impossible situation and that she would write instead to the salary remuneration committee of the main board. Madge received two letters from the main board. One came from a board member who thanked her for her grievance, saying, "We will look into it." The second came from the chairman of the company who met with Madge to deliver the letter and a veiled threat,

He told me, "You should be prepared to take the consequences if you are going to take the matter further. Think very carefully about heightening this matter." When I said nothing, he then passed me a letter.

The letter informed Madge that the board had rejected her grievance but valued her as a person and an employee. Although Madge requested to meet personally with the remuneration committee, her request was denied.

During this interview with the chairman, Madge told him that she expected the remuneration committee to reject the grievance but that she intended to have an independent expert look at her job and her comparator's, the male board member who was being paid double Madge's salary, to establish whether the pay disparity was justified. A few days later, Madge was told by the chairman that the internal board, her male colleagues, had voted unanimously that Madge should leave the company.

It is clear that the managing director had no intention of investigating Madge's claim. Three months after she had contacted the Equal Opportunities Commission, it decided to take up her case for equal pay, victimization, and unfair dismissal. Madge's company was required to submit detailed records to the industrial tribunal about directors' salaries and answer questions about sex discrimination. Madge submitted detailed job descriptions for her role and for her male comparator's role and a three-year human resources plan to demonstrate that her role had responsibility and influence at least equal to her comparator's. The company submitted its version of her job description. But the company eliminated several important elements.

They completely eliminated any responsibility I had had for health and safety for the organisation. I introduced health and safety in all of the offices and stores, conducted risk assessments and monitored the whole process. My comparator had a job selecting clothing, mine was selecting people. I argued that selecting people was equally as important to selecting clothing.

It became clear to Madge during the proceedings that her company would stall, claim not to have documents, and when forced to give information grossly distort the truth. In the end, Madge won her case on all counts and she received a record settlement.

Katherine, a marketing manager, was called into a meeting to ostensibly discuss her development. For several months she had been pushing for the organization to use her skills more fully. Instead of a development discussion she found two senior-level managers, the marketing director (her manager) and the human resource director, sitting around a conference table with a redundancy agreement already typed up and ready for her to sign. Katherine was told that she had to take redundancy as her position was no longer required by the company. When she asked how she could file a grievance, she was told that there was no basis on which to file a grievance because this was simply the company exercising its right to restructure departments. It was clear to Katherine that her manager had enlisted the support of the human resources director to get rid of her.

Despite the fact that the company had an employee relations manager, a position designed to advise on issues of employment (including redundancy), this individual was not brought into the process. Because management had no wish to establish lines of communication with Katherine, the employee relations manager, who might have been involved, heard about Katherine's redundancy from the company's receptionist.

Patricia, also a marketing manager, was told she would have to take redundancy because she was "unsuitable" for the position into which her job had evolved. She described the redundancy as a set-up between her manager, the sales directors, and the personnel director, who conducted the redundancy discussion with her. The redundancy discussion occurred shortly after she filed a complaint against one of the sales directors for sexual harassment.

Fiona's appeal for a fair job evaluation was yet another example of procedural elements, such as grievances, appeals, and complaint procedures, being tools of the patriarchy. When Fiona's bid for a promotion was turned down, she was told she could appeal to the same group, the overwhelmingly male job evaluation committee, that had rejected her previously.

I had little faith that anything would change, especially since I was not allowed to attend my appeal meeting. For all I know they may not have even discussed my appeal. I had to justify all of my reasons for the promotion in writing whilst they provided me with no written reasons why I was not fit to be promoted.

Elizabeth encountered a situation in which the human resources department seemed in collusion with her manager before hearing all of the facts about her case. Before Elizabeth met with her manager to discuss her grievance, she discovered that the personnel manager had met with him privately for two hours to brief him about how to handle the meeting. Elizabeth, her manager, the personnel manager, and one of Elizabeth's trusted colleagues attended the grievance meeting. During the grievance hearing, the human resources manager and her manager were sitting close together and across from Elizabeth.

It seemed an obvious power play with the two of them opposing me across the table. I thought they are in this together and this [the grievance meeting] is simply a formality.

Elizabeth's manager made several statements about her failing to follow his procedures with respect to paperwork. Elizabeth explained that several others in the department had not completed the paperwork, yet they were allowed to attend work-related conferences and to engage in development opportunities. In the middle of the meeting, Elizabeth's manager produced a thick file,

My manager dropped a thick file on the table in front of us and said, "Just to show you how troublesome you are I have memos from people who have worked with you." I had never seen or heard of these memos before and someone told me afterwards that he had asked his buddies to write things. I reminded them that in every appraisal I had had since joining I had exceeded my targets.

During the meeting, Elizabeth's friend persistently had to ask Elizabeth's manager to stick to facts rather than his opinions about Elizabeth. The human resources manager said nothing when Elizabeth objected to the file turning into evidence "out of the blue." After a short recess, the grievance hearing continued. She recalled the rest of the meeting, "My manager apologised to me. He agreed to review my application for senior consultant and said that he would work on rebuilding our relationship." The next day, Elizabeth and her manager met for breakfast.

He said he didn't really care what I had said in the meeting the day before. He didn't care that I had a grievance. He was still going to continue to do what he wanted and he wanted me to do the bits of paper work anyway. So I said, "Really what you are saying is you just said those things for the record and everything is going to continue as before." He said, "Yes." I said, "Unless you are willing to negotiate and to compromise and to try to work things out in terms of how we communicate, there is no communication."

It was clear to Elizabeth that the human resources manager was not interested in investigating her claims of unfair treatment and intimidation. Her manager was told to apologize, but given no other stronger form of punishment. The same type of harassment continued as before; Elizabeth's manager found fault with her over insignificant items and continued to deny her any development opportunities. Elizabeth knew that the personnel manager was not interested in monitoring her manager's behavior because the personnel manager felt that his apology was sufficient. In the end, Elizabeth could not endure the constant intimidation and she resigned. Millett (1970) noted that patriarchal societies often treat obvious offenders of women's rights leniently as a message that society tolerates and even condones abuse against women.

Shortly after Elizabeth left the organization, her manager was demoted. Elizabeth discovered that within a space of three months two other women had filed a grievance against the manager during his probationary period in his new management role. The grievances concerned her manager's condescending attitude toward women subordinates and his constant bullying behavior. It is worth noting that the organization overlooked all three grievances without seeing a pattern in his behavior or punishing him in any way. After Elizabeth handed in her resignation, the organization began to take notice of the problems that her manager had caused. "I guess they finally recognised that he wasn't right for the job. It is interesting that they *only* demoted him when in the meantime he caused three good women to leave," Elizabeth remarked.

When Mary asked about the grievance procedure she was told that she would have to submit her reasons to her new manager, the woman who had displaced her and who had asked her to take redundancy. Any appeal of her manager's handling of the grievance would go to her manager's manager, the personnel director. Both individuals had put undo pressure on her to take redundancy and the personnel director had threatened to produce negative letters in her personnel file if she didn't accept their terms. She was also told that at any future meetings to discuss her redundancy terms she would not be permitted to have legal representation present because "the company did not allow it." The grievance procedure was hardly unbiased; however, Mary said she intended to take her grievance forward via the board. She telephoned to make an appointment to see the company president who said, almost before she could describe why she wanted to meet with him, "We can meet but don't expect that I can do anything more for you in your situation." It was obvious to Mary that after she indicated to the personnel director that she would take the matter higher, he had quickly intervened to speak to the president. After this point, Mary endured many instances of intimidation and bullying by the personnel director.

The introduction of the Employee Relations Bill in the United Kingdom now suggests that employees are entitled to take what it refers to as a "companion" with them during the disciplinary and grievance proceedings. This legislation has some interesting caveats in favor of the employer. First, the companion may not be a solicitor, but he or she may be a fellow employee or trade union official. The companion is not allowed to answer questions on behalf of the employee. Second, the bill applies to dismissals rather than redundancies; therefore, if the dismissal is labeled as a "redundancy" (as in Mary's case) employees are not entitled to have an advocate with them (Aiken, 1999).

Special Problems Associated with Equal Pay Cases

Madge was extremely lucky to have won her case. In 1991, the Equal Opportunities Commission (EOC) received 17,363 inquiries from the public about equality issues, but was only able to provide assistance to 161 cases (Figes, 1994). The U.K. government has not willingly addressed equal pay legislation; it has been forced to address the issue by the European Commission. In 1981, the European Commission started infringement proceedings against the U.K. government, alleging that it had not enabled employees to claim equal pay for work of equal value, as the Treaty of Rome, Article 119, laid down. The U.K. responded with the Equal Value Amendment in 1983, which tagged equal value issues onto existing legislation.

In practice, employers can use delaying tactics. Dr. Pam Enderby, a speech therapist and head of a hospital department of speech therapy, began her case for equal pay against Frenchay Health Authority in 1986. After numerous delays, it took more than 11 years for her to win her case. Figes (1994) documents several practices that put obstacles in women's way when they try to pursue claims of equal pay. First, a male comparator must be found who has not been subjected to the same allegedly unfair treatment. Second, if an employer has a job evaluation scheme, it often gives the appearance that differential treatment of men and women is based on nonbiased assessments of responsibilities. However, in job evaluation schemes, higher levels of demand are often assigned to traditionally male activities. For instance, the responsibility of managing budgets usually awards an individual more points in a job evaluation scheme than does managing customers, a more typically female activity. Because supervision is typically considered a male activity, it is easy to see how Fiona's organization suggested that her manager was making decisions for her. How was Fiona to prove that he had not been heavily supervising her decisions unless he was willing to say he had not?

In 1993, the government responded to the EOC's proposal for strengthening equal pay legislation by failing to acknowledge that job evaluation schemes can be in themselves discriminatory and should not be used as a defense against equal pay claims (Figes, 1994). Often the "material factor defence" (p. 181), which suggests that a woman's pay was determined by a separate nondiscriminatory collective bargaining unit that was different from her male comparator's bargaining unit, is used. However, in Enderby's case, the European Court of Justice ruled that different collective bargaining units or arrangements cannot be used as justification for unequal pay. The "red circling of male salaries" and "market forces" (Figes, 1994, p. 182) are other defenses used by employers to fight equal pay claims. If a comparator is found, the employer suggests that he was moved from another job for extenuating circumstances but kept on the same salary as he had before the move. The employer may argue that "market forces" made it necessary to pay the male more.

Part of adjudicating equal pay claims is the appointment of an independent expert to examine the demands of the jobs in question. Although regulations require this report to be written within 42 days, according to EOC estimates it takes about 12 months for the reports to reach the tribunal. Employers deny access to premises and use other means to obstruct the process (Figes, 1994, p. 183).

SACKING OUT OF THE BLUE: PURPORTED REASONS FOR TERMINATION

The women profiled in this book were unprepared for termination. Despite troubles at work, many of the women felt that they were protected by their good performance and by their commitment to their organizations. Being taken by surprise left them at an extreme disadvantage; they could not prepare counterarguments and they were often pressured to make an immediate decision about accepting redundancy. Because they had already been marginalized in their organizations, they had no power base from which to pull together support from others. Furthermore, in many of the termination discussions, the patriarchy arranged to outnumber the women by having two representatives at the discussion. Two members of management demonstrate to the woman that she is isolated in her attempt to challenge the patriarchy and lend weight to the reasons for her dismissal. In all the cases, the women were given what they believed to be fallacious reasons for their terminations, including euphemisms such as "it is just not working out" or the "need to restructure the organization" to serious charges of lack of performance and disloyalty.

A few days after Madge, a personnel director, had filed a grievance against her organization because of unequal pay, she was called to the managing director's office where the managing director and the chairman dismissed her. The meeting had not been scheduled and the managing director simply said that he wanted to have a chat with her. She did not expect the chairman to be there.

They said that in view of the fact that I had taken action they had irretrievably lost trust and confidence in me. They said the internal board had voted unanimously that I should go. They said I was being suspended for two weeks and that I would be dismissed at the end of the month. And that they were going to offer me a year's salary to drop the case.

Madge told them that they were dismissing her simply for exercising her statutory rights, she was under contract with them for at least two years, and this was victimization, unfair dismissal, and breach of contract. After she collected two personal items from her desk and in full view of her staff, she was escorted out of the building by the managing director, a man she had worked with for seven and a half years.

The managing director and the chairman attempted to completely isolate Madge by suspending her from work. They ignored her claims of unequal pay and instead charged her with disloyalty in her attempts to supposedly sully the reputation of the managing director by making claims to the board that he had promised her equal pay.

Katherine, a marketing manager, was called into an unscheduled meeting just as Madge had been asked to attend a meeting at short notice. After several incidents in which Katherine felt her manager was putting distance between her and him, her manager called her into a meeting with the head of human resources ostensibly to discuss her development plan.

He said totally out of the blue, "we've been thinking about your position and I really don't think there is any future for you here." It was as sudden as that with very little explanation offered. He then went on to say he didn't think I'd been particularly busy—that I wasn't working enough. I was shocked and upset as I'd been putting in extremely long hours—10 hour days.

As in Madge's case, Katherine did not expect to find a second individual at the meeting. She felt that the cards were stacked against her because the head of human resources was present. Both individuals had colluded in her dismissal and there seemed little point in objecting; they had made up their minds about her termination.

The owner of the consultancy where Caroline worked called an unscheduled meeting of the administrative people and Caroline. They were all told that they should contact the new owners to determine whether they would be hired and what their terms would be. Although the male consultants in the organization had been part of the negotiation and had been protected by Jim, the owner of the firm, Caroline was left to fend for herself in negotiating a new position.

Patricia, a marketing manager, had complained about several instances of harassment from the sales directors with whom she worked closely. Out of the blue, she was called into the personnel director's office one morning and told that her job had been restructured into a larger role. She asked if she might apply for the position but was told that she was the "wrong type of person." The position was given to one of the sales directors who had no marketing experience.

In less than two weeks after Lesley, the head of a large engineering division, had stood her ground about wanting to restructure her own division, Lesley's managing director called her in and said, "It just isn't working out. I would like you to leave." Lesley knew that her managing director was acting on instructions from the vice president. In three days, Lesley had devolved responsibility to her team of managers and left the company with what she felt was a generous severance package.

Fiona, manager of sales management development, had prepared a lengthy appeal to a job evaluation committee to be promoted to what she felt was justifiably a director-level job. Her manager, who had formerly been supportive, discouraged her from making the appeal and he was the individual who had to present her case. She was not allowed to be present at the appeal hearing. As Fiona recalled,

I do not even know how or if my case was presented. In the end I made things difficult for them and for my boss whom I expected to support my appeal as he knew the work I'd been doing. They clearly didn't expect an appeal and didn't want to promote me to the level that I should have been at given their own criteria. In the end, the human resources director and my manager called me in to say the position was no longer required and that my manager would manage the programmes that I put into place.

Fiona knew that she was making things difficult for the board, but felt that they would eventually recognize that her work was of equivalent value to the other directors. She did not expect to be dismissed, especially given the fact that her performance had been significantly above average according to the company's performance appraisal system.

Diane, a finance director, was made redundant at 1 year, 11 months, and 2 weeks of service, just two weeks short of employment protection. Her managing director called her into his office one morning and said that he would no longer require her service because the accounts no longer warranted a full-time person. Prior to the sacking meeting, Diane had been worn down by constant bullying and harassment tactics. She recalls not having the energy to fight the managing director any longer and felt that the ostensible reason for her termination was a difficult one to rebut.

Mary, head of training, was taken by surprise twice. In the first instance, her job was restructured and her management position taken away and, in the second, she was made redundant. After Mary's team had delivered the culture change program, she was called in to meet with the personnel director, an individual who had grown closer and closer to the board. The personnel manager told her that her job had been restructured and that one of his managers would be taking over its management from her. Mary was shocked,

He wouldn't give me a reason for the change. He just said that the organization had changed the role and that Linda, the compensation manager—someone on his team—would now be managing my department. I was to report to this person along with the seven people I had managed. I let him know I was not happy with this and expected to know why I hadn't even been allowed to apply for the position. I also said I couldn't understand how Linda got the job as she had no experience in training or in managing a team.

Several months after the restructure and after returning from her holiday, the personnel director and her new manager called Mary in for a discussion. They told her that they had been unhappy with her work since joining the new team and suggested that she consider redundancy. There was, they said, no real role for her.

My first reaction was to object to the allegations of lack of performance. I looked at my new manager and said she had given me no real work on which to judge my performance. She said she was not confident that I could do project work at a lower level so she had deliberately not given me any. I said that I had had no negative feedback. She then said that Mike, one of the field managers with whom I had worked closely, had complained.

Mary tried to defend herself against these allegations by saying that she and the sales director had had a very good and open relationship. She suggested that she should go directly to the sales director to discuss the allegations. The personnel director warned her not to go to the sales director, saying that this would be "unprofessional conduct." The meeting ended with the personnel director saying, "You should seriously consider the offer [of redundancy], you wouldn't want a negative letter in your personnel file." Mary asked him if this was a veiled threat and reminded him that he couldn't do that because there had been no history of poor performance. The personnel director tried to pressure Mary into agreeing to a severance amount at this meeting. After he tossed out a few figures, Mary suggested that these were too low and requested that he put his proposal in writing. He refused to do so, saying this was unnecessary. Mary insisted that she needed more information before agreeing to anything. Finally, he suggested that they meet again in three days after Mary had had time to think about his "serious" offer.

Mary's diary entries describe in detail how she was terminated and how the personnel director made allegations against her of unsatisfactory performance, although there had not been any evidence of poor performance. In fact, during the time when she was supposedly underperforming, Mary had received compliments from sales managers on her programs.

During the time Mary was considering the personnel director's proposal for redundancy and her agreeing to go quietly, she was subjected to constant harassment and bullying by the personnel director. These incidents of harassment are well documented in her diary entries.

Karen, a total quality manager, had had several disagreements with her manager over taking on a new position. He had once threatened to dismiss her but had rescinded his decision. She felt that they had patched up their arguments and she was resolved to try to forge an amicable working relationship. As agreed before any of the difficulties between them began, Karen went to Tunisia for a two-week vacation. Upon her return she had another altercation with her manager.

As soon as I arrived he called me into his office. He said, "You were supposed to be here yesterday. You basically knocked off a day of work." I explained that I had not planned to be back until today and would certainly take the day as a holiday. He then said that our relationship had broken down since Christmas and we couldn't possibly work together. I suggested that we needed to try to work it out. That perhaps we needed to meet more often. He said that he didn't want to try. I then said, "I'm going to fight you." He said, "You haven't got anything to fight with." I stood up to leave and he yelled at me, "I haven't finished yet." I said, "Well I have. There is nothing more to say." Then he stood up and physically threatened me. He stood right next to me and pushed his finger into my chest. I sat down and said "O.K." I thought he was right on the edge and would hit me.

I was frightened and traumatized. I can remember a kind of stare-down as if we were two children. Eventually he started talking again.

Karen agreed to take a severance payment based on her length of service. A few weeks before she was dismissed, the British standards organization awarded her company the BS5750, a prestigious quality award. Karen and her department were largely responsible for the achievement.

BUYING OFF WOMEN

Companies would prefer to buy women off, usually for more than they would have had to pay a woman if her case had gone to an industrial tribunal and the outcome favored the woman. Though expensive, buying women off allows the patriarchy to continue its practices of discrimination, and avoid unwanted publicity, because the legal system will not be brought in to interfere with the company's practices. When women accept settlements they are sometimes forced to sign "gag" clauses to prevent them from talking to the media about their case or are required to sign clauses that stop them from taking any further legal action against their employer for unfair dismissal or sex discrimination. Furthermore, if a woman settles out of court and then talks about her case to the press, she risks a libel action.

Moreover, women know the pain they will have to endure through a long, protracted legal battle. Companies have financial resources to fight legal cases, whereas individuals generally do not. As Figes (1994) points out, a woman who presses a claim under the equality legislation has to be "superhuman" to win. "In 1990/91, out of a total of 12,423 cases, just 319 sex discrimination and 198 equal pay claims went to an industrial tribunal. . . . There is no legal aid for cases considered by the industrial tribunal. In 1991, success evaded all but seventy-eight of the sex discrimination cases, and just ten of the claims for equal pay" (p. 166). Even if a woman succeeds in her bid for justice the rewards are minimal and the protection she might receive from further victimization from her employer are absent. Until the European Court of Justice ruling in 1993, the statutory ceiling on compensation awarded was £11,000, with the average award in 1991 at only £1,142 (Figès, 1994). The tribunal has no power to reinstate a woman to her former position and is not interested in monitoring the company's possible future discriminatory practices. In short, it treats each case as an isolated incident. None of the 70 women who successfully fought their cases in Leonard's study (1987) said her terms and conditions had improved as a result.

With the exception of two, the women profiled in this book accepted out of court settlements. Fear of not being able to secure another position, worry about receiving a lower settlement than the one offered by their companies, and exhaustion were commonly cited reasons for accepting a settlement. Many of the women felt they had been physically and emotionally worn down by the systematic abuse they had endured and did not have the energy to engage in yet another battle.

Katherine accepted a redundancy payment calculated on her number of years service with her employer. Because she had several years with the company and wanted to "get on with her life" she decided not to challenge the decision. She also feared what would happen if potential future employers discovered that she had taken her former employer to an industrial tribunal. Karen also accepted redundancy terms. She expressed similar reservations about taking legal action against her employer. Lesley indicated that her severance package was "generous" and she also suggested that she "needed to move on quickly from what had been an exhausting job." Fiona's experience was similar to the others. She said,

I was worn down by the whole appeals process and discouraged by the outcome. I didn't have much confidence in the fairness of systems and couldn't risk the potential negative outcome of a tribunal.

Diane took redundancy but because she had less than two years service (23 months and 2 weeks) and under the law she was not entitled to any cash payment. She indicated that she was exhausted from the "game playing" that had occurred over the months leading up to her termination and couldn't be subjected to more of it. Over the years in high-level positions she had accumulated enough money to start over. Like many of the others, she indicated the need to put the experience behind her, "I wanted to get on with my life and use some time to be with my father who was getting older."

Mary contacted the Equal Opportunities Commission and a solicitor who specialized in employment law.

I was told by the EOC and my solicitor that I could have a case of unfair dismissal. My solicitor said, however, that given what I'd been offered as a severance, I'd be lucky to get more from a tribunal. She said it would depend very much on the judge and how generous he would want to be.

Walby (1990) discussed how the state enforces practices of patriarchy in employment both directly and indirectly as a means of limiting women's power. Low settlements, as predicted by Mary's solicitor in her case of unfair dismissal, and difficult cases to prove without evidence beyond a shadow of doubt, as in sexual harassment cases, are two examples of such patriarchal control.

In the end, Mary decided to settle her grievance and she negotiated a severance payment with the help of her solicitor.

The grievance process wore me down. I was mentally and physically exhausted from the bullying. I don't think I could have faced several months of preparing a tribunal case. I sort of regret not having the energy for it, but I couldn't afford to take the financial risk. In the end, they made me sign a statement that I wouldn't sue them for sexual harassment or unfair dismissal—that I had no further claims from them if I accepted the money. I regret that too, because it was too easy for them. They couldn't be held accountable for their actions.

Although Patricia had been sexually harassed and had witnesses to the effect, she decided not to take her employer to an industrial tribunal.

I was so tired of working in these types of environments and couldn't face the idea of more antagonism. I didn't want to see any of them again and surely if I went to tribunal I would have to. I needed a complete break and decided I would spend more time with my children.

Caroline was not technically bought off, but she was sold off cheaply to another organization. When she contacted her prospective employers, she discovered that her former colleagues (the three male consultants and the owner) had suggested that she could be brought in to the new company inexpensively. They offered her half of her former salary, with no medical benefits. When she challenged this decision, her new employers said that they wanted to see how much work she would bring in and felt it necessary to put her on a probationary standing at first. Eventually the new CEO told Caroline he couldn't sustain her salary because the other male consultants were so expensive. Caroline saw no alternative but to resign; her colleagues had taken her clients to make her look less attractive as a partner in the business and then she was told that she couldn't be paid as much as they were because they were so expensive!

These cases have several characteristics in common. First, the women felt psychologically battered and physically exhausted to the extent that they could not find the energy to fight their cases further. Second, they were aware that they were being manipulated by the system in terms of settlements that offered them no choice but to accept. Third, they expressed both a strong desire to rid themselves of any future contact with their organizations and the need to find something more meaningful and positive in their lives.

With the exception of Madge's case, which became public in her organization and in the newspapers, the organizations suggested to their members that these women resigned "for personal reasons." Mary discovered that the human resources director told other employees that she had left to pursue "academic interests." which was in her words "a total fabrication of the truth." Walby (1986) argues that women leave the workforce because of breakdowns in agreements between themselves and their employers or the unions. Moreover, individual decisions to leave obscure the deeper questions about what led women to leave.

THE "RESERVE ARMY" OF COMPLIANT REPLACEMENTS

In some cases, the profiled women were replaced by more compliant women who would not challenge the patriarchal nature of their organizations. The phenomenon of a reserve army of compliant replacements was noted in Millett (1970) as a means of ensuring the continuation of the patriarchy. McKenna (1997) and Kanter (1977) describe a compliant woman as one who allies herself with the power structure to receive an accepted identity, yet at the same time becomes a hostage to the majority group.

In contrast to more compliant women, the women described in this book often challenged the current thinking of their organizations and stood up to sexist procedures. Throughout her tenure in the position, Mary remembers challenging ways in which the company conducted its promotional process and in particular questioning one of her peers—the personnel director. Their areas often overlapped; for example, her team implemented an assessment process for sales managers that his team designed.

I was unhappy with the assessment exercises and I told David [the personnel manager]. I said that they disadvantaged women because the characteristics they were designed to look for were typically masculine. Like "takes charge of a meeting" or "is able to take decisions." I suggested that looking at the quality of decisions was more important than measuring the speed with which they are made. He was also using a psychometric test to look for character traits that had not been proven to distinguish successful candidates from average ones. I thought we needed more data on our managers before we used a test as a predictor. I wanted to revamp the process and reminded him that out of nearly 140 branch managers we had no women. I also thought the assessors, especially the sales director and some of the current sales managers, consciously or unconsciously, thought the role was more suitable for men.

Mary also remembers challenging senior management about the work schedules imposed on her team. Various members were beginning to become ill as a result of an unreasonable schedule. She suggested borrowing some other individuals who could serve as alternates so that people did not "burn out."

I used the analogy of the athlete who had run too many miles. You could do a marathon once but couldn't be expected to do it time and time again without a break. I was told they weren't allowed to take holidays during the 9 month project, but I had figured out a way to give them the odd day without compromising the programme. I think senior management was annoyed with me for reworking their schedules.

Mary had the reputation as a forceful person with opinions. She wanted to help the organization change from a traditional hierarchical one to one in which individual contributions were recognized and valued. In part the culture change program was intended to educate managers about empowering employees, something about which Mary felt passionately.

On reflection, Mary believed she had been displaced by a woman the organization found nonthreatening and more stereotypically feminine than herself.

She was younger and they could pay her considerably less money whereas I was older and at the top of the pay scale for my grade. She wouldn't disagree with anybody or debate issues with her superiors. She was also overtly feminine and flirtatious with men who were in higher jobs. She routinely hugged and kissed men on the cheek when she saw them which was something I could never bring myself to do.

Katherine knew her role had gradually been changing and that her manager had been easing her out of the organization. She felt it had more to do with her manager's inability to deal with a strong woman than her work performance or the actual work that needed to be done.

The senior vice president and my boss saw me as a maverick and I didn't fit in. They wouldn't find a role for me even though I had years of industry knowledge.

Katherine's replacement was far from a maverick. She was younger than Katherine and was brought in at a salary less than Katherine had formerly been paid.

When Fiona was made redundant she was told by her manager that he would be taking on her responsibilities. For a few months, he did manage the role; as it became evident that he could not cope with the additional responsibility, the organization sought a replacement for Fiona. The company promoted a younger woman with less experience and at a lower grade level than Fiona had been.

Of course I talked to friends who had been working with me about Jane. They said she always agreed with everything and wouldn't rock the boat. I knew her and thought of her as a young aspiring person. Compared to me she was softer and less outspoken.

The women who had been displaced by younger, more compliant women recognized that by comparison they were more confrontational, outspoken, and perhaps less able to play the stereotypically "feminine" role. Although they did not use the word "androgynous," they described their mode of behavior as both masculine and feminine. They reiterated that they would not flatter men, use their "feminine wiles," or otherwise try to manipulate situations based on their gender. Perhaps the masculine side of their behavior, characterized by strong opinions and a desire to have an impact, offended and threatened their male superiors.

This attitude against strong women has been noted elsewhere. Male managers in local government were identified as fearing competition from competent female managers who they viewed as belonging in a subordinate role in their organization (Young and Spencer, 1991). A pacesetting style of leadership was viewed by male subordinates more critically when used by female rather than male managers (Hay, 1993). This seems to indicate that women's desire to play the role of change agent in their organizations is less tolerated than a man's desire to play a similar influential role.

The idea of compliant female managers is predominant elsewhere in business and government. Sue Maddock, of the Manchester Business School, interviewed female managers in local government. She found half of them felt they had not been outspoken or challenging when they were lower down the ranks and thought that they had been selected because they were "soft, tame options" (Figes, 1994, p. 60).

CONCLUSION

The profiled women's cases are similar in many respects. All the women demonstrated substantial success in their early careers and enjoyed promotions to middle or senior management levels. Their curriculum vitae show increased levels of responsibility and influence. However, each woman was stopped just when she reached a level where she *should* have been able to have influence both inside and outside of her functional specialty. At a point when these women demanded too much from the hierarchy, they were suddenly told that their performance was poor or their attitude was "wrong." What they wanted was fair treatment, assignments worthy of their skills, and treatment similar to their male colleagues. It is highly unlikely that their performance was actually substandard or their attitude poor. Up until they began making demands from their organizations, these women were performing well enough to be promoted. They demonstrated commitment by working long hours and holidays. The majority of them reported working harder and longer than their male counterparts.

When these women were displaced by someone else, the individual was either an accepted part of the hierarchy (as in Patricia's case) or someone who would not threaten it (as in Mary's and Katherine's cases). Patricia was displaced by one of the sales directors, who had no marketing experience but fit with the already established male group of directors. Katherine and Mary were replaced by younger, stereotypically more feminine and less experienced women; women, who in Katherine's and Mary's perception, would not "rock the boat" by challenging the well-established rituals of men.

In these cases, the corporate personnel departments often acted as a tool of the patriarchy. Instead of adjudicating cases of unfair treatment, the personnel managers and directors had already sided with the hierarchy. In Madge's case, the chairman and managing director never bothered to investigate her claims of unequal pay. Elizabeth discovered that her manager and the personnel manager had met privately to discuss her grievance. If an effort to investigate Elizabeth's claims had really been made, Elizabeth should also have been interviewed by the personnel manager. Katherine, like Elizabeth, felt that the human resources director played the role of aiding and abetting her manager. "He [Katherine's manager] was very chummy with the human resources director. During the redundancy discussion she was there to help him. She never interviewed me to see if there was another place for me in the organization. She obviously wasn't there as an impartial observer," Katherine recalled.

These cases demonstrate the imperviousness of female subordination; men do not see any advantages to making the fundamental changes necessary to help women and women are not in the positions of power necessary to change well-established modes of operation. In addition, women are in such few numbers and isolated from one another. Change often occurs when a group can exert enough pressure on a social system. One comment from Patricia exemplifies the problem of being isolated as a woman, "I didn't have anyone to go to for redress. If something doesn't seem right or fair it probably isn't. Unfortunately, I don't think an individual can turn a culture around."

CHAPTER 7

Patriarchy and Personality

◆◆

How did the women profiled in this book respond to the circumstances in which they found themselves? To what extent did they consider their fate inevitable or avoidable? How did their character, temperament, personality, and their own choices play a role in their treatment and termination? And, finally, to what extent did they come to believe during or after their termination that their fates were sealed by a patriarchal institution as opposed to their own choices?

My conclusion is not the neat compromise that personality and individual strategy share equally with the patriarchy causal responsibility for the termination of these women, still less the skeptical conclusion that we cannot disentangle these two causal forces in order to apportion causal force between them. Rather, the experiences of these women, together with what we know independently about the management styles expected of successful women, suggest that patriarchy operates along two apparently independent pathways: first, through the institutions that constrain women and, second, by initially demanding male traits and strategies of women managers and then punishing the women when these traits and strategies threaten the patriarchy.

The pattern of severe horizontal segregation in modern business results in a class of women managers who find themselves at the interface between the largely female world of subordinates and the almost entirely male world of managers. The women in this book rose to their management positions as a result of their class backgrounds, education, successes in prior work assignments, and a constellation of character, personality, and other psychological traits. These factors distinguished them from women whose work trajectory did not carry them as far as the glass ceiling, which separates men and women at the interface between subordinates and managers. It is a natural supposition that, like most successful male managers who are terminated, these women were "let go" because of personal conflicts that might reflect psychological traits. If this supposition were warranted, then individual idiosyncratic factors peculiar to these ten women would more fully account for their management experiences than such broad-scale forces as a monolithic patriarchy.

In fact, these women's own characters, and the strategies they chose both to advance in their professions and to deal with the male-dominated work environment, did have a role in their termination. But the more one reflects on the role of character and strategy, the more evident it becomes that without these traits and strategies the women would never have reached the interface at which they were stopped. There is much empirical and qualitative evidence to suggest that to secure positions across the threshold in senior management women must adopt styles and embrace values that once they have penetrated the glass ceiling make them threats to the hegemony of the patriarchy.

THE DOUBLE-BIND

Much research on differences in management style between men and women indicates that men view the work environment as a competitive one in which responsibilities and authority are hierarchically organized. Aggressiveness, assertiveness, and individual ownership of projects, initiatives, and working units are required for success and central to moving up toward the highest reaches of management (Helgeson, 1990; Rosener, 1995; Still, 1988). For example, Still identifies the following four factors that are "believed to distinguish successful [male] from unsuccessful [male] managers." Effective managers (1) project an aura of command free from emotionality, (2) project a conservative image of establishment stability, (3) exhibit an urbane social style, and (4) are self-reliant, independent, aggressive, and dominant. By contrast, women are "known" to be (1) submissive, dependent, noncombative, noncompetitive, sensitive, gentle, and yielding; (2) emotional and sometimes tearful and hysterical; (3) incapable of making "hard decisions" and "understanding the bottom line"; and (4) more family oriented than career oriented (Still, 1988, pp. 40–41).

To the extent that men's characteristic perceptions of the structure and values of the modern business organization are more accurate than women's, this difference in management styles must inevitably hamper women's attainment of positions in senior management. The male-dominated hierarchy cannot understand or accept the cooperative strategies women employ, and such successes as these strategies secure are not attributed to the women who secure them just because their styles do not make ownership as clear-cut as male management styles do. Accordingly, women are often encouraged to adopt more masculine, aggressive, and competitive management styles to get ahead. Doing so is held to make male managers more comfortable with female ones, because men can understand and respond to them appropriately, and to enable women managers to secure better treatment in the largely male environment of the management bureaucracy. Much of the literature of professional advice to women managers is aimed at depersonalizing the business environment for women so they can learn to recognize that apparent hostility, uncooperativeness, and the asymmetrical exercise of power is not directed at them because they are women, but is just an endemic feature of life to which all managers are exposed.

Reworking one's personality, character, and interpersonal strategies is no easy matter. Indeed, for many women, as for men, it is advice impossible to follow. Patriarchy theory would lead us to suspect that women are as forcefully socialized to accept a male-dominated hierarchy in both private and public spheres as men are. Thus, this sort of advice to adopt male strategies may have all the usefulness of the proposal that a left-handed person begin, as an adult, one day to write with the right hand. If getting to the middle and upper reaches of institutions that are already male dominated requires an androgynous style not available to most women, regardless of other qualifications, it will be no surprise that there is a firm glass ceiling through which few women can move.

Consider what happens to women who follow this advice and adopt male management strategies, or, more likely, women who are already disposed by upbringing, education, or socialization to adopt the interests, aspirations, temperament, and values required for success in modern business. It is these "male" character traits, strategies, and choices that bring women up through the interface between mainly female labor and largely male management. Without them, the women would have remained at the lower echelons of the organization and been unnoticed. Once they arrive across this interface, their personalities and approaches to interaction with men begin to constitute threats to the patriarchy.

This dilemma has been recognized in the management literature as the double-bind. Nichols (1994, p. 9) reminds us of Ann Hopkins, the Price Waterhouse consultant who was denied partnership in the firm even though she had adopted a male management style. She billed more hours and generated more business than any other candidate up for promotion at that time. She was told by the chairman that she should "take charge less often," appear more feminine, and wear more makeup.

Nicholson and West (1988) report a study in which Deborah L. Rhode, a law professor at Stanford University, examined a large number of sex discrimination cases and discovered that women had been denied promotion either for being too ambitious and argumentative or for being old-fashioned and reserved (p. 9).

Women managers expect that their work environment will require a male management style of them. Duerst-Lahti and Johnson (1992) studied senior educational leaders and asked male and female administrators to analyze their own leadership style. Female top-level administrators avoided feminine traits, while men did not. Women in the study tried to adopt traits and styles deemed to be more valued by their organizations: masculine traits. Yet men in their organizations were not comfortable with women adopting these traits. Duerst-Lahti and Johnson used the term "transgendered" to mean that a particular trait or behavior exercised by both men and women will be understood differently when used by men and women. They found that the appropriate degree of assertiveness for men was viewed differently from the appropriate degree expected for women leaders. Women seem to be confined to a more limited range of appropriate assertive/aggressive behavior than men. On a continuum from passive to aggressive, a woman's behavior is expected to be closer to the passive end than is a man's. She is not considered unusual if she is fully passive, yet is highly likely to be labeled in an unflattering way for being seen as too aggressive. Duerst-Lahti and Johnson (1992) concluded that gender perceptions and gender stereotypes intrude upon our assessment of supposedly gender-neutral traits.

In another similar study of leadership and managerial styles (Kelly, Hale, and Burgess, 1991), tolerance for the traits of dominance and intimidation was different for men than for women; dominance and intimidation were positive traits for male managers whereas they were seen as inappropriate traits for women managers. Instead, "being attractive" seemed a requirement for women to be viewed positively.

And yet, as Still (1988) notes, women must "give into the inevitable and accept the male managerial model as your role guide" (p. 42). The result, as Morrison et al. (1987) describe it, is a process of personal cognitive readjustment that never ends for a woman. Unlike men, women operate within a narrow band of acceptable behavior. They must constantly assess the appropriateness for them of behaviors they see exhibited by their male peers. For example, success for a woman may depend on toning down masculine behavior with a more feminine style and on being ambitious but not expecting equal treatment (Morrison et al., 1987). But how easy is it to endlessly readjust?

The women interviewed for this book could not do it. They overstepped the degree of assertiveness acceptable for a woman. Because they repeatedly behaved like their male colleagues in terms of assertive/aggressive behavior, they were not only labeled in an unflattering way but were also eased out of their positions.

Although these women's male management styles played a role in their termination, these same styles were also obligatory for their attaining visibility and some status within their organizations. These women could not solve the double-bind dilemma by switching to a more feminine style, a role that they had never been socialized to play. Are they exceptions, or is the rare senior women manager the solitary female with chameleon-like qualities able continually to readjust personality to navigate the patriarchy?

THE ILLUSION OF EMPOWERMENT

The ten women profiled in this book described their early career and university experience in terms of accepting and taking responsibility. They saw opportunities and acted on them. This early sense of self-confidence, success in their studies, and a desire to work autonomously may have caused them to feel themselves empowered once they came into employment, when in fact their organizations had not actually bestowed real power to them.

For example, in her early career Lesley had been an excellent student of physics, had earned scholarships to study space science, and had run her own laboratory. These early experiences allowed her a great deal of autonomy and she felt highly accomplished and equal, if not intellectually superior, to her male colleagues. When asked about how she felt about working in a non-female environment she commented,

I was completely comfortable with it, it did not worry me much at all. . . . I was the manager of 11 systems engineers. I remember doing an interview with *Electronic Times* and they said was I worried about it [being female and managing men] and I said no because I have a knack for getting people to like working for me.

Unwisely, Lesley assumed an empowered stance with the new vice president when outlining her plan for reorganizing her department. Despite knowing ahead of time that he "was not universally liked" and that there were "ghastly stories circulating about his personality," she chose to present ideas that conflicted with his own ideas about retraining current staff to be software engineers. Although she was most qualified to work out a plan for reduction of her staff because she more than anyone understood their relative skills, she proceeded incautiously in the expectation that it was her *right* to decide on this matter. The right to make the decision did not depend on qualifications; rather, it depended on deference to the hierarchy.

Like Lesley, Karen had acted empowered during her university and early career days. For instance, she approached a university without having earned A levels and managed to talk her way into it. Once admitted, she assumed leadership roles within the university and when she worked in higher education, she had been reasonably autonomous within her role as a lecturer. As she moved into the business world, she continued to assume that she would be allowed to make decisions on her own. While a total quality manager at British Steel, she managed to hold her own on the shop floor of an all-male manufacturing unit. She had acted as though empowered and it had paid dividends in terms of career advancement, until she reached a more senior level. Karen's assuming additional responsibility and having an opinion about efficiency practices within British Steel had been accepted because at her low to middle level of management she did not pose a threat to the hierarchy. However, when she assumed she could influence a board decision to change her job description, she misread the degree to which the organization was willing to let her act according to her own wishes. Not only did she embarrass her boss by her lack of compliance, she also challenged the authority of the board.

Elizabeth acted as if she were empowered to ignore aspects of her job that she felt were unimportant, specifically paperwork and the completion of her expense report; her manager felt these tasks could not be postponed. As she reasoned, she was the top income earner in the consultancy and her manager should judge her on her success with clients. She repeatedly ignored his requests for the paperwork, assuming that client contact, high productivity, and additional business were more important. After a meeting in which they had exchanged unpleasant words, Elizabeth's boss finally volunteered to show her how to complete the necessary account information for which he had been asking. Instead of agreeing to learn about the system with his assistance, she suggested that it was late and she "did not feel up to it and was upset from their meeting." However justified she might have been in her complaints about his style and treatment of her, she aggravated the situation by not agreeing to do the paperwork and learn the account management system when he finally volunteered to show her.

Patricia's early career success and independent character led her to act empowered in the various positions she held. She recalls her father telling her that she could do anything she set her mind to and, as a teenager, she fully expected and wanted to support herself after finishing university. Achieving at university, traveling extensively, and obtaining repeated job promotions at a young age imbued her with self-confidence and assertiveness. She carried these traits to the workplace. When she saw her budget transferred to the sales directors she could not remain silent; she became outraged and let her superiors know it.

When they realized that they had been deceived and self-deceived about the degree of their empowerment, many of the women responded with anger and began to register complaints. The unresponsiveness of their institutions increasingly alienated these women from their superiors.

INCAUTIOUS ACTIONS AND DIRECT CONFRONTATION

As the double-bind literature suggests, it is at periods of potential job risk that women must assess the appropriateness of behaviors they see evinced by their male colleagues. Some of the women conspicuously failed to do this. They acted incautiously when bringing their complaints forward. Their lack of diplomacy, direct style, and unwillingness to seek compromise in terms of their situations may have backed their relative bosses into corners.

Elizabeth, for example, when attending her grievance meeting with her boss, a personnel manager, and a colleague explained her boss's communication style in direct and disparaging terms, "I don't like being called a 'bright girl' which I find patronizing." On another occasion at a one-to-one meeting with her boss, Elizabeth again directly confronted what she believed to be his lack of communication skills.

I asked him to stop talking to me as if I were a child at which point he shouted at me and said, "Well stop acting like one." I said that I would like to remind him that he was my manager, not my father or God and not even my father spoke to me this way, and that I would like to be treated with some respect and as an adult.

During another one-to-one meeting, Elizabeth expressed to her boss that she found his style "inflexible, imposing, and harassing." On still a fourth occasion during a meeting with his team, Elizabeth confronted him publicly. After her boss interrupted her as she was attempting to clarify something with the group, she said, "Please refrain from patronizing and interrupting me. I would appreciate the opportunity to finish asking my question." This public confrontation undoubtedly proved embarrassing to him and probably made reconciliation between them impossible.

Although Elizabeth appears to have been justified in her complaints, she did not try to negotiate a peace with her manager. Instead she confronted him without any attempt to use nuanced language in her accusations of his behavior.

Like Elizabeth, Diane directly confronted her boss, the chairman and a man she did not respect, in front of others. In her journal entry she reflected on the conversation she had with the chairman about their communication problems,

Eventually he came to the real point that I was rude to him in front of junior staff. I said that I felt we had a very jokey relationship and that both of us were "rude" to each other. He said, "but you mean it" to which I replied that I was joking in just the same vein as himself and that if he wanted me to stop joking then he had to as well. This caused him to totally backtrack. He didn't want to give up that right.

Diane acknowledged that elements of her personality were too confrontational but she seemed unable to control this aspect of her character. Rather than diplomatically choose the appropriate moment or refrain from asking a question that might embarrass or catch her superiors off-guard, she seemed to delight in being direct,

I'm assertive. I'm strident. I want to get somewhere. Those sorts of things for a woman are not seen as being a good team player. There are different rules for women. I am a very good team player, but I come out with comments. People always say, "Why do you ask the awkward question or the large question? The one that can't be answered." . . . I would go into meetings and say, "Come on let's bring things out on the table."

Not only was Diane direct, she may have been seen to usurp her chairman's role in controlling what information would be shared and what information would be kept confidential or private.

In retrospect, Fiona felt that she had not been diplomatic enough with her immediate manager after he explained that her job evaluation appeal had been turned down. She told him she was demotivated, felt embittered by the job evaluation committee's decision, and that she found it difficult to work with Jim, a colleague who had been promoted during the same job evaluation proceedings. She told him that she resented being asked to do Jim's work and help him design his programs when she had been effectively "passed over." Fiona said, "In retrospect this [her talking to him openly] was probably a mistake as I was demonstrating my continuing disgust at what had happened and the role he played in it." Soon after her frank discussions with her boss, Fiona described her contact with him as "increasingly infrequent" and when it did occur, it was "strained." If she had kept her feelings to herself and at least on the surface accepted her situation perhaps she would not have been terminated.

The direct and unequivocal communication style adopted by these women has been independently noted to hurt rather than help women managers. A study of 300 male and female executives, director level to chief executive officer (CEO), in the United States suggested that women create obstacles for themselves by being blunt, forthright, and transparent. They may dig their heels in when challenged and may defend their beliefs too vociferously (Hagberg, 1999). Professor Linda L. Carli asked 229 undergraduates to rate female and male speakers on their persuasive abilities. She found that men were influenced more by women who speak tentatively than those who speak assertively (cited in Nichols, 1994, p. 10). Yet, tentative approaches would never have led the women profiled in this book across the horizontal barrier into the male preserve of management.

MENTORING AND THE HIERARCHY

The importance of mentors and networks, and their paucity for women managers, has been discussed in Chapters 2 and 5. In 1987, Morrison et al. studied successful male and female managers. The women were in positions ranging from one level below general management to senior vice president. Both men and women were considered by senior management to be successful managers with high potential for the future. The successful women managers reported that their credibility was enhanced by senior-level executives taking an interest in promoting their success, whereas successful men in the same study did not appear to need this type of endorsement to progress. Every successful female general manager was described by senior executives from her company as having significant sponsorship from upper management. This help involved advice, counsel, support, and feedback. Successful women were supported by good bosses who visibly demonstrated confidence in them and let others know of their talents. These supportive bosses encouraged risk taking, helped women get promoted, and gave them challenging assignments. In Morrison et al.'s study (1987), 51% of the women reported developmental help from others, bosses, and other senior executives, while only 18% of men reported direct help from senior executives. Arnold and Davidson (1990) found that both successful men and women use mentors to gain access to formal power networks within their organizations.

Unlike the women in Morrison et al.'s and Arnold and Davidson's studies, the women profiled in this book did not have champions in the senior management ranks. Many had come from other organizations with a track record of success, but failed to secure senior management "sponsorship" for their actions in their new environment. Why were these women unable to secure sponsorship? Recall Morrison et al.'s (1987) point about the female manager's need to engage in a process of never-ending cognitive readjustment. Unlike Morrison et al.'s cases of successful women managers, the women profiled in this book did not tone down masculine behavior with a more feminine style.

Moreover, the women expected and demanded equal treatment. There is independent evidence that such demands are correlated with the stigma of an "unsuccessful" female manager. Leonie Still (1988) conducted oral histories with 50 female managers in Australia. She reported that successful women have faced prejudice, stereotypical reactions, and discrimination but did not complain or become resentful. Women, on the other hand, who became determined to end the discriminatory treatment they received, voiced their concerns, and demanded equality turned out to be unsuccessful. Moreover, women who seemed able to subordinate their own value system to that of their organization were otherwise identified as "successful."

The women profiled in this book, however, were unable to silence their own value system; many said they fought a battle because they were "right" and were concerned with justice. They reached a point where they demanded that their ill-treatment be addressed; often they voiced their concerns to senior management; and they finally could no longer sit quietly and endure unequal treatment, harassment, or bullying. They assumed that they would be treated equally to their male counterparts when they reached senior levels and were determined to redress their situations; this determination to seek fairness and their outspokenness may have cost them their jobs.

A reasonable conclusion, therefore, is that these two factors—unwillingness or inability to engage in cognitive readjustment and insistence on equitable treatment—prevented them from securing sponsorship and having their experience and talents fully recognized. In short, these women were terminated because the institution of modern business initially called for a masculine style and then punished them for retaining it.

Some of the women found it difficult to acknowledge the "superiority" of their bosses and the highest levels in the hierarchy of their organizations. In part, this lack of respect was generated from the ill-treatment they received from their male colleagues and superiors and in part from their genuine distaste for hierarchical power. At times these women even acted impertinently toward individuals whom they considered unworthy of praise or unintelligent. Diane recognized her impatience with the hierarchy in the following entry from her journal,

I have tried to get on with the directors., but my basic problem is that I don't respect them. . . . It may be because of my competitive streak, but I've got to get over it because this may be a problem that I've always had. I get on with those below, but not those above because I don't recognize their "superiority."

In another journal entry she revealed how little she respected the chairman, "My real view is that I see him as an idiot and I am respecting him less and less at each swipe." When informally advising a young woman who reported to the sales manager on how to deal with him, Diane clearly advised her to assert her individuality rather than be "political" in explaining to him how to accurately predict sales.

She was concerned that it wasn't what Rob [the sales manager] wanted. I tried to impress on her she had to do the job she could see was there on the basis that she was a better judge than Rob and do things that would look good on her CV [curriculum vitae] in 2 years. If a new sales manager came in would she want to be viewed as a PA [Personal Assistant] to her boss or a Sales Coordinator who had sorted out the department?

Diane did not understand a basic fact of organizational life; that is, that she and others at her level were not and would never be considered equal to the chairman in terms of their degree of authority, their right to make decisions, and their general status. Because she viewed herself as intellectually superior to the chairman, she found it impossible to play into the hands of the hierarchy.

Karen admitted she had little time for what she saw as the political side of the hierarchy. Her early career aim was to be a director but she confided, "Once I saw how they operated, I changed my mind. I don't think I'd enjoy the political side of a directorship. It goes against my value system."

Patricia also confided that she had been unprepared for the "ruthlessness and politics" at senior levels and felt that she would never be prepared to play the games necessary to survive in what seemed an inhospitable environment.

Madge discussed how she could not bring herself to be a "yes" person in terms of dealing with her superiors.

I could not bring myself to do what my colleagues felt they had to do to succeed or stay in their jobs and that was to flatter men, not about their appearance but about their skills and experience. I neither saw these skills in depth nor felt that if they were there they needed other people to bolster them.

What these women failed to recognize was that men in their quest to move up within the hierarchy may be willing to play the games these women felt they could not. In addition, playing these games may be easier for men because they are socialized from an early stage in their careers to play them. To their advantage, men may flatter their male bosses in an attempt to gain favor and may more readily accept the hierarchy as a fact of their professional lives. This willingness to flatter executives, play their games, and generally not "rock the boat" by disagreeing was noted by Chris Argyris (1966) in his study of executive and subordinate communication behaviors. Male executives (CEOs) demonstrated three basic values: significant human relationships are the ones that deal with achieving the organization's objectives; cognitive rationality is to be emphasized, and feelings and emotions should be played down. Human relationships are most effectively influenced by unilateral direction, coercion, control, rewards, and penalties that sanction all three of these values (p. 89). The women profiled in this book seemed to misunderstand these basic values. First, at times, they placed their own principles and values above the organization's objectives. The value of "justice" and fair treatment featured predominantly in these women's minds above the organizational norms of secrecy about how the promotional process works and top-down decision making. Second, they were not careful about revealing their emotions and feelings about the treatment they received. Third, they did not understand the "chain of command." Fiona tried to appeal her job evaluation even when her manager suggested to her that he could not influence the hierarchy. In the Argyris study (1966), subordinates did not challenge their boss's opinions even when they disagreed and when delivering "bad" news found euphemisms to describe failing projects. The direct, confrontational communication style so prevalent in the profiled women did not exist between the male CEOs and their subordinates in the Argyris study. Even after 30 years since Argyris' first study, today's corporations, in spite of change management programs, have made little progress toward empowering their employees (Argyris, 1998).

NAÏVETÉ ABOUT THE GRIEVANCE PROCESS

Filing a complaint or a grievance will naturally change the "implied" employment contract. In organizations, people are hired with the unstated expectation that they will outwardly exhibit a positive mental attitude even if this positive attitude is mere appearance. When an individual files a grievance or makes a complaint, the implied harmony of the organization has been challenged. The public complaint calls attention to everyone in the organization that the possibility of unfairness exists. Once this happens, organizations seek to rid themselves of individuals who will become a constant reminder to those around them of possible discrimination and recourse under the law. The women profiled in this book seemed to think their employers would deal with their cases and not penalize them for their protests. They naively believed that the organizations would admit the injustice and correct it, and became outraged when their employers made their lives difficult. This naïveté about how organizations really operate led them to act incautiously during the grievance process.

The backlash against women once they file a grievance has been noted elsewhere. Attorney Catherine Broderick complained to her employer, the Securities and Exchange Commission, about her supervisors giving raises and promotions to those with whom they were having affairs. After she complained, her performance appraisals were downgraded. When she won her suit and was promoted to a management position, she seemed surprised to find that she was not given more responsibility. Price Waterhouse consultant Ann Hopkins was denied partner and told to wear makeup, walk and talk more femininely, and wear jewelry. She won a suit giving her $371,000 in back pay and was promoted to partner, but she finds that she is always identified with the suit and has made enemies within Price Waterhouse (Saltzman, 1996).

CONSCIOUS OR UNCONSCIOUS AWARENESS OF SUBORDINATION AS A SOCIAL SYSTEM?

In Chapter 3, a number of important unanswered questions are identified for patriarchy theory, including those about the detailed workings of patriarchal institutions and how it is that the norms of the patriarchy are internalized by participants in its institutions. Are men and women who interact in ways that systematically subordinate the latter conscious of this subordination? If they are, how do they rationalize or justify it? Or is the patriarchy invisible even to those who enforce it and those upon whom it is enforced? These are crucial questions for any one who contemplates ameliorating the treatment of women and seeks means to do so. Some of what the profiled women reported about their own experiences and the conclusions to which they came after their termination sheds light on these questions.

The degree to which the women attributed their own subordination to a larger social system outside of their control was a function of several different factors. First, the women who were isolated from other women, who did not discuss their situation with other women who had similar experiences, or who did not seek legal counsel and redress were more apt to blame themselves and their choices for their misfortune or to see their treatment as an isolated instance involving an unreasonable individual supervisor, much as men see termination in a personal context (Gould, 1986). Those who did seek counsel and redress through external agencies such as the Equal Opportunities Commission, those who discussed their situations openly with others, and those who engaged in reading about organizational culture and feminist ideology came to understand their situation as a system of female subordination by men.

Caroline discussed her situation with several other women who had been through similar experiences. She described having time to reflect on what had happened to her and felt that men band together against women, even when they do not like one another. Even though she recognized an unfair system and did not feel that this system was likely to change, she wanted the security of working for a company rather than going out on her own.

Madge sought help from the Equal Opportunities Commission and discussed her situation with a solicitor specializing in employment and discrimination cases. No doubt her perspective on her own situation was influenced by forces outside herself. As she became involved in these outside agencies her awareness of a patriarchal system of management increased. After the Equal Opportunities Commission asked for an independent report on Madge's case, she said she had begun to see her case as "One rule for them, one rule for us [women]" and "Jobs for the boys." Although she did not want to be labeled a "feminist," she described an unfair system where injustices existed for women but not for men.

Madge's perception of her situation also changed as she began receiving media attention. She was approached by the woman's editor of a national newspaper and by the BBC for a program about discrimination of women at work. In the newspaper interview, she indicated that women are making some progress, but that it has been insufficient and too slow. She said that there are still severe gaps in pay between men and women. She felt that if people fail to address inequality issues, many companies will face severe problems as the result of discrimination claims. These outside contacts broadened her understanding of her situation by demonstrating to her that her case was not unique.

Like Madge, Diane sought external contacts as she moved through the management hierarchy. When Diane began studying for her MBA degree she read about organizational culture and power and cultivated friendships with lecturers and students in her MBA program. Her study broadened her understanding of organizational issues such as who in the organization has power and who is subordinated by whom. Diane became so interested in the concept of power, in fact, that she later wrote conference papers and presented them at Hull University and the British Accounting Association. These papers reflect how power dimensions influence decision making in organizations.

Diane's journey into organizational culture and power influenced the way she viewed her own situation; she perceived her case not as an individual one but rather as the result of male domination and control. When asked about how she viewed her climb up the organizational hierarchy, she replied,

It gets harder the higher and the older you get. You are fine at certain levels as a "bright girl." They [men] can handle that. If you are going into jobs where there had always been a woman there well then don't worry about it. It's when you go into their [men's] territory at a higher level that they don't like it, especially if you won't know your place. You're supposed to be bright but not too bright. You can't overshadow them [men]. You need to constantly acknowledge, in little ways, their superiority to you.

Fiona's experience changed her perceptions of how organizations inherently operate. Although she did not use the word "patriarchy" to describe institutionalized subordination of women, she did acknowledge that after her termination, when she went to work for another company, her aspirations about progressing up the hierarchy had changed. She also recognized that she had more power and commanded more respect and more money when she operated outside the confines of an organizational hierarchy.

I have no illusions now. I don't put in near the effort that I used to. I still am considered a good employee but I hold no illusions of progressing to my potential. . . . I do the odd bit of consulting for other companies. It's funny how as an outsider I am well respected and get paid a lot of money for a day's work. I have thought a lot about this. I don't pose a threat to the men when I am not part of their organization.

Katherine seemed ambivalent about the "real" reasons for her dismissal. At times, she seemed to recognize a patriarchal system and at times she seemed to blame herself. On the one hand, she attributed her failure to the inability of women to break into what she called "a male system of entitlement" and she recognized the collusion of the personnel department in her dismissal. On the other hand, she expressed women's failure to figure out the organizational dynamics as the reason for their lack of success. In the end, she described her redundancy as the decision of one man, her immediate manager, who seemed to see her as a threat.

Whether these women sought outside support was a function of the severity of harassment or bullying behavior that they endured. Those who endured systematic abuse over a long period of time (several months, for example) and those who were subjected to blatant bullying or sexual harassment were more likely to seek redress outside of their businesses and came to see their experiences as institutionally and not personally determined. Madge and Diane fell into this category as both had endured several months of systematic abuse by their organizations.

Of course, it might well be that when these women sought redress outside their companies, their counselors encouraged them to seek deeper explanations for their problems than a miscreant boss or their own personal and "political" mistakes. However, what is known about the differences between their experiences and those of successful male managers who were terminated undercuts this suggestion. Gould (1986) found that terminated successful male managers were adept at organizational survival and that "with few exceptions, the difficulty was sharply tied to a clash with one individual in the organization—the boss" (p. 16). Nothing like the patterns described in Chapters 5 and 6 emerges in the data about successful male terminations. The experiences documented in the previous two chapters make it plain that whether the women recognized it or not, their treatment was not simply the result of personal incompatibilities. Post-termination reflection did not create but rather enabled them to discover the nature of the patriarchal system in which they had operated, regardless of whether they came to use the word "patriarchy" or not.

Once they sought advice or legal counsel, or read books related to exploitation of women, some of the profiled women began to reconstruct what had happened to them. Many of the women talked about the mixed emotions of relief, anger, and frustration: relief to discover that their problems were not unique to them and that they were not the result of some dark personality flaw; anger at their sense of impotence against a system that is inherently unfair to women; and frustration at their inability to change that system.

Some of the women did not go through this self-reflective stage that led to examining larger gender issues in society. These women tended not to seek other women out, discuss their situations openly, go through counseling, or contact employment solicitors or outside agencies such as the Equal Opportunities Commission (EOC). The majority of the women profiled in this book tended to either blame themselves for their ultimate dismissal or blame the actions of one or a few men. McKenna (1997) suggests that women deal with the pain of conflicting male and female values by going into a state of denial. This denial does not become a problem for them until they see their personal and professional interests at odds. McKenna describes Ellie's realization of this process of denial,

I didn't see that I had slowly come to identify with a value system that ultimately wasn't going to recognize all of me or serve my interests. But in the early days I was also single and childless and young, and I was being nicely rewarded with money and power and position. There was, as yet, no point where my professional and personal interests differed. (1997, pp. 70–71)

Most of the profiled women had not considered their environments to be disadvantageous to women until they, themselves, were subject to unfair treatment. Even then, they did not attribute their situations to systematic discrimination and subordination of women in general. Karen and Elizabeth analyzed their situations in terms of the actions of sexist bosses. They did not subscribe the actions of their bosses to larger patriarchal forces. Similarly, Lesley assessed her termination in terms of the lack of support from her boss who she felt needed to defend her area with the vice president from abroad. She looked to herself and to a degree blamed herself for acting assertively.

Tom [Lesley's boss] was under pressure from the guy in the States who didn't know me and who obviously couldn't handle me. I mean it's a fault and I try to dampen it down but at the end of the day if you've spent 25 years of your life building up your self-confidence, well I'm afraid men will have to handle it. I'm not going to back down.

After being fired, Lesley said "I acted professionally and kept the situation to myself. I told my team a good story and preserved Tom's reputation for the good of the engineering division." Lesley said she spent the first month after being fired "wandering around Watford" and reading romance novels. She then approached an outplacement firm and began looking earnestly for work. Counselors in outplacement are unlikely to help a woman reflect on the process that led to her termination. The focus of outplacement counseling is not to examine the past, but to look for future employment and to repackage oneself for the best job possible. Outplacement counselors naturally do not look for larger organizational barriers to advancement because they are in the business of keeping individuals motivated to rejoin the workforce.

Like Lesley, Patricia blamed herself for her termination, yet she also seemed to understand that there were forces operating in the culture that would be hard to overcome. She expressed this ambivalence about the causes of her being fired in two different parts of one interview. In the first case, she said,

The last thing I thought was that it was my fault. I do feel it was my doing. I was foolish. . . . Because I complained about things, I was deliberately left out of the loop. I should have tried to be more political.

Later in the same interview, she seemed to recognize that forces larger than herself were responsible. She remarked,

Mine [her firing] was disguised redundancy. Really the culture has to change. Women should look for early warning signs and trust their intuition. If something doesn't seem right or fair, it probably isn't. I don't think an individual can turn a culture around.

The difference between successful and unsuccessful women managers is that the former do not make an issue out of their unequal treatment; they soldier on, making the most of a system that subordinates women. What makes these women successful? It could be that success is simply survival at levels of senior management in which few woman can survive. If Morrison et al. (1987) is right, success is a matter of continuous cognitive readjustment to remain nonthreatening and appear compliant. As discussed in Chapter 6, the reserve army of compliant female replacements learns to know its place and will not challenge the hierarchy. These women may well identify themselves as successful; yet by remaining at lower levels of management and adopting strategies and making choices that minimize their exposure to patriarchal discipline, they reinforce the effectiveness of the patriarchy.

CONCLUSION

In Chapter 3, it is noted that the patriarchy theory is silent about how the norms that accord power to a hierarchy of males actually work to produce women's subordination. What are the practices of the social institution through which the patriarchy operates? Are these practices recognized by participants for what they are? Does the patriarchy operate through recognized self-conscious strategies of individual men and women or the unnoticed impersonal operation of an autonomous structure? These are questions that any theory of the modern business enterprise as a male hierarchy must answer. In Chapter 5, eight different dimensions of patriarchal enforcement are identified. Seven of these eight dimensions are ways in which males enforce subordination, acting from specific norms that sanction certain practices. It is important to bear in mind that corporate discipline is not enforced on males in the same way.

In the ten cases discussed in this book, assignment of the fundamental causes of termination took two forms: the majority of women recognized a tough, "macho" environment but still blamed themselves for not overcoming it or blamed isolated sexist men, while only four—Madge, Diane, Fiona, and Caroline—recognized systematic patriarchal forces at work. What distinguishes these women from the rest is not their backgrounds, but their contact with external agencies and friends who opened their eyes to other explanations and literature about power and equality issues.

These women's narratives do not suggest that the patriarchal structures, which channelled their experiences, were the result of conscious choices of individuals who set out to enforce a male-dominated hierarchy. To some extent, indeed, the men with whom they interacted were as much victims as enforcers of the patriarchy. Some are recorded as even attempting unsuccessfully to escape its exigencies. Recall that Fiona's manager initially tried to support her proposal in a job evaluation committee but was forced by other men to "close ranks" against her and Madge's female colleague felt powerless to help her fight the board. In these women's narratives, it seems clear that both genders are unwilling victims of a system they usually cannot recognize while they are still operating within it. Along with the patriarchy, participants in social processes act on many other norms that reflect the role of class: social, economic, race, or asymmetries of power. The degree to which people recognize their actions as driven by identifiable norms is highly variable and often only arises as the product of special kinds of education and instruction. Even more than others, patriarchal norms are likely to remain invisible, especially in a society that formally endorses equality.

This invisibility suggests early and thorough internalization of the norms of the patriarchy. Even the androgynous style required to move up toward senior management is not so much imposed on the women profiled in this book as it is eagerly adopted from a relatively early age. It appears that shaking free of the traits encouraged by a patriarchal system requires nothing less than the enforced recognition that the institutional setting and one's responses to it are both creatures of such a system. At this point, at least among women, the patriarchy becomes visible if not less powerful.

Like most people who are not terminated, the profiled women often did not recognize that their treatment was being meted out in accordance with institutionalized norms common to all business organizations. Accordingly, most of the women did not generally experience or describe their work environments as patriarchal. Rather, during their working period and even through the experience of termination, most analyzed the experience as reflecting individual choices that made them at least in part agents in the drama of their dismissals. A good deal of the aversive gender differential treatment was viewed as individual sexism, which the organization did not suppress. For many of the women, even subsequent reflections suggested that they thought matters might have gone differently had they chosen different strategies in their careers.

Their termination experiences reflect the interaction of other features they shared in common—personal, psychological, and behavioral, along with patriarchal constraints in which they operated—to bring about termination. In the case of Madge, Fiona, Diane, and Caroline, once circumstances provided an opportunity to rethink the processes through which they went, they began to recognize patriarchal forces that first limited their potential and then sealed their fates. Even though the others did not express recognition of a system of subordination, there is much evidence that it was responsible for the outcomes they experienced. We need to divide the pre-termination experiences of women from the process of actual dismissal. In the period before their actual job loss, and indeed throughout their careers moving up the management ladder, the women profiled in this book were subjected to a subordination that was largely not volitional. That is, men who made their lives difficult did not do so predominantly or exclusively because they saw these women as identifiable threats to the dominance of a male hierarchy at the level of middle to senior management. The patriarchy made it easy or permissible for men to respond to women managers in ways that reflected the institutionalized inequality of all women throughout the economy. It was in the final stages of termination that male colleagues, co-workers, and bosses viewed these women as potential threats to their power and acted from motives of ensuring the continued dominance of a patriarchy within their business environments.

Successful women managers who lose their jobs represent a crucial test case at the borderline of horizontal segregation in modern management. For it is at the frontier between the almost entirely male hierarchy of management and their predominantly female support staff that men come face to face with women of largely the same class, race, education, and aspirations for leadership, responsibility, and reward. That there is a patriarchy in operation in modern management is manifest in the experiences of the women featured in this book. When these successful women managers break through and then are pushed back beneath the glass ceiling, their stories can tell us much about the ways in which a patriarchy operates and what becomes of women who confront it.

CHAPTER 8

The Present and the Future

◆◆

my
critique

This book has examined the subordination of women in modern business organizations through the experiences of ten senior women managers. The mechanisms that reinforce power to control these women were explored in Chapter 5: verbal communication patterns of men that minimize the contributions of women or publicly demean them, withholding of information, denial of status, lack of mentoring and networks, intimidation tactics, the double-bind women experience when they try to assert themselves, and the closing of ranks when women challenge the organization by formally raising issues of discrimination or unfair treatment. In Chapter 6, discussion centered on how the patriarchy punishes women when they object to unfair treatment and how eventually it imposes the ultimate sanction: termination of women who seriously threaten its hegemony.

The popular dual systems approach to the interaction of the patriarchy and capitalist modes of economic organization suggests that both often work together to subordinate women. As Hartmann (1979, p. 230) notes, "the . . . mutual accommodation between patriarchy and capitalism has created a vicious circle for women." But as Walby (1988, 1990) and Witz (1992) both show, sometimes capitalism and the patriarchy come into conflict. There are some historical circumstances in which the interests of capital have been served by reducing or eliminating the subordinate role that the patriarchy imposes on women (in war, for instance). And in some areas of contemporary corporate life, the benefits to the business of such relaxation of inequalities may be considerable. One might suppose that the promotion of highly competent women through the glass ceiling and into the highest levels of management would provide critical benefits in circumstances of strong competition among corporations. In the 1970s economists following Gary Becker (1975) argued that forces encouraging economic efficiency would eventually lead to the disappearance of racial discrimination in employment and elsewhere. Because of the extra production costs it imposes and the inability to hire the most qualified candidates for positions that it also requires, racial discrimination should price itself out of highly competitive markets. Economic rationality alone could on this view be expected to reduce if not eliminate such inequities. Similarly, discrimination with regard to gender would end. It is in these circumstances that capitalism and the patriarchy may be expected to move in opposite directions. Some studies of the increased penetration of women in vertically segregated work during war time indirectly support this view. As the cost in productivity of excluding women from industrial labor rose during both world wars, capitalist economies at least temporarily broke down barriers to women's participation in the labor force. But as victory reduced the costs of subordination, women left the labor force in large numbers (Summerfield, 1984).

This conflict between patriarchy and capitalism arises only rarely and, when it does arise, invariably the power to ensure continued subordination overwhelms capitalism's power to fully exploit the talents and abilities of women. If economic rationality at least sometimes encourages eliminating restrictions to the employment and progress of talented women, why wouldn't organizations eliminate these restrictions? Certainly it would be in the best interests of organizations to promote talented people, whether they are male or female. Why is the patriarchy resistant to incentives of economic efficiency?

Like capitalism, the patriarchy constitutes a well-established social system, one that existed long before capitalism, and has either been insulated from capitalism's impact or has shaped capitalism to subordinate women. Marxist-feminist scholars like Hartmann argue that patriarchy's historical priority to capitalism has its sources in the power it gave men to organize. Hartmann (1979, p. 207) notes, "before capitalism, a patriarchal system was established in which men controlled the labour of women . . . and in doing so men learned techniques of hierarchical organization and control." But patriarchy's domination of social relations even prior to the period of capitalist social organization cannot have been manifest solely in the greater facility it provided men to organize. As Witz argues, "if the maintenance of patriarchal relations depends so crucially on the *organized* pursuit of exclusionary strategies [of discrimination against women], then 'patriarchal capitalism' could hardly have been said to exist before 1900" (1992, p. 27). The patriarchy is a historically prior and more pervasive system of social relations in which men are provided with many resources to maintain their gender dominance throughout a great range of economic, political, legal, and other changes in society.

As a social system the patriarchy has shown remarkable resilience over long periods. It is an ancient, yet flexible, and almost ubiquitous way in which societies have been organized. Its historical persistence, cross-cultural universality, pervasiveness within cultures, and the very different forms it takes suggest that as a social system patriarchy is both robust in its resistance to and accommodation of change. To some extent the systematic character of male domination is illustrated by the processes that the ten cases reported in the last three chapters.

HOW THE PATRIARCHY WORKS

In sexist organizations, good performance at or above the glass ceiling often can lead to termination because it threatens the patriarchy. In these organizations, men and women comply with the patriarchy whether or not they are in sympathy with it. Sexist men, those actively encouraging the patriarchy by their discrimination, harassment, and bullying of women, either are given a punishment so weak as to be ineffective or are not punished at all. In either case, the message to other men and to women in the organization is that it is acceptable to subordinate and the organization will turn a blind eye to those who engage in discriminatory practices. In this book's study, several men fell into this category; two examples demonstrate how this phenomenon operates. Recall the situation where Patricia, a marketing manager, tried in vain to assert herself in the face of constant humiliation. Patricia's manager and the sales manager who harassed and publicly humiliated her were never punished. They were only required to give Patricia a pro forma apology. Madge, a human resource director for a large retail organization, endured similar humiliation, yet Madge's managing director was never punished for his unfair treatment of her even when an industrial tribunal intervened and agreed with Madge's claims of victimization. Instead, Madge's managing director's fellow board members rallied around him to show their solidarity for his actions. As Collier (1995) notes, men exert control over women when they see them try to enter the male preserve or when they see them object to their subordinated status. This control may be exercised in the form of harassment or intimidation.

Male behavior patterns in the form of harassment and intimidation obviously disadvantage women, but so too do institutionalized practices such as recruitment methods and fast-track management trainee programs. Gender differences in the acquisition of on-the-job training have been reported by Olsen and Sexton (1996). Men receive more on-the-job training than women when they enter a job and acquire more training through their careers. These gender differences in on-the-job training significantly affect the male/female wage gap.

Occasionally nonsexist men will try to advance the status of women in organizations but will be discouraged from doing so. They may make female appointments for positions, support the training of women at work, or identify female mentoring projects. However, at the point where women begin pushing up against the glass ceiling and demanding their rights, even nonsexist men will find the costs of supporting women too high. These men will encounter severe pressure to conform to the patriarchy and "not rock the boat." Their own careers may be placed in jeopardy for not following the rules and the mores of the patriarchy. A few examples from the cases in this book illustrate how the patriarchy forestalls nonsexist men's efforts to advance women in corporations. Lesley's immediate manager, the managing director of an engineering firm, was unable to intervene on Lesley's behalf to save her position. The managing director had promoted Lesley to lead one of the largest engineering divisions in the company. He had been very supportive of her until she began challenging the vice president's opinions. At this point, the managing director withdrew his support.

I had a feeling he [the managing director] was being lent on extremely heavily and he had his own career to back up and just basically wasn't prepared to lose it. He had to look after his own family.

Fiona's manager had a similar dilemma. He supported Fiona up to the point when she demanded a fairer job evaluation. When the job evaluation committee refused to endorse a higher grade level, he would not fight the committee. Karen's manager had agreed that an increase in salary was fair for the new position Karen would assume. However, when Karen's manager encountered resistance from the board of directors he would not support her. In fact, her manager told the board that Karen would accept the position at the salary level she had rejected.

In addition to the pressure that the patriarchy exerts to prevent nonsexist men from acting individually to help particular women, there are further factors preventing men from acting as individuals in support of women as a class. Thibaut and Kelley (1967) notes, "the environment always applies the rule that 'winner takes all', whether the winner is an individual or a coalition. Second best receives nothing" (p. 215). The risks are too high for men to act autonomously. Closing ranks with other men at least ensures that men will win collectively. The collective win is always preferred to losing everything.

It is easy to see how men are controlled by institutionalized sexism. Also, the patriarchy regulates women. Women are allowed to operate below the glass ceiling where they are "doers" and "implementers" rather than "decision makers" and "strategists." Often when women assert their rights to be involved in decisions and strategy alongside men, they come to be labeled "difficult" women. The strong, assertive styles of these women coupled with their competent performance threatens the grip of the patriarchy, which responds by finally forcing these women out of their organizations.

In organizations, a second type of women co-exists with the "difficult" woman. She is the compliant subordinate. These women comprise a "reserve army" for the patriarchy. The patriarchy gives some concessions to this group of women because these concessions do not threaten its underlying character or control. For example, flexible working hours and child care programs do not reduce the real power that men have in organizations. In fact, it can be argued that these programs increase men's power over women by making it easier for the patriarchy to more easily retain a reserve army of women.

In Chapters 5 and 6 members of this "reserve army" of compliant women were encountered. Katherine's replacement was a woman eager to assume Katherine's former role at a reduced income and status level. Like Katherine's replacement, Mary's successor was more than willing to assume her role at a salary less than what Mary was earning.

The mechanisms of the patriarchy's control are imposed on men and women: verbal communication patterns that exclude or demean women, withholding of information, denial of status, lack of real mentoring experiences and the absence of networking, intimidation, the double-bind that women experience when they try to assert themselves, and men being forced to close ranks as women threaten to take action. The patriarchy's control mechanisms in organizations are most likely not limited to the ones described in this book. Indeed, more research may uncover other mechanisms that are used to keep women in their place.

IMPLICATIONS

If the patriarchy is a persistent structural system, one whose causal force often overwhelms other systems such as economic and legal ones, then incremental legal changes and isolated political resistance to it, even if successful, will not rapidly destabilize it. Indeed, the patriarchy controls the legal system. It can make compensating adjustments to prevent the legal system's use as a threat to patriarchal domination. The weakness of legal initiatives reflects the law's dependence on the patriarchy. For example, government initiatives such as Britain's Opportunity 2000 have not threatened the underlying character of male dominance in organizations. Signing up for Opportunity 2000 is not mandatory for organizations. The monitoring and control over those companies that have chosen to participate has been lacking. Wendy Richards examined the role of Opportunity 2000 in general in organizations and specifically within the National Health Service. She believes there appears to be no specific guidance given to member organisations as to the type of equal opportunities measures they should be pursuing . . . there appears to be no method of exerting control over the implementation of programmes by participating organisations; this is particularly clear from the campaign's first annual report. (1996, pp. 91–92)

A condition of joining the European Union by both the European Parliament and the European Commission is an equal opportunity policy. While all countries in the European Union have a nondiscrimination clause in their constitutions, the enforcement of such policies has been lacking. The only gender discrimination case ruled on in a central or eastern European country was a Hungarian case involving an advertisement seeking a young man for employment (Commission of the European Communities, 1999).

Moreover, Dickens (1994) suggests organizations have promoted the equal opportunity agenda for three reasons: to avoid a penalty, to ensure a steady supply of women in the workforce for lower-level positions, and to promote their image as equal opportunity employers.

Although the U.K. Parliament has enacted the Sex Discrimination Act and the Equal Pay Act, and the U.S. Congress has passed similar equal employment legislation, the real enforcement of these laws is problematic. Research suggests that often women feel too threatened to report harassment, fearing that they will be further victimized (University of St. Thomas, 1993; Swiss, 1995 cited in Rheem, 1996). In spite of the law against sex discrimination, harassment continues to be a problem in the workplace (Cockburn, 1990; IRS, 1992). Women still comprise the lower echelons of business organizations and make significantly less than men; often cases of harassment remain unpunished or are punished at a level that does not provide the incentive for organizations to change or be overturned by judicial processes. As firms have tried to lower their labor costs, women have suffered. Two thirds of all part-time workers in the United States are women and women comprise the majority of temporary workers without employment benefits (Milkman, 1995). In a study of 325 women managers, 50% said they advanced more slowly than their male colleagues, 68% felt that they were held to a higher standard than men, 62% said they had experienced gender bias, and 69% had experienced language demeaning to women. Perhaps most worrying was the female managers' perception that there is a gap between their organization's equity policies and its actual practices (Swiss, 1995, cited in Rheem, 1996). The attainment of equality is very difficult because it requires not just a change in law but a change in cultural consciousness.

If the legal system were a real remedy wouldn't we have seen more progress than we have? Employment remains segregated and unprotected for women; in the European Union women account for 80% of part-time workers without the employment protection afforded permanent full-time employees. Women's employment continues to be concentrated in the service sector where 80% of women workers in the European Union work. Women's share of clerical jobs has increased rather than decreased (Commission of the European Communities, 1999). In most countries, women's participation in management ranges from only 10% to 40% (ILO, 1997). The actual figures are probably below those reported because management statistics include "administrative workers," a class that may include many without managerial responsibilities. The dearth of women managers is noted in several recent studies. For example, in Switzerland in 1996, women held 10% of management positions in sectors representing 80% of professional workers. Another Swiss study of 97 organizations indicated that 9% of management jobs were held by women, yet more than one quarter of these companies employed no women managers at all (ILO, 1997). A survey of 343 German organizations, employing around 1.14 million workers, reported that only 7% of their technical and managerial staff were women (ILO, 1997). In the former Soviet Union an International Labour Organization study found that not more than 6% of heads of enterprises nationwide were women (Posadskaya and Zakharova, 1990). Where women have been successful reaching the upper levels of management, it has been in areas considered to be less strategic and central to the organization. Personnel and administration represent the highest growth areas for women managers in the United States, France, and Finland (ILO, 1997).

Conditions vary somewhat between legal environments in different countries. In the United Kingdom, there has been little incentive for organizations to change their discriminatory practices. Some positive changes in U.K. law have occurred, however. In 1993, the ceiling on compensation for successful sex discrimination claims was removed. In 1999, the qualifying period for unfair dismissal claims was reduced from two years of continuous service to one year and the compensation sum for dismissal raised from £8,925 to £50,000 (Aiken, 1999). Although these changes are positive, companies can subvert the law by labeling an unfair dismissal as a redundancy and by settling with women out of court. The burden of proof in an unfair dismissal case will rest on the individual woman who is unlikely to have the resources to fight a corporation.

By contrast to the U.K. legal system, in the United States there have never been ceilings on discrimination case awards. Furthermore, in the United Kingdom class action suits are illegal, preventing women from having a collective voice against discrimination at work. In the United States, where class action suits are permissible, in 1996 Mitsubishi Corporation was fined in a class action suit of female assembly line workers for routine harassment. Other class action sex discrimination suits have been filed against State Farm Insurance, Publix Grocery Stores, Lucky Stores, and Northwest Airlines. In 1999, a class action suit was lodged against Merrill Lynch in the United States for its alleged discrimination against female brokers. Issues in this case include the funneling of clients and leads to male brokers, lack of access to training for women, and lower salaries paid to women with similar or better qualifications than that of men. Also in 1999, Winn Dixie grocery chain settled a discrimination lawsuit for $33 million after approximately 50,000 employees claimed that they had been discriminated against based on their race or gender (Winn Dixie grocery, 1999).

There have been attempts to reduce the systematic discriminatory effects of regulation which do not appear to be biased against women, but which are. However, these attempts have difficulty succeeding. For example, the concept of indirect sex discrimination—the principle that equal treatment shall mean that discrimination will not occur on the grounds of sex either directly or indirectly—has been problematic in the United Kingdom and has not served women well. As von Prondsynski and Richards (1995) note, the potential for using indirect discrimination as a tool for labor market reform has been minimized because of its interpretation in the Sex Discrimination Act of 1975,

in the United Kingdom this potential has been partly thwarted by the wording of the statutory definition in the Sex Discrimination Act 1975. Under this definition a "requirement or condition" is indirectly discriminatory if the employer "cannot show [it] to be justifiable irrespective of the sex of the person to whom it is applied". [footnote S.I.(1)(b)(ii) of the 1975 Act.] The use of the term "justifiable" gives all sorts of hostages to fortune. (p. 120)

The case of *Clymo v. Wandsworth London Borough Council* provides an example of this kind of interpretation. The Wandsworth London Borough Council was not found to indirectly discriminate against women for refusing to make job sharing available for managerial posts. The employment appeal tribunal ruled that the Wandsworth Council had made a reasonable managerial decision, which was justifiable for the running of the business (von Prondsynski and Richards, 1995). Clearly the court's interpretation of what is "reasonable" and "justifiable" under the law makes the prohibition of indirect discrimination unenforceable.

As this case illustrates, organizations often go unpunished for indirect discrimination. In the United Kingdom, punitive damages for sexual harassment and unequal pay are not high enough to change the behavior of organizations. Furthermore, as this book suggests, many organizations prefer to buy women off cheaply rather than engage in public legal battles. If the legal system, exemplified by governmental policy and employment law, were at the forefront of equality issues unjust laws would already have been changed. For example, women in Western countries are penalized by the social security system for interrupted work lives. Long, continuous employment are necessary for social security benefits and unemployment benefits in many Western European countries. Governmental policy has not addressed the working mother with young children. Child care subsidies, vouchers for state-approved child care, tax breaks for child care, and more generous parental leave policies would be evidence of such support. In June 1999, the Swiss people voted down by 61% a bill allowing for 14 weeks of paid maternity leave. At the same time, in Switzerland men are provided 3 weeks annual paid leave for military service. We can see that legal and political systems do not respond well to advancing women's rights, but why? Legal and political systems are stifled by men who, just as in business environments, regulate women at or below the glass ceiling. Although more than 40% of law students at universities in the United States and the United Kingdom are women, the number of women practicing law is low—only about 12% in the United Kingdom. The profession remains male dominated and limits the type and quality of work available to women solicitors and barristers (Spencer and Podmore, 1987).

When women begin to demand equality and start to make gains the dominant political culture responds by resisting their initiatives. This was evident in the reaction to the 1997 Labour Party initiative in Britain to shortlist only women candidates for its winnable constituencies. Members of the party vehemently protested, saying that this action violated men's rights and would be the introduction of a much dreaded quota system. In central and eastern Europe as women gained parliamentary seats and a more equal footing with men in education,

These factors have, in some countries, led to a backlash in the transition period, with the promotion of the traditional role model for women within the male bread-winner family. The backlash has been accompanied by increased pressures on women, with the closing of childcare facilities following the dismantling of large State-run enterprises and the rising costs of childcare. (Commission of the European Communities, 1999, p. 30)

Susan Faludi has documented a similar attitude in the United States where women's gains have consistently been met with a backlash since the 1980s. Electoral patterns illustrate this backlash,

For the first time in American history [in 1980], a gender voting gap emerged over women's rights issues. For the first time, polls found men less likely than women to support equal roles for the sexes in business and government, less likely to support the Equal Rights Amendment—and more likely to say they preferred the "traditional" family where the wife stayed home. Moreover, some signs began to surface that men's support of women's rights issues was not only lagging but might actually be eroding. (1991, p. 61)

Faludi presents a convincing argument showing the effects of the backlash; for example, men have rejected equal employment principles on the grounds that women have unfairly taken over the labor market, cheating men out of jobs that they deserve. In November 1996, California referendum 209, called the "Civil Rights Initiative," effectively made affirmative action illegal. The initiative gained 60% approval. Another form of backlash against women creeping into management positions in the United Kingdom is the pervasive requirement of many British firms that candidates for board-level positions must have had prior board experience in a public company. This effectively eliminates women from consideration and explains the scarcity of female board members in the United Kingdom (Adler and Izraeli, 1994).

In the United States, a large scale, longitudinal study was conducted with 8,534 men and 7,779 women tracking their job advancement to managerial positions between 1981 and 1987 (Maume, 1999). The study revealed several interesting differences between men's and women's job progression. Older women were better able than younger women to demonstrate their skills, whereas age presented no obstacle for men. Women's promotional chances declined as their tenure increased with an employer. It seems the longer a woman remains with an employer at one salary grade, the more apt she is to be stuck there. Men benefitted from organizations where there were more women than men; in these female dominated environments, men were apt to be promoted more often than women. Conversely, once placed in typically female roles, women in female dominated and male dominated environments did not receive the training or education to move up.

THE POSSIBILITY OF CHANGE

By examining other major social changes we may gain an insight into the difficulty of any concerted attempt to reduce the subordination of women in business environments. In the United States, at least two social movements made significant gains over limited time periods. The civil rights movement and resistance to the Vietnam War both attained outcomes resisted by the dominant political forces. The success of these highly charged movements required political organization and a critical mass of people opposed to the status quo. Organization was possible because this critical mass could be mobilized. Communication was readily organized because the target population was easily identified and targeted. Speeches, leaflets, and marches were efficiently transmitted and commanded the attention of a sufficient number of people.

The movement for gender equity in middle- and senior-level management jobs has none of these advantages. More generally, Turner and Killian (1957) suggest that there are four conditions necessary for a nondominant group to defeat a dominant group. The minority group must:

1. already possess some political control
2. have justification for extending their control

3. are able to mobilize the means of mass communication or the source of information

4. have support from other minority groups.

Both the civil rights movement and the Vietnam anti-war movement had these characteristics. For example, some members of Congress supported the civil rights movement at its inception so the movement had some influence. There was a strong moral justification for providing equal rights for all citizens. Education about the equal rights movement was mobilized through churches, television, and newspapers and other minority groups with collateral interests rallied to the cause. Much the same was true for the anti-war movement, although universities and students played the role borne by churches and African Americans in the civil rights movement.

By contrast, fighting against sexism and providing true equal opportunity for women in business organizations is difficult because most of Turner and Killian's (1957) four factors are absent. Because women are in such scant numbers at the top of organizations they do not possess control or power; because they have no control, they cannot mobilize the sources of information and communication in their organizations. And again, because they are isolated from one another, women find it impossible to organize and to garner support from other groups. Women in organizations, especially at the middle and senior management level, are separated from one another, whereas students on American campuses are not. Furthermore, women may not be prepared to be militant because their livelihoods depend on their continued employment. Such risks did not usually concern civil rights activists and students.

The few women who have made it to the upper reaches of organizations often disassociate themselves from gender equity issues. Their own fragile status and their wish to associate with and be thought of as similar to their male peers makes them hesitant to support or be identified with feminist principles. Many female managers and senior administrators in universities have remarked in private and public that they do not wish to be labeled "feminists"; they feel the term would be unhelpful to them in their careers. Some women enjoy their status as a successful minority, taking pride in the attitude that they came up the hard way without help from anyone else. Like successful women at the top, talented women at the middle are often unhelpful to other women, but for different reasons. Successful women at the middle management level hoping to reach senior management often see other women as competition. After all, in companies where there are a minuscule number of positions available to women at the top, it makes sense that women competing for these places will in the worst case sabotage one another and in the best case not offer support. The unwillingness of successful women to speak out against sexist practices makes change even more difficult. When challenged by assertive women, men who want to continue sexist practices can direct attention to the few successful women and claim that their success and their lack of complaints prove the absence of workplace discrimination.

If women are unable to find help from within their organizations, could they find support from an external source? Could the trade unions be the answer? Here we can look to the United Kingdom, where trade unions are stronger than in the United States. The trade union movement in the United Kingdom has had the power to oppose the patriarchy, but it has not served women well in terms of helping them organize themselves or by demanding equality in the workplace. Even when female members of the union have become more vocal about women's issues, the union leaders have not represented their interests. In fact, the trade unions allowed men to organize the patriarchy at work (Walby, 1986, 1990). The United Kingdom and Ireland have weak or uneven collective bargaining compared to Denmark, Germany, Italy, Belgium, and the Netherlands. Moreover, women have traditionally been concentrated in sectors where trade union membership is low such as retailing, catering, and clerical work and where collective regulation is limited. Clerical and administrative staff often are not covered by collective agreements, whereas male-dominated industries such as construction and agriculture are regulated by agreements (Rubery and Fagan, 1995). Women's participation in unions is growing and unions of female workers are growing very fast in the service industries. However, these jobs are pink-collar jobs with little if any upward mobility. An international survey of unions reported that despite the fact that women constitute most of the new members, they do not have proportional representation in trade union leadership (ILO, 1999). According to this survey, the top four reasons for women rejecting union membership were their lack of understanding of how unions could help them, fear of reprisals from employers, conflicting family responsibilities, and the male-dominated culture of unions (ILO, 1999). If, over time, the power of union leadership shifts toward women, we may see some positive outcomes. In addition to the problems faced by women attempting to organize to undermine sexist practices, the character of subordination itself makes concerted opposition difficult. The male power structure is spatially distributed and diverse in its operations. How does one target all business organizations? In addition, organizations provide material incentives for males to maintain the subordination of women. Competition for promotions is reduced if a significant proportion (for example, women) of the potential workforce is ineligible. The patriarchy also provides small incremental rewards to compliant women; junior staff may move along the career ladder up to the glass ceiling, where they provide ready substitutes for women who seek to break through it.

WOMEN-DOMINATED PROFESSIONS

One might hope that as women begin to dominate professions numerically, the power imbalance between men and women will disappear. Several authors have suggested that women's status in the workforce will improve once they reach a critical mass (Kanter, 1977; Rustad, 1982; Martin, 1988). At least some research has shown that this is unlikely because of the entrenched sexism in society. In fact, an examination of four predominantly female occupations—nursing, librarianship, elementary school teaching, and social work—shows that, rather than being victimized for their maleness, men in these professions are considered more marketable than women, are given preferential treatment, and are often tracked into higher-level jobs within these professions (Williams, 1998). If men do experience discrimination in these professions, it comes from outside, rather than inside the organizations, in the form of stereotypes. The public may assume male nurses are gay, male librarians will be considered "wimpy," and male elementary teachers report disbelief from other men outside the profession in their choice of such a low-status profession. Unlike the tokenism experienced by women in male-dominated professions, the tokenism experienced by males inside female-dominated professions seems to work in men's favor. Both the men and women interviewed in Williams' study recognized that men are often given preferential treatment in hiring and promotions, are accepted by supervisors and colleagues, and "are well integrated into the work place culture" (1998, p. 296). Similarly, male prison officials working in female-dominated prisons reported no opposition from female staff or supervisors, yet female workers in male prison establishments were admitted by male wardens "only under order of the law and often after considerable resistance" (Zimmer, 1988, p. 70).

Kathlene's research (1998) on gender dynamics in politics sheds light on the behavior of men in female-dominated professions. The interaction between men and women in the Colorado state legislature, a state with one of the highest proportions of women legislators, suggested that male committee chairs used their position of power more than female chairs to control committee hearing discussions. In addition, male chairs delayed witness testimony often by questioning female sponsors during their introduction of a bill. However, when women held the power as chair, male witnesses often displayed verbal aggressiveness by interrupting the female chair. Overall, male legislators displayed gender power by dominating discussion and by focusing more on men than on women. This verbal dominance increased when the proportion of women in committee hearings increased or when a bill was sponsored by a woman (Kathlene, 1998). This research, as well as Williams' study (1998) of men in female-dominated professions, implies that simply adding more women to the employment hierarchy, even at relatively senior levels, is no guarantee of gender equity.

Beyond business and government, the academic environment provides more evidence of the phenomenon of men controlling female-dominated professions. Title IX legislation in the United States prohibits sex discrimination in educational institutions that receive federal funds. When Title IX was passed in 1972, few people anticipated its far-reaching consequences, especially in the area of male-dominated athletics. Within just a few years, women's participation in college athletics doubled and coaching women's athletic teams began to have much higher visibility. With the subsequent tighter enforcement of more equal funding in sports, coaches of women's athletic teams, although still underpaid compared to coaches of men's athletic teams, experienced a rise in their salaries. At this juncture, what had been almost entirely a female job became a majority male profession. In 1996, only 47.4% of coaches of women's teams were females, down from 90% in 1972 when Title IX was enacted. The status of women athletic administrators has fared even worse since the passage of Title IX; today only 19.4% of women's programs are directed by a female, while in 1972 more than 90% of women's programs were under the direction of a woman (Acosta and Carpenter, 1998). As the resources, power, status, and remuneration of administrative positions in women's sports became more significant, the patriarchy arrogated control of these positions from women to men.

THE GLOBAL ECONOMY AS A SOURCE OF CHANGE

Many American firms are planning to or have already expanded their presence in foreign markets. Can women managers expect to benefit from the global economy? In an age of mergers and acquisitions that often occur internationally do women have more opportunity? Globalization should open opportunities for talented women, but it is unlikely to do so. If the male-dominated power structure exists in the international economy women are likely to fair poorly. For example, when downsizing occurs at management grades, women are likely to be more adversely affected than men. A recent acquisition of Amoco by British Petroleum left many women downgraded from director-level positions to manager positions and from manager positions to supervisors, while it left most male directorships and male managers' positions intact. Although women have steadily increased their employment rates in the European Union in the 1990s, their incomes are significantly less than men's earnings. Women spend on average eight hours fewer per week than men in paid work, their hourly wage is lower than men's, and they are less likely to earn premiums for overtime or pay increments for seniority (Rubery et al., 1998). A recent study of 686 major North American firms with operations outside of North America found women to hold only 402 of 13,348 international management positions (Adler, 1994).

Three myths about women prevent their progress in holding international positions: women do not want to be international managers, women in dual-career marriages are poor candidates for overseas assignments, and cultural barriers in foreign countries may prevent women from succeeding. None of these common beliefs is borne out by fact. When 100 international female managers were interviewed, 97% said that their assignments were successful and most of their companies promoted them because of their experience abroad. A North American woman in a foreign country is often expected to act like a foreigner and she is not held to the standards of a local woman. It seems that an American woman abroad is classified by the foreign culture as an American business person first and a woman second. This is especially true if the woman's American colleagues present her to the foreign nationals as someone with credentials to be taken seriously. Most of the women profiled in this book indicated that they encountered more prejudice from their home companies than the foreign nationals because their companies viewed them as a high risk compared to men in overseas assignments. These myths concerning potential female ex-patriots reflect another device of the male power structure: the practice of preventing women from breaking through in a new area where women are not already present.

FUTURE PROGRESS

What can produce the broad social change required to weaken the patriarchy's control? Only changes that undermine the patriarchy in its fundamental cultural and social forms will have significant impact. As women become entrepreneurs and business owners we may see more support for equality in women-owned work environments. A good example of a successful woman entrepreneur who has made a difference in the lives of many women is Mary Kay Ash of Mary Kay Cosmetics. Her first objective in founding the company was to provide opportunities for women; she had worked in direct selling and corporate environments and had repeatedly been passed over for promotion. Evidence of her commitment to women rests in Mary Kay's employment statistics; 70% of managers at Mary Kay are women and several senior-level positions are filled by women including vice presidents of finance, product marketing, marketing communications, quality assurance, the research guidance testing department, and the legal department (Dodge, 1999; Whiddon, 1999). Avon Corporation also has provided opportunity for women. As part of the diversity efforts at Avon, the owners realized that offering opportunities for women in entry-level jobs would have little impact on the overall progress of women. Instead, Avon made it a policy to bring women into management at the senior level. Of Avon's officers, 32% are women and four sit on the board of directors: Susan Kropf, the president of Avon US; Edwina Woodbury, the chief financial officer; and Christina Gold, the executive vice president of direct selling development. Andrea Jung was recently promoted from the president of global marketing and new business to Avon's first female CEO. Company-wide, 86% of Avon's managers are women. An obvious fact about both Avon and Mary Kay is that they are marketing products for women that are best understood by women. As models of women-organized and-controlled businesses, Avon and Mary Kay could be replicated in other industries and in small businesses, in particular.

Immigrants launched their own small businesses because prejudice and other barriers made it difficult for them to succeed in mainstream business organizations. The experience of immigrants in the United States provides a powerful example for women. Women are realizing that the best way to succeed is to control their own destiny; women own or control about 6.5 million small businesses and are starting small business ventures at twice the rate of men (Zellner et al., 1994). The majority of economic growth in the United States comes from small business. Some estimates suggest that 80% of jobs for college graduates in the United States will come from small businesses of less than 500 employees (Byrne, 1993). This is where women should focus their efforts. Could law firms started by women partners provide a more woman-friendly atmosphere and more opportunity for women lawyers? Could a company focusing on financial services for women provide both sound advice for women at all stages and circumstances in their lives as well as offer career opportunities for women? Women with commercial backgrounds may find better opportunities starting up businesses that offer products with particular appeal to women. Moreover, they could attract and hire primarily women, moving the most talented ones to the very top.

Catalyst, a U.S. research organization whose mission is to work with business to effect change for women, makes several recommendations for breaking the glass ceiling for policy makers, employers, and for individual women. In studying corporations that have advanced women, Catalyst (1999) found that successful initiatives included removal of cultural and environmental barriers to advancement, early identification of high-potential women, leadership development programs that provide meaningful assignments and that emphasize lateral moves and line experience, support of families that seek to balance work and family commitments, and support from the highest level of corporate management. Catalyst (1999) notes that because biases against women are embedded in corporate cultures, systematic strategies are needed rather than ad hoc, isolated approaches. Its recommendations for policy makers include advocating further research on women, expanding the U.S. Department of Labor's glass ceiling audits to include women in field sites and other locations outside of corporate headquarters, disseminating information and benchmark data on organizations and the status of women within them, and improving statistical procedures for tracking the progress of women. For example, the Bureau of Labor Statistics groups together administrative, managerial, and executive positions, which makes it difficult to know the actual number of women managers. Finally, policy makers should increase financial support for academic programs that will raise the number of women in nontraditional fields such as science and engineering.

Catalyst recommends that employers conduct internal research on the barriers that women face and conduct departure surveys to find out the reasons for turnover. It suggests that top management commit to retaining and advancing women and that senior management sponsor action plans intended for employee development. In addition, it recommends that employers benchmark their efforts against those of similar companies and develop a range of initiatives to eliminate attitudinal biases that exist in the workplace. Many of these recommendations involve communication of commitment to women—through training, information sessions, or further education. Finally, employers should hold managers accountable for the progress of gender-related initiatives and measure the changes and improvements against the organization's goals.

Catalyst suggests that each woman should choose an employer carefully, learning about the employer's representation of women in senior management and the criteria the organization uses to measure success. In addition, women should identify the skill set necessary for advancement and try to obtain line assignments within the company structure. Seeking out additional highly visible tasks, finding a mentor, networking both internally and externally, taking on high-risk assignments, and seeking feedback are also suggested. Finally, women are cautioned to remain flexible and to establish their own support system of family and friends. Catalyst's recommendations make sense; however, they are only possible to implement in organizations that are already committed to the idea of helping women advance.

Like Catalyst, the International Labour Organization in Europe has made recommendations for advancing women. One of its central tenets is "gender mainstreaming"—the recommendation to put gender on the agenda of all policy formulation and business practices. The idea of gender mainstreaming came from the U.N. Beijing World Conference on Women in September 1995 with an emphasis on governments conducting "gender impact analysis" in the development of economic and social policies. The concept is transferable to businesses; people in organizations should regularly discuss the impact of gender in all facets of the business and in all of their interactions—in job assignments, in product development, in promotional decisions, and in the dynamics of meetings. Bringing gender to the forefront of conversation, rather than keeping it in the background or making it a taboo subject altogether, may begin to foster women's rights.

When women do not find organizations that meet their needs or career aspirations, working as independent entrepreneurs, unattached to the encumbrances of any organization, can be an effective strategy. If women are subject to discrimination as part of the institutional practices of companies, perhaps they would be more successful working for corporations as consultants from the outside. Many of the women featured in this book said that this approach proved to be successful. When women do not confront the patriarchy head on and are not viewed as competition by senior-level men, they are able to operate more effectively. Mary explained,

I am now working for companies and charging an extremely good daily rate. I think they see me as an ally in this situation and yet the same men that hire me and pay me well won't promote women from within their own organizations. What is going on here, I ask myself? They seem to truly value my skills as long as I am not part of their own organization. I'm non-threatening.

If women begin training themselves in skills that are highly valued in the marketplace, such as information technology, software development, and biotechnology, and then market their skills as independent consultants or business owners they may find their work more rewarding, both financially and otherwise, than if they worked for a firm.

Once women position themselves as either business owners or independent contractors, they may market their products and services through the Internet. The Internet can help women in their entrepreneurial efforts by being both a customer communication medium and a marketing vehicle. It provides a level playing field because the significance of gender is minimized in electronic commerce. The kind of antics that characterize meetings that disadvantage women need not happen when they have time to plan their approach, when their gender is less obvious, and when the customer is focused on their product and is not face to face with individual women. Furthermore, the Internet can be a means of inexpensive support for women who are or who want to become entrepreneurs. Examples of successful women entrepreneurs, free advice, chat rooms, organizations that support women in business, and information about obtaining venture capital are just a few of the resources that can be obtained over the Internet. In non-Internet communication, face to face dialogue between men and women can become fraught with power politics. As a communication vehicle in business, the Internet offers a potential opportunity to revise the way people communicate in general. Because interactions can be anonymous, genderless, and unemotional and because small companies can present themselves just as professionally as large multinational ones, business will become a more equitable arena for women.

Education is a long-range strategy for equality; unlike taking control of one's career, however, it takes time and generations for its effects to be felt. If both sexes are educated from a very early age about the importance of equal opportunity and if, because of this education, attitudes change, which in turn produce stronger laws relating to equality of women and stronger penalties for breaking those laws, then we may see some real progress. However, education is unlikely to have a significant, large-scale impact that produces change fast enough. In the short term, education cannot sufficiently challenge the legal and political system. Gun control legislation in the United States provides a good example of this phenomenon. Even the countless examples of the danger of guns and despite that school systems provide educational programs to encourage nonviolent solutions to conflict and alienation, the U.S. legal and political system will not effectively address the problem with stringent gun legislation. No amount of information alone will change the status quo.

The strategies described in this section—private consulting, entrepreneurship, advocating change in sympathetic business organizations, work in corporations serving women, and electronic commerce—have produced some reduction in the degree of women's subordination in industrial economies, particularly in the United States.

In a way, the measurable decline in gender inequality in the United States is something that the patriarchy theorist should expect. Recall the claim from Chapter 3 that patriarchal social institutions persist because they have enabled men to arrogate a disproportionate share of scarce resources throughout recorded history and before it. In an increasingly affluent economy in which scarcity is persistently reduced, the need for men to dominate resources and control women is diminished. When there are more resources for everyone, it is easier for men to share slices of the pie. In the United States there are a small number of cases of women breaking the glass ceiling and the statistics of women entering the executive suite are improving, albeit very slowly. Why they should be improving at all suggests that men no longer feel the need as strongly to dominate all economic resources. The fact that in the United States women have experienced more progress breaking through the glass ceiling than, for example, women in Britain, can be attributed to a more affluent society, especially among those who work in the business world. The difference in per capita income in Britain versus the United States is significant; in 1997, Britain's per capita income was $17,980 and in the United States it was $27,600 (World Almanac and Book of Facts, 1997, pp. 829, 831). Comparison of executive salaries in the two countries suggests even greater disparity. Senior management positions in the United States often offer double the remuneration than those in the United Kingdom. When men at middle and senior levels in organizations feel highly compensated for their work, there will be less need to keep women down. Accordingly, we should expect the patriarchy to weaken.

In a developed Western democracy the weakening of the patriarchy may well involve a negative feedback process that further weakens it. That is, the level of affluence reduces the need for men to dominate all resources and allows women a more visible and vigorous role in the economy as well as a greater share of its rewards. This greater share is then itself deployed by women to increase their economic, legal, and political power. This, in turn, results in a further weakening of the patriarchy and another cycle of closer approach to real gender equality. For example, despite the pro forma similarity of the British and American common law tradition, women in the United States have more successfully secured legal remedies to discrimination. The greater effectiveness of the law in countering female subordination is itself the result of a weakening of the patriarchy.

If this analysis is cogent, the patriarchy may turn out to be a long-lived, but nevertheless impermanent, feature of human society.

Appendix: Research Methodology

◆◆

For the reader who wants a better understanding of how I proceeded with the research and why I chose a qualitative approach, I offer this appendix. Both the positive aspects and the potential pitfalls of my research methodology are discussed.

QUALITATIVE ANALYSIS AND THE MEANING OF TERMINATION

Quantitative analysis has already established employment patterns of segregation and subordination of women. It does not, however, tell us much about how discrimination affects individuals or the informal operations of organizations that disadvantage women. Qualitative studies can begin to identify some of the causes for the differences in the treatment of women as well as uncover the meaning of a social process, institution, or experience, both for the participants and, if possible, for the social institution itself. Only a qualitative analysis of the sort used in this book can hope to uncover these wider meanings. It does so by asking subjects to reflect on the significant events in their own managerial experiences and to identify their meaning; that is, how they and other participants made sense of them, understood and interpreted their consequences, and what these events indicated about how others viewed them.

Little substantial quantitative examination of the phenomenon of senior women leaving management has been reported, and only one substantial qualitative study of this phenomenon (Marshall, 1995) was found. Even the one qualitative study does not focus on termination, but reports largely on women managers leaving employment voluntarily. A great deal of quantitative and survey research on unemployment already exists, as well as some useful quasi-experimental studies of sexual discrimination in the workplace, at both nonprofessional and professional levels. While survey research captures specifics such as age, sex, length of time out of work, and financial status and is a convenient method for dealing with large populations, it provides at best only a very partial insight into the meaning of job loss and the differences in how this process affects men versus how it affects women and whether termination is the result of different causes among men and women, especially among the ranks of otherwise apparently successful managers. Understanding how a group of women experienced job loss, the meaning they gave the experience, and how their companies have dealt with their specific cases can provide a firmer foundation for subsequent quantitative research.

A qualitative study of women's termination is valuable independently of its upshot for the formation of quantitatively testable hypotheses. In the United Kingdom in recent years much of the most significant research and many revealing discoveries about differences between the social experience, status, and roles of men and women have been the result of qualitative approaches. U.S. studies have illuminated how women experience the division of domestic work when both partners work outside the home and in the area of women's health issues (Hochschild and Machung, 1989). An increasing number of these insights have had ramifications for policy in both the public and private sphere.

Qualitative research on the position and role of women in industrial society has made visible a variety of activities, responsibilities, and roles almost exclusive to women that had hitherto been unnoticed or unvalued by society at large or by social scientists. For example, domestic work in the home, child care, and labor in the informal economy were widely ignored until qualitative social scientists began to focus on them and show their significance for women's and men's lives. By taking participants' perceptions seriously such studies also uncovered both the feelings and the reality of oppression, dissatisfaction, and inequality that characterize many women's social and domestic roles.

Moreover, qualitative studies of women's experiences and the significance they attach to them has had effects similar to cross-cultural interpretative social science. Just as cross-cultural study leads to the recognition of ethnocentric bias both in everyday life and in the social scientist's own theoretical approach, so too qualitative approaches to women's experiences have revealed limitations, inadequacy, and discriminatory dimensions of concepts, categorizations, working assumptions, and explicit and implicit theory in a male-dominated society, institution, or scientific discipline. One can expect similar outcomes when qualitative methods are applied to the study of women's experiences in dealing with business organizations, and the management theory and practice that pervade it. Consider, for example, how a male-oriented conception of leadership style might blind one to the strengths of a less competitive, more cooperative approach with which women are often more closely associated.

It is particularly remarkable that, as some qualitative studies have shown, the subjective weight of gender differences overwhelm other apparently more salient factors in human interactions. West (1988) showed that in medical settings a female physician and a male patient will find themselves in a relationship reflecting gender dominance more powerful than occupational role dominance. If gender can be this powerful in a health care context, its potential to deform relationships in non–life-threatening circumstances, such as corporate management, may be even greater.

A qualitative study of sufficient adequacy and credibility should be able to help construct a more balanced interpretative understanding of contemporary human institutions. This should make it possible to enhance the experience and the contribution of all participants. Finch (1986) has developed and illustrated the role that qualitative research can play in the framing and improvement of public policy. As Walker (1985, p. 19) notes, "qualitative research can offer the policy maker . . . a theory of social action grounded on the experiences—the world view—of those likely to be affected by the policy decision."

In my research, a qualitative approach, which includes the women's own narratives, enables any one interested in the phenomenon of termination to pursue a longitudinal treatment of it. The reader is guided through the women's personal journeys, which occurred over several years. The narratives provide access to their feelings and thoughts about their terminations on two separate occasions. It would be difficult to track the feelings of the women over time with a survey instrument, unless the subjects were willing to write lengthy answers to questions. Surveys are usually used to capture data that can be easily quantified using statistical analysis procedures. Yin (1989, p. 18) describes the purpose of survey research: "These strategies are advantageous when the research goal is to describe the incidence or prevalence of a phenomenon or when it is to be predictive about certain outcomes." The purpose of this book, on the other hand, was not to predict outcomes but to ask "how" and "why" questions and to reconstruct the participant's understanding of a critical event in management's treatment of her as a woman.

CRITICISM OF A QUALITATIVE APPROACH

Qualitative research has been criticized on at least four counts: for the bias that the researcher brings to the subject that must interfere with the interpretation process, for adequacy and credibility of the data, for ethical treatment of subjects, and for the lack of objectivity between researcher and the participants in the research. Sensitivity to these criticisms affected how I approached my research.

I had to consider my own life experiences and perspective. I have strong views about equality in the workplace and I support women's efforts to gain entry into senior management positions. I have also worked in business for several years, in both the United States and England, and have seen the effects of sexism in business environments in both countries. I needed to recognize my perspective and be careful not to impose an interpretation on events that may support my views but be inaccurate. Guba and Lincoln (1994) note that we cannot deny our biases, but suggest that reflexivity about the research subject is important to minimize their influence. By pouring over the data and thinking about possible connections and interpretations, we can overcome the effect of bias. Olesen (1994) suggests that feminist qualitative scholars would call "bias" a misplaced term. Rather, biases are resources that the researcher can evoke to guide her or him in gathering data and understanding her or his own interpretations of it. Again, Olesen suggests that the researcher needs to be sufficiently reflexive about her or his views.

I tried to achieve this reflexivity by reading and rereading transcripts of the interviews I conducted to see if different insights emerged, by talking to others about my interpretations of the data, and by searching for other plausible explanations outside my initial interpretation. Additional reading about economic exploitation and race, class, and gender discrimination led me to ponder various explanations. On several occasions I asked myself whether these women deserved to be fired. Had they provided me a clever rationalization for true incompetence and lack of performance? Evidence to the contrary emerged from performance appraisals, promotions, and evidence of their commitment and hard work.

I also shared a draft of my interpretation with specialists in industrial relations and women in management. Discussion with these experts challenged me to return to the narratives to seek further nuances in their accounts. I again reread the original transcripts and discovered other themes and dimensions I had overlooked in my quest to understand how women who did not deserve to be fired were "let go." Especially important in determining each of their fates was the personality of these women. Their impatience, incaution, and indifference to politics of their organizations contributed to their termination. The emergence of this theme, as I looked back on the material with the help of others noticing things that had escaped me, reflects how reflexiveness can mitigate bias.

In addition to the pitfalls of bias, qualitative research has been criticized for its lack of adequacy and credibility. Actively looking for negative cases to refute one's theory is one way to deal with this charge. Triangulating the data (finding different data sources) is another means of improving its adequacy. Finally, taking accounts back to respondents and using the women's voices improved their adequacy. In the end, these ways of dealing with credibility and adequacy of stories does not change the fact that they are interpreted first by the storyteller herself, and second by the interpreter of the story. The truth I was searching for was an understanding of how my research subjects experienced and made meaning out of their terminations. In an effort to uncover this truth, I triangulated the data by including diaries, e-mail correspondence, and performance reviews. This additional data added to the credibility of the women's stories in the sense that their accounts remained consistent from one type of data to another. I did not actively seek negative cases; on the other hand, I did not select out cases that did not confirm the patterns that were emerging. Perhaps the most important part of establishing credibility is using the women's voices. In remaining faithful to the women's voices, I used their exact words to describe a phenomenon and was careful not to eliminate data that seemed to contradict my findings. A certain amount of inconsistency lent credibility to their stories; for example, it seemed natural that the women would not remember every detail, especially when reflecting on events that had taken place several months before the time of the interviews.

The final criticism of qualitative research concerns lack of objectivity between researcher and participant. Unlike quantitative research, qualitative research assumes and welcomes an interplay between researcher and participant in the making of meaning (Lincoln and Guba, 1985). The question often debated is how much interplay is desirable? During my research, I chose to involve the participants in the crafting of their accounts by asking them to add to and edit the transcripts wherever they chose. Sharing the written interviews enhanced adequacy and credibility, by ensuring that my reports accurately reflected the meanings participants found in their experiences. They reframed ongoing experience in light of new questions and learning that they experienced from thinking about their situation over time. This reflexivity of participants provided additional understanding of the mechanisms of control in business organizations. I chose not to involve them directly in identifying the patterns in their accounts because they were not as well acquainted with the various explanations for women's subordination as I had become and they might have objected to some of my findings. For example, I believe they mishandled some situations on a tactical and interpersonal level and were too direct, incautious, and confrontational with influential people in the business setting. The women may have denied these criticisms of their personal styles and felt offended by my labeling their behavior in this way.

THE RESEARCH PROCESS

My sample encompassed professional women trained in common fields such as human resources, finance, marketing, and sales. All had worked in a variety of industries and locations in Britain. I looked for female middle or senior managers who had reached a level in their careers marked by a substantial degree of authority and responsibility. This authority and responsibility might be evidenced by management of staff, responsibility for a budget, decision-making power, and by identification with a peer group of substantial rank. By selecting individuals from a variety of careers, geographic locations, and industries, I hoped to capture what is common to professional women's experiences regardless of their occupation, their geographic location, or the industry in which they worked. Women in this study came from both the manufacturing and service sectors, representing companies in the financial services, retail, printing, aerospace, and food processing areas.

Locating women for this study was not an easy task. Women in senior management positions are few and far between and those who have been forced out of their organizations naturally would be reluctant to discuss the details of their termination with a complete stranger. Nevertheless, companies that specialize in executive outplacement, governmental agencies, career counseling companies, national newspapers, and managers of organizations in which the women worked helped me identify potentially suitable subjects who would be willing to talk to me. Two London-based executive outplacement companies helped locate subjects. With the approval of the women concerned, both firms agreed to send me curriculum vitae of displaced women executives. I regularly scanned national newspapers for stories about women in management. One of my research subjects, a top female executive, was featured in an article about equal pay in a prominent national newspaper. I wrote to the women's editor of the newspaper to request the woman's address. The editor agreed to ask her if she would allow me to contact her. The woman (Madge in the book) was more than happy to tell me her story. In addition, I used my professional network and contacts at the Equal Opportunities Commission to find suitable interviewees. I talked about my research with my work colleagues and friends. Often these individuals suggested people I could contact.

From a potential pool of women whose employment had been terminated, I deliberately sifted out those who had a variety of low-paid service jobs. Sometimes I contacted an individual by telephone to find that she did not fit my criterion of a senior- or middle-level manager with substantial accountability. During each initial telephone conversation I tried to establish how much accountability and responsibility the woman had had, if she had been given budgetary responsibilities, and if she managed people. I discovered that the title "manager" did not always mean the same thing in all organizations. Some so-called managers had little authority and were themselves heavily supervised. These individuals, who were really first-line supervisors with the title "manager," were excluded from the study. I also sifted out women who had been made redundant, along with others, because of massive layoffs. I rejected six potential subjects because they were too low in the hierarchy of their organization for the purpose of my study as well as other women who had been laid off as a result of downsizing. I selected women with several years' work experience, and with progressively more difficult and responsible positions. In short, I wanted to study career women who had made the same kind of sacrifices and investments in their careers as many men have made.

Obtaining a racially mixed sample proved extremely difficult. It is rare to find minority women in the upper reaches of management. From contacts I had in the management consultancy field, I did locate a Jamaican woman who fit my selection criteria and who agreed to participate in the study. Two other minority women were contacted; however, both were held to "gag" clauses, which forbid them to discuss their cases, by their former employers.

DATA COLLECTION

The ten women's narratives were gathered by in-depth interviews. I interviewed each woman twice for approximately two to three hours during each encounter. The first interview helped me establish background information about each woman. At the initial interview, I asked questions about the woman's job progression, the reason for her job loss, and her attitude toward work and family and her value system. If I had not been able to obtain a curriculum vitae before the first interview, I collected one at this time to gain insight into the woman's background and her career progression before losing her job. The second interview allowed each woman to go into more detail about her termination experience, explaining the events leading up to the dismissal and the individuals involved.

As part of the interview process, I asked each woman to read the interview transcripts relevant to my interview with her and to edit them, adding nuance and description wherever appropriate. Many of the women commented that reading their interviews was therapeutic, made them think about their organizations and what had happened to them, and helped them plan for the future in terms of choosing the next stage of their careers. As I read their additions, I noted that the women had varying degrees of self-awareness about their situations. Some were very aware of gender and power relations in their organization and others were less aware. Some seemed to evaluate their situation and the events leading up to it as an isolated event that happened only to them, not as part of a system. As Lincoln notes (1994), all feminist qualitative research shares the general assumption that subjects will be involved in the creation of the data. The involvement, rather than distancing, of subjects in making meaning is encouraged in feminist scholarship for several reasons; first, it enriches the data available for interpretation and, second, it is more ethical and empowering to openly share information with subjects (Olesen, 1994).

When the women returned edited versions of the transcripts of my field notes, some of them wrote covering letters to explain how they felt after reflecting on their situations. For example, Madge confided in a letter to me, "It is ironically a year ago today that I was dismissed. I have been thinking carefully about my emotions up to that day. I now see that I had lost all respect for them [her co-directors] and no working relationship can survive without mutual respect." In the same letter, she explained that she was being featured on a News at 10 program about male discrimination in the workplace. Diane also wrote to me indicating that she had been reflecting on her termination. In her letter, she mentions books she has read to help her think about power and gender. "I wonder whether some of these issues are to do with patriarchy. Vic Seidler has cornered a market in male orders, and one book I have is *Unreasonable Men: Masculinity and Social Theory* by Routledge [sic] (1994)." I logged these conversations and letters by date and individual and incorporated them with my field notes. These informal contacts helped me to evaluate how some of the women (Diane and Madge, in particular) had a conscious awareness of patriarchal operations in corporations. These informal conversations and letters became data for several of the chapters.

My work experience as a human resource professional helped in many ways with the research. First, I had been trained to interview job candidates and knew how to verify answers to questions, check for inconsistencies, and look for indicators of successful experience. Many times during my career, I had selected or recommended for selection senior-level men and women. Second, as a former employee relations manager, I had listened to disgruntled employees and learned what to look for in terms of legitimate and illegitimate complaints. In short, my experience as a human resource professional assisted me in establishing the credibility of the women's stories.

In addition to the interviews, I collected any documents and information the women were given by their employers when they were terminated. These materials included legal documents or redundancy and dismissal policies. The documents, as well as the women's opinions about them, provide insight about the legal and bureaucratic framework through which the termination of successful women is effected. Three of the subjects volunteered to give me lengthy diaries of their experiences leading up to their terminations; one volunteered to give me e-mail correspondence that she wrote during her employment; and several gave me copies of their performance review documents. These proved valuable additions to the interviews because they were written during or shortly after events occurred in the women's work lives.

Lincoln and Guba (1985) draw a distinction between two types of material culture: documents and records. Documents are intended to be personal and private; records are for public consumption. I secured both types of material in the form of private diaries, letters, e-mail correspondence, and public performance appraisal records. Both types of data lend further insights to the experiences of the women, but in different ways. The diaries, letters, and e-mail correspondence evoke feelings about events that are happening to these women, perhaps in a way that they would not be willing to share publicly, while the performance reviews constitute a public record, suggesting how the organization objectively measured the women's performance. They substantiate these women's assertions that they had been unjustly treated, and they assured me that poor performance was not the reason for the women's terminations. Performance reviews show that these women had, as their interviews and curriculum vitae suggest, achieved a great deal. These documents also suggest that when an organization wants to dismiss an individual, performance reviews are not taken seriously; they are simply irrelevant.

DATA ANALYSIS

I conducted a case by case analysis by looking at each of the women's interview data individually to see what themes emerged. The adequacy of each theme was evaluated by the number of times the woman addressed the theme and by the nature of the theme. For example, several times during the interview process Lesley mentioned her philosophy of participatory, nonautocratic management using different examples such as,

The best authority you can have is that which other people concede you without you asking for it.

If you try to impose your authority there are numerous ways people can get around you, but they don't do that if they have respect.

We [Lesley and her direct subordinates] always had our argument behind closed doors, but we came to consensus on what we had to do. It was not an autocratic set-up.

I could reason that Lesley believed strongly in and practiced a participatory management style because of two factors: her interview accounts did not contain contradictory evidence and she spoke about her participatory management style many times, in different contexts and in different situations. Many of the women could not tell me precisely how many times something happened. For example, Diane, Madge, and Elizabeth said that men "often" or "all the time" took credit for their ideas in meetings of various kinds; however, they could not tell me the exact number of times these incidents occurred. They were able to recall several examples of how and where these communication difficulties occurred, which gave me confidence that they had, in fact, occurred frequently.

Cross-Site Analysis

After analyzing several cases I began to examine their relationship to one another. Building meaning from the data across several cases is called "cross-site analysis" by Miles and Huberman (1994). I accomplished this cross-site analysis by constructing a large matrix of themes I found in the majority of the cases. For example, key themes such as "communication," "denial of status," and "bullying behavior" were repeated across interviews. In forming this large matrix, the adequacy of a theme depended on the number of times the women described its occurrence, the number of women reporting it, and whether or not there were contradictions or opposing themes present.

During this cross-site analysis several patterns emerged that indeed indicated a management patriarchy. In particular, the women cited disturbing communication patterns that left them at a disadvantage compared to their male colleagues, framing effects that suggested unconscious bias against women in the promotion and job evaluation process, the way in which information was handled or withheld, and the manner in which meetings were conducted.

Clustering and Unclustering Data

As I constructed a large matrix, it became clear that some situations belonged in different categories from those in which I had originally placed them. This clustering and unclustering of themes is an important part of the data analysis stage (Miles and Huberman, 1994). It allows one to see different possibilities with the data and keeps one from forming conclusions too quickly. An example of unclustering occurred when I was working with the theme "communication." I had initially placed incidents where the women had had information withheld from them under this category. On closer inspection, the nature of these occurrences was different from those in the communication category. This is because withholding information was more covert than the incidents described under "communication," where the women seemed to know either immediately or shortly after an incident that their ideas had been ascribed to men. They discovered, usually by inference rather than direct observation, that they had been cut out of meetings, bypassed in the opinion-gathering process, and left out of important discussions in which decisions or policies were made.

In the process of clustering and unclustering themes, I noted that many themes interacted with other variables. For example, as women became more assertive in their roles and demanded equal participation, they became marginalized. It is significant that the incidence of "withholding information" increased or first occurred after women tried to establish or assert their authority in their role. Similarly, "test designed to intimidate," another theme, interacted with the women's assertiveness. As the women became more assertive, they were intimidated more frequently, in public as well as in private. I found that "assertiveness" correlated with being verbally "dressed down," "intimidation tactics," and "sexual harassment" while "lack of mentoring and lack of networks," "denying resources," and "denying status" did not seem to begin when the women became more assertive. These categories seemed to be present from the time the women took their positions in either middle or senior management.

Looking for Negative Evidence

Looking for contradictions in the data and for rival explanations to phenomena is an important, albeit unnatural, part of the qualitative research process. In this study, it was difficult to look for rival case studies; that is, women who had been fired for incompetence. It is unlikely that women would respond to solicitations for stories about being fired for just cause. Instead, I asked the women in my study for performance reviews to ensure that they had not been fired for incompetence. Their record of achievement through promotions along with performance data suggested that their terminations were for reasons other than incompetence.

Looking for negative evidence took the form of revisiting my typed transcripts after constructing these matrixes. Even at this stage, it is not too late to revisit what qualitative researchers often call field notes. I discovered that certain personality effects contributed to the women's terminations. Although patriarchy still figured predominantly in the treatment of the women, their ultimate fates rested to some degree on their lack of caution, outspokenness, and lack of acknowledgment of hierarchical practices. This raised a question for me as to why so many of these women shared similar personality characteristics. I later sought explanations for this in my conclusion. Analyzing the transcripts of Diane and Lesley, I discovered additional material that I had missed. Initial evidence suggested that Diane was mistreated and unjustly fired. With further analysis of the transcripts, I saw that, although Diane was unfairly dismissed, even Diane herself recognized that her personality negatively affected her situation. She concedes that she was "strident" and "confrontational" and behaved in a "non-female" way that she suggested was threatening to men. Diane said, "I could not help myself," even though she knew this style did not help her situation. When revisiting Lesley's case, I found examples of where Lesley had admitted that her personality, particularly her stubbornness, got in the way of her interactions with her male colleagues. She said, "Tom [Lesley's managing director] if he had to make people redundant was right to get rid of me because I would have fought him every inch of the way and would have made his life a misery." Lesley recognized that her desire to be "right" and to be principled in her decision making made her a thorn in the side of her boss. Although these personality characteristics do not justify the terminations of these women, they do explain why less-confrontational, compliant women in organizations survive.

The Making of Metaphors

As Miles and Huberman (1994) suggest, qualitative researchers should think and write metaphorically to help communicate complex social realities. This is done as a data-reducing strategy and it helps the researcher see larger constructs and theories in which the data might fit. Miles and Huberman stress that the process of making and using metaphors must not happen too early in the data-gathering phase, otherwise the researcher may fall in love with a metaphor that does not actually fit. In writing up the themes of my analysis, these metaphors emerged out of the data and became conceptual frameworks for linking the experiences of the women. For example, "closing ranks" is a metaphor to describe men's loyalty to one another and their banding together to support one another no matter what they may feel individually. The "reserve army," a Marxian metaphor, was appropriate for describing how successful women can be replaced by other women as a compliant form of labor. Finally, "network" is a metaphor used to describe the complex web of interconnections among employees that is established more frequently among men. The "network" metaphor in my study describes how men help one another, share information, and exclude women. The "glass ceiling" metaphor, now very familiar to the general public, suggests a barrier that women can see through but not penetrate. The "concrete ceiling," a metaphor applied to women of color, suggests a barrier so profound that no light can penetrate it. As I worked with the data, these metaphors suggested constructs or theoretical frameworks and, I hope, provided the reader with memorable mental pictures of the ways in which the experiences of these women were similar.

Moving toward Explanation

As qualitative researchers write up data, they begin to move from description to explanation. I began to examine my themes to see if and how they related to one another and if they fit into a larger conceptual framework. I looked for what these themes had in common, how they were different, how the women's individual actions and behaviors interacted with the themes, and whether or not the themes occurred in a chronological sequence. The themes in Chapter 5 (verbal and written communication, withholding information, denying status, denying resources, lack of mentoring and networks, tests designed to intimidate, the double-bind, and closing ranks) and the themes in Chapter 6 (promises unfulfilled, responsibilities denied, allegations of poor performance, isolation and stigmatization, victimization and sexual harassment, the grievance procedure, sacking out of the blue, buying off women, and the reserve army) led me to examine various theories: Marxist ideology, human capital theory, dual systems theory, and patriarchy theory. Up to this point, I had read a great deal about the psychological impact of redundancy on terminated employees, especially men. I began to read more generally about women's subordination, labor economics, and the nature of power. This additional reading illuminated the data; I returned to the transcribed interviews on several occasions and reread them to see if and how power, forces in capitalism, gender relations, class differences, and the individual differences in the women's personalities accounted for the patterns I uncovered. Of these theoretical frameworks, patriarchy theory seemed to encompass all of the themes suggested by my data. Individual themes may lead one to competing theories. For example, examining the theme "denying resources" may suggest human capital theory because resources may be allocated on the basis of a person's productivity. The "reserve army" theme may suggest the Marxian account of the exploitation of weaker economic classes by stronger ones. "Denying status" may suggest differences explained by social class theory. However, evidence within my cases and more general evidence on differential treatment of men and women in modern management settings showed the limitations of each of these theories. The one theory encompassing all these themes and not suffering from the limitations of the others is patriarchy theory.

A FINAL NOTE

Some things remain a mystery. Could these women have avoided their fates by being more cautious? Do men who fall outside the norm, for example, gay men, threaten the patriarchy in the same way that women do?

More qualitative studies on the impact of termination on both men and women need to be done in order to shed light on the similarities and differences in the treatment of men and women. More studies are needed to differentiate the experiences of white women from women of color and to differentiate the experiences of women operating in different cultures. Additional research will also help organizational leaders better understand the legal and non-legal consequences of their companies' grievance procedures and dismissal practices. Leaders in organizations could learn more about the obstacles facing women if they conducted thorough "exit" interviews with women, whether they leave voluntarily or involuntarily. Although this involves extra effort and expense, employers will better understand the relationship between organizational culture and women's propensity to leave.

Bibliography

Abelson, R. (1999, August 22). A push from the top shatters the glass ceiling. *The New York Times*, p. 1, 23.

Abrams, K. (1994). Title VII and the complex female subject. *Michigan Law Review*, 92 (8), 2479–2540.

Acker, J. (1990). Hierarchies, jobs, bodies: A theory of gendered organizations. *Gender and Society, 4*, 139–158.

Acosta, R. & Carpenter, L. J. (1998). *Women in Intercollegiate Sport*. Unpublished manuscript, Brooklyn College Department of Physical Education and Exercise Science.

Adkins, L. (1995). *Gendered Work*. Buckingham, England: Open University Press.

Adler, N. J. (1994). Women managers in a global economy. *Training and Development, 48* (4), 31–36.

Adler, N. & Izraeli, D. (1988). Women in management worldwide. In N. Adler & D. Izraeli (eds.), *Women in Management Worldwide* (pp. 168–185). New York: Sharpe.

———. (1994). Where in the world are the women executives. *Business Quarterly, 59*, 89–94.

Aiken, O. (1999, March 11). Accompany matter. *People Management*, 27–28.

Alban Metcalfe, B. (1989). What motivated managers: An investigation by gender and sector of employment. *Public Administration, 67*, 95–108.

Alexis, M. (1974). The political economy of labor market discrimination: Synthesis and exploration. In A. Horowitz, & G. Von Furstenberg (eds.), *Patterns of Discrimination*, vol. II, Lexington, MA: Heath.

Alimo-Metcalfe, B. (1994). Gender bias in the selection and assessment of women in management. In R. Burke & M. Davidson (eds.), *Women in Management: Current Research Issues* (pp. 93–109). London: Paul Chapman.

Allan, M., Bhavnani, R. & French, K. (1992). *Promoting Women: Management Development and Training for Women in Social Services Departments*. London: Department of Health, Social Services Inspectorate.

Argyris, C. (1966, March–April). Interpersonal barriers to decision making. *Harvard Business Review*, 84–97.

———. (1998, May). Empowerment: The emperor's new clothes. *Harvard Business Review*, 98–105.

Arnold, V. & Davidson, M. J. (1990). Adopt a mentor—The new way ahead for women managers? *Women in Management Review and Abstracts*, 5 (2), 10–18.

Arroba, T. & James, K. (1987). Are politics palatable to women managers? *Women in Management Review, 3*, 123–130.

Arrow, K. (1972). Models of job discrimination. In A. Pascal (ed.), *Racial Discrimination in Economic Models of Race in the Labor Market*. Lexington, MA: Heath.

Baack, J., Carr-Ruffino, N. & Pelletier, M. (1993). Making it to the top: Specific leadership skills—A comparison of male and female perceptions of skills needed by women and men managers. *Women in Management Review, 8* (2), 17–23.

Bagguley, P. & Walby, S. (1988). *Women and Local Labour Markets: a Comparative Analysis of Five Localities*. Lancaster: University of Lancaster.

Banks, M. E. & Ackerman, R. J. (1990). Ethnic and computer employment status. *Social Sciences Computer Review, 8(1)*, 75–82.

Barron, R. D. & Norris, G. M. (1991). Sexual divisions and the dual labour market. In D. Leonard & S. Allen (eds.), *Sexual Divisions Revisited* (pp. 153–177). London: MacMillan.

Bartram, D. (1992). The personality of UK managers: 16PF norms for short-listed managers. *Journal of Occupational and Organizational Psychology, 65*, 159–172.

Becker, G. (1964). *Human Capital*. Chicago: University of Chicago Press.

———. (1975). *Human Capital*. New York: Columbia University.

———. (1985). Human capital, effort, and the sexual division of labor. *Journal of Labor Economics, 3, 1, par 2 (January)*, 533–558.

Bernard, C. & Schlaffler, E. (1997). "The man in the street": Why he harasses. In L. Richardson, V. Taylor & N. Whittier (eds.), *Feminist Frontiers IV* (pp. 395–398). New York: McGraw-Hill.

Berry, J. (1996). Women and consulting: The downside. *Journal of Management Consulting, 9* (1), 34–38.

Bierema, L. (1996). How executive women learn corporate culture. *Human Resource Development Quarterly, 7* (2), 145–164.

Boyer, I. (1995). *Balance on Trial: Women's Careers in Accountancy*. London: Chartered Institute of Management Accounts.

Brass, D. J. (1985). Men's and women's networks. *Academy of Management Journal, 28*, 327–343.

Braverman, D. (1974). *Labour and Monopoly Capital*. New York: Monthly Review Press.

Brenner, O. C., Tomkiewicz, J. & Schein, V. E. (1989). The relationship between sex-role stereotypes and requisite management characteristics revisited. *Academy of Management Journal, 32* (3), 662–669.

Brett, J. M., Stroh, L. & Reilly, A. (1994). Turnover of female managers. In M. J. Davidson & R. J. Burke (eds.), *Women in Management: Current Research Issues* (pp. 55–64). London: Paul Chapman.

Brewster, C. & Rees, B. (1995). Supporting equality: Patriarchy at work in Europe. *Personnel Review, 24,* 19–40.

Brockbank, A. & Traves, J. (1996). Career aspirations—women managers in retailing. In S. Ledwith & F. Colgan (eds.), *Women in Organisations* (pp. 78–98). Basingstoke, UK: MacMillan.

Brosman, M. & Davidson, M. (1994). Computerphobia—Is it a particularly female phenomenon. *The Psychologist, 7,* 73–78.

Brown-Johnson, N. & Scandura, T. (1994). The effect of mentorship and sex-role style on male-female earnings. *Industrial Relations, 33,* 263–274.

Brownmiller, S. (1976). *Against Our Will: Men, Women and Rape.* Baltimore, MD: Penguin.

Burke, R. J. (1995). Incidence and consequences of sexual harassment in a professional services firm. *Employee Counselling Today, 7* (3), 23–29.

Burke, R. J. & McKeen, C. A. (1989). Developing formal mentoring programs in organizations. *Business Quarterly,* winter, 69–76.

———. (1994). Career development among managerial and professional women. In M. Davidson & R. Burke (eds.), *Women in Management: Current Research Issues* (pp. 65–79). London: Paul Chapman.

Byrne, J. A. (1993). Enterprise: How entrepreneurs are reshaping the economy—And what big companies can learn. *Business Week/Enterprise 1993,* Special Issue, 11–18.

Cain, G. C. (1991). The uses and limits of statistical analysis in measuring economic discrimination. In E. P. Hoffman (ed.), *Essays on the Economics of Discrimination.* Kalamazoo, MI: W.E. Upjohn Institute for Employment Research.

Caputi, J. & Russell, D. (1997). "Femicide": Speaking the unspeakable. In L. Richardson, V. Taylor & Whittier, N. (eds.), *Feminist Frontiers IV* (pp. 421–426). New York: McGraw-Hill.

Carothers, S. C. & Crull, P. (1984). Contrasting sexual harassment in female and male dominated occupations. In K. Brodkin-Sacha & D. Remy (eds.), *My Troubles Are Going to Have Trouble With Me* (pp. 219–228). New Brunswick, NJ: Rutgers University Press.

Catalyst. (1999, July 13). Women of color report a "concrete ceiling" barring their advancement in corporate America [summary of research findings on the World Wide Web]. Retrieved July 30, 1999, from the World Wide Web: http://www.catalystwomen.org.

Chiplin B. & Sloane, P. J. (1982). *Tackling Discrimination in the Workplace.* Cambridge: Cambridge University Press.

Cleveland, J. N. & Kerst, M. E. (1993). Sexual harassment and perceptions of power: An under articulated relationship. *Journal of Vocational Behavior, 42,* 49–67.

Cockburn, C. (1983). *Brothers: male dominance and technological change.* London: Pluto Press.

Cockburn, C. (1990). Men's power in organizations: "equal opportunities" intervenes. In J. Hearn & D. Morgan (eds.), *Men, Masculinities and Social Theory* (pp. 72–89). London: Unwin Hyman Ltd.

Coe, T. (1992). *The Key to the Men's Club: Opening Doors to Women in Management*. Corby, Northants: The Institute of Management.

———. (1993). Unlocking the barriers to women in management. *Executive Development, 6* (5), 15–17.

Collier, R. (1995). *Combating Sexual Harassment in the Workplace*. Buckingham, England: Open University Press.

Collinson, D. & Collinson, M. (1989). Sexuality in the workplace: The domination of men's sexuality. In J. Hearn et al. (eds.), *The Sexuality of Organization* (pp. 91–109). London: Sage.

———. (1996). "Its only Dick": The sexual harassment of women managers in insurance sales. *Work, Employment and Society, 10,* 29–56.

Collinson, D., Knights, D. & Collinson, M. (1990). *Managing to Discriminate*. London: Routledge.

Commission of the European Communities. (1999). *Equal Opportunities for Women and Men in the European Union—1998*. Brussels: Commission of the European Communities.

Connell, R. W. (1987). *Gender and Power: Society, the Person and Sexual Politics*. Cambridge: Polity Press.

Corcoran-Nantes, Y. & Roberts, K. (1995). We've got one of those: The peripheral status of women managers in male dominated industries. *Gender, Work and Organisation 2* (1), 21–33.

Cotton, J. L. & Tuttle, J. M. (1986). Employee turnover: A meta-analysis and review with implications for research. *Academy of Management Review, 11,* 55–70.

Court, G. (1995). Creating a culture for equality. *Opportunity 2000: Toward a Balanced Workforce*. London: Business in the Community.

Davidson, M. & Cooper, C. (1983). *Stress and the Woman Manager*. New York: St. Martin's.

———. (1992). *Shattering the Glass Ceiling: The Woman Manager*. London: Paul Chapman.

Davis, E. (1996). Women at the top. *HR Focus, 73,* 18.

Delphy, C. (1984). *A Materialist Analysis of Women's Oppression*. London: Heinneman.

Denzin, N. (1978). *The Research Act: A Theoretical Introduction to Sociological Methods*. New York: McGraw Hill.

Department of Employment UK. (1990, April). *Employment Gazette*. London: H. M. Printing Office, 186–195.

———. (1997, January). Labour market trends. *Employment Gazette 105* (1), 1–28.

Dex, S. (1988). *Women's Attitudes Toward Work*. Basingstoke, UK: MacMillan.

Dickens, L. (1994). Wasted resources? Equal opportunities in employment. In K. Sisson (ed.), *Personnel Management* (2nd ed.) (pp. 253–298). Oxford: Blackwell.

Di Tomaso, N. (1989). Sexuality in the workplace: Discrimination and harassment. In J. Hearn et al. (eds.), *The Sexuality of Organization* (pp. 77–90). London: Sage.

Dodge, K. (1999, May 19). Personal communication, Mary Kay Cosmetics.

Doeringer, P. B. & Piore, M. J. (1971). *Internal Labor Markets and Manpower Analysis*. Lexington, MA: Heath Lexington Books.

Duerst-Lahti, G. & Johnson C. (1992). Management styles, stereotypes, and advantages. In M. E. Guy (ed.), *Women and Men of the States* (pp. 125–156). Armonk, NY: M. E. Sharpe.

Duncan, K. C. (1996). Gender differences in the effect of education on the slope of experience-earnings profile: National longitudinal survey of youth, 1979–1988. *American Journal of Economics and Sociology, 55* (4), 457–471.

Dwyer, P., Johnson, M. & Miller, K. (1996, April 15). Out of the typing pool into career limbo. *Business Week*, 92–94.

Edwards, R. C., Gordon, D. M. & Reich, M. (1982). *Labour Market Segmentation*. Lexington, MA: Lexington Books.

Ellis, V. (1988). Current trade union attempts to remove occupational segregation in employment of women. In S. Walby (ed.), *Gender Segregation at Work*. Milton Keynes, England: Open University Press.

Ellison, R. (1989). Labour force outlook to 2001. *Employment Gazette, 97,* 159–217.

Equal Opportunities Commission. (1988). *Local Authority Equal Opportunity Policies: Report of a Survey*. Manchester, England: EOC.

Equal Opportunities Review. (1995). *Junior barristers face sex discrimination, 60,* 5.

Eurostat. (1991). *Labour Force Survey*. Luxembourg: Eurostat.

Faludi, S. (1991). *Backlash: The Undeclared War against American Women*. New York: Crown.

Ferber, M. A. & Green, C. A. (1991). Occupational segregation and the earnings gap: Further evidence. In E. Hoffman (ed.), *Essays on the Economics of Discrimination* (pp. 145–165). Kalamazoo, MI: W. E. Upjohn Institute for Employment Research.

Ferrers, T. (1995). Australia. *Chartered Accountants Journal of New Zealand, 74* (1), 84–86.

Figes, K. (1994). *Because of Her Sex: The Myth of Equality for Women in Britain*. London: MacMillan.

Finch, J. (1986). *Research and Policy: The Uses of Qualitative Research in Social and Educational Research*. Lewes, England: Falmer Press.

Firestone, S. (1970). *Dialectic of Sex: The Case for Feminist Revolution*. New York: Morrow.

Goldthorpe, J. H. (1983). Women and class analysis: A defense of the traditional view. *Sociology, 17,* 465–488.

Gordon, D. M. (1989). *Theories of Poverty and Unemployment*. Lexington, MA: Lexington Books.

Gordon, D. M., Edwards, R. & Reich, M. (1982). *Segmented Work, Divided Workers*. Cambridge: Cambridge University Press.

Gould, R. (1986). *Sacked: Why Good People Get Fired and How to Avoid It*. New York: John Wiley and Sons.

Graf, L. & Hemmasi, M. (1995). Risque humour: How it really affects the workplace. *HR Magazine, 40* (11), 64–69.

Gregg, P., Machin, S. & Szymanski, S. (1993). The disappearing relationship between directors pay and corporate performance. *British Journal of Industrial Relations, 31* (1), 1–9.

Guba, E. & Lincoln, Y. (1994). Competing paradigms in qualitative research. In N. Denzin & Y. Lincoln (eds.), *Handbook of Qualitative Research* (pp. 105–117). Thousand Oaks, CA: Sage.

Gutek, B. (1989). Sexuality in the workplace: Key issues in social research and organizational practice. In J. Hearn et al. (eds.), *The Sexuality of Organization* (pp. 56–70). London: Sage.

Gutek, B. A. & Dunwoody, V. (1987). Understanding sex in the workplace. In L. Stromberg, C. Larwood, & B. A. Gutek (eds.), *Women and Work: An Annual Review* (pp. 249–270). Beverley Hills: Sage.

Hadjifotiou, N. (1983). *Women and Harassment at Work.* London: Pluto Press.

Hagberg, J. (1999, June 15). Barriers women face: Risk, rescue & righteousness [article on the World Wide Web]. Hagberg Consulting Group. Retrieved July 11, 1999, from the World Wide Web: http://hcgnet.com.

Hakim, C. (1979). *Occupational Segregation: A Comparative Study of the Degree and Pattern of the Differentiation between Men and Women's Work in Britain, the US and Other Countries.* London: Department of Employment.

Hammer, J. (1990). Men, power and the exploitation of women. In J. Hearn & D. Morgan (eds.), *Men, Masculinities and Social Theory* (pp. 21–42). London: Unwin Hyman Ltd..

Hammond, V. (1994). Opportunity 2000: Good practice in UK organizations. In M. Davidson & R. Burke (eds.), *Women in Management: Current Research Issues* (pp. 304–316). London: Paul Chapman.

Hansard Commission. (1990). *The Report of the Hansard Society Commission on Women at the Top.* London: The Hansard Society.

Hartmann, H. (1979). Capitalism, patriarchy and job segregation by sex. In Z. Eisenstein (ed.), *Capitalist Patriarchy and the Case for Socialist Feminism* (pp. 206–247). New York: Monthly Review Press.

Hay Management Consultants. (1993). *Trent Regional Health Authority: Managerial Styles and Climate of Men and Women in Trent RHA.* London: Hay Management Consultants.

Hegewisch, A. & Mayne, L. (1994). Equal opportunities policies in Europe. In C. Brewster & A. Hegewisch (eds.), *Policy and Practice in European Human Resource Management* (pp. 216–229). London: Routledge.

Heilman, M. E., Block, C. J., Martell, R. F. & Simon, M. C. (1989). Has anything changed—Current characterizations of men, women, and managers. *Journal of Applied Psychology, 74* (6), 935–942.

Helgeson, S. (1990). *The Female Advantage.* New York: Doubleday.

Hemenway, K. (1995). Human nature and the glass ceiling in industry. *Communications of the ACM, 38,* 55–62.

Hochschild, A. & Machung, A. (1989). *The Second Shift: Working Parents and the Revolution at Home.* New York: Viking.

Holden, K. & Hansen, W. L. (1987). Part-time work and occupational segregation. In C. Brown & J. Pechman (eds.), *Gender in the Workplace* (pp. 217–246). Washington, DC: Brookings Institution.

Holton, V., Rabbetts, J. & Scrivener, S. (1993). *Women on the Boards of Britain's*

Top 200 Companies. Berkhamsted, England: Ashridge Management Research Group.

Howe, E. & McRae, S. (1991). *Women on the Board.* London: Policy Study Institute.

Hutt, R. (1985). *Chief Officer Profiles: Regional and District Nursing Officers, IMS Report No. 111.* University of Sussex, England: Institute of Manpower Studies.

Hyman, R. (1990). Patriarchy at work, S. Walby. *English Historical Review, 105,* 230–231.

Ibarra, H. (1992). Homophily and differential returns: Sex differences in network structure and access in an advertising firm. *Administrative Sciences Quarterly, 36,* 422–427.

International Labour Organization (ILO). (1997). *Breaking Through the Glass Ceiling: Women in Management.* Geneva: ILO.

———. (May, 1999). *The Role of Trade Unions in Promoting Gender Equality and Protecting Vulnerable Workers.* Geneva: ILO.

IRS Employment Review. (1992). Sexual harassment at the workplace. *IRS Employment Review, 513,* 6–15.

Jago, A. G. & Vroom, V. H. (1982). Sex differences in the incidence and evaluation of participative leader behaviour. *Journal of Applied Psychology, 67,* 776–783.

Johnson, J.E.V. & Powell, P. L. (1994). Decision making, risk and gender: Are managers different? *British Journal of Management, 5,* 123–138.

Journung, C. (1984). Patterns of occupational segregation by sex in the labour market. In Schmid, G. & Weitzel, R. (eds.), *Sex Discrimination and Equal Opportunity.* Aldershot, England: Gower.

Junior barristers face sex discrimination. (1995). *Equal Opportunities Review, 60,* 5.

Kahneman, D., Slovic, P. & Tversky, A. (1982). *Judgement under Uncertainty.* Cambridge: Cambridge University Press.

Kanter, R. M. (1977). *Men and Women of the Corporation.* New York: Basic Books.

Kathlene, L. (1998). Position power versus gender power: Who holds the floor. In G. Duerst-Lahti & R. M. Kelly (eds.), *Gender Power, Leadership and Governance* (pp. 167–193). Ann Arbor: University of Michigan Press.

Kelly, R., Hale, M. & Burgess, J. (1991). Gender and managerial/leadership styles: A comparison of Arizona public administrators. *Women and Politics, 11* (2), 119–139.

Kesler, S. B. (1975). Actuarial prejudice towards women and its implications. *Journal of Applied Social Psychology, 5,* 201–216.

Kirkup, G. (1992). Social construction of computers: Hammer or harpsichord. In G. Kirkup & L. Smith-Kellar (eds.), *Inverting Women: Science, Technology and Gender* (pp. 276–281). Cambridge, U K: Polity.

Korn-Ferry International & UCLA Anderson Graduate School of Management. (1993). *Decade of the Executive Woman.* Los Angeles: Korn-Ferry International.

Kottis, A. P. (1993). The glass ceiling and how to break it. *Women in Management Review, 8,* 9–15.

Kram, K. E. & Isabella, L. (1985). Mentoring alternatives: The role of peer relationships in career development. *Academy of Management Journal, 28,* 110–132.

Krueger, A. (1963). The economics of discrimination. *Journal of Political Economy, 71,* 481–486.

Lacayo, R., Holmes, S., & Sachs, A. (1988, November 14). A hard nose and a short skirt. *Time, 132,* 98.

Lach, D. H. & Gwartney-Gibbs, P. A. (1993). Sociological perspectives on sexual harassment and work place dispute resolution. *Journal of Vocational Behavior, 42,* 102–115.

Leonard, J. S. (1987). The interaction of residential segregation and employment discrimination. *Journal of Urban Economics, 21* (3), 323–346.

Lincoln, Y. S. (1994). Feminist in qualitative research. In N. Denzin & Y. S. Lincoln (eds.), *Handbook of Qualitative Research* (pp. 158–179). Thousand Oaks, CA: Sage.

Lincoln, Y. S. & Guba, E. G. (1985). *Naturalistic Inquiry.* Beverly Hills, CA: Sage.

Lipman-Blumen, J. (1984). *Gender Roles and Power.* Englewood Cliffs, NJ: Prentice Hall.

Lloyd, C. (1975). *Discrimination and the Division of Labor.* New York: Columbia University Press.

MacKinnon, K. (1979). *Sexual Harassment of Working Women.* New Haven, CT: Yale University Press.

Maddock, S. J. & Parkin, D. (1993). Gender cultures: Women's choices and strategies at work. *Women in Management Review, 8,* 3–9.

Management Services (1996). Women executives forge ahead. *Management Services, 40* (6), 3.

Mann, S. (1995). Politics and power in organisations. *Leadership, 15* (2), 9–15.

Marchetti, M. (1996). Memo to men: Shut up! *Sales and Marketing Management, 148* (2), 28.

Marks, A. (1984). *Exit Miss Jones.* London Alfred Marks Ltd. (available from Industrial Society).

Marshall, J. (1994). Why women leave senior management jobs: My research approach and some initial findings. In M. Tanton (ed.), *Women in Management: A Developing Presence* (pp. 185–201). London: Routledge.

———. (1995). *Women Managers Moving On.* London: Routledge.

Martin, S. (1988). Think like a man, work like a dog, and act like a lady: Occupational dilemmas of policewomen. In A. Statham, E. Miller & H. Mauksch (eds.), *The Worth of Women's Work* (pp. 205–221). Albany: State University of New York Press.

Mattis, M. C. (1990). Dismantling the glass ceiling, pane by pane. *The Human Resources Professional,* fall, 5–8.

Maume, D. J. (1999). Glass ceilings and glass escalators. *Work and Occupations, 26* (4): 483–509.

McCall, M. W., Lombardo, M. M., & Morrison, A. C. (1988). *The Lessons of Experience.* New York: Lexington Books.

McKenna, E. P. (1997). *When Work Doesn't Work Anymore: Women, Work and Identity.* New York: Delacorte Press.

McRae, S. (1996). *Women at the Top: Progress after Five Years.* London: The Hansard Society.

Miles, M. & Huberman, A. (1994). *Qualitative Data Analysis: An Expanded Sourcebook* (2nd ed.). Thousand Oaks, CA: Sage.

Milkman, R. (1995, December). Economic inequality among women. *British Journal of Industrial Relations, 33,* 679–683.

Miller, J., Fry L. & Labovitz, S. (1975). Inequities in the organizational experiences of women and men. *Social Forces, 54,* 365–381.

Millett, K. (1970). *Sexual Politics.* Garden City, NJ: Doubleday.

Mincer, J. & Polachek, S. W. (1974). Family investment in human capital: Earnings of women. *Journal of Political Economy, 82,* 76–111.

Morris, B. (1997, July 21). If women ran the world it would look a lot like Avon. *Fortune,* 74–79.

Morrison, A. C. (1992). *The New Leaders.* San Francisco: Jossey-Bass.

Morrison, A. C. & Von Glinow, M. A. (1990). Women and minorities in management. *American Psychologist, 42,* 200–208.

Morrison, A. M., White, R. P., Van Velsor, E. & Center for Creative Leadership. (1987). *Breaking the Glass Ceiling.* Reading, MA: Addison-Wesley.

Morrison, A. M., White, R. P. & Van Velsor, E. (1992). *Breaking the Glass Ceiling* (2nd ed.). Reading, MA: Addison-Wesley.

NEDO (National Economic Department Office). (1990). *Woman Managers: The Untapped Resource.* London: NEDO.

Newell, S. (1993). The superwoman syndrome: Gender differences in attitudes towards equal opportunities at work and towards domestic responsibilities at home. *Work, Employment and Society, 7,* 275–289.

Nichols, N. (1994). Whatever happened to Rosie the riveter? In N. Nichols (ed.), *Reach for the Top* (pp. 3–12). Boston: Harvard Business Review.

Nicholson, N. & West, M. (1988). *Managerial Job Change: Men and Women in Transition.* Cambridge: Cambridge University Press.

Office for Public Management. (1994). *Getting More Women to the Top in the Housing Association Movement—a Practical Guide.* London: Office for Public Management.

Ohlett, P., Ruderman, M. & McCauley, C. (1994). Gender difference in managers' developmental job experiences. *Academy of Management Journal, 37,* 46–67.

Olesen, V. (1994). Feminism and models of qualitative research. In N. Denzin & Y. Lincoln (eds.), *Handbook of Qualitative Research* (pp. 158–174). Thousand Oaks, CA: Sage.

Olsen, R. N. & Sexton, E. A. (1996, January). Gender differences in managers' developmental job experiences. *Academy of Management Journal 37,* 46–67.

Pateman, C. (1988). *The Sexual Contract.* Cambridge: Polity Press.

Perrow, G. L. (1986). *Complex Organizations.* New York: Random House.

Peters, T. (1988). *Thriving on Chaos.* New York: Alfred Knopf.

Posadskaya, A. & Zakharova, N. (1990). *To Be a Manager: Changes for Women in the USSR* (Discussion paper no. 65). Geneva: Training Policies Branch, International Labour Organization.

Post Secondary Education Opportunity. (1998, October). Where are the guys? *Post Secondary Education Opportunity, 76* 1–8.

Powell, G. N. (1988). *Women and Men in Management* (1st ed.). Newbury Park, CA: Sage.

———. (1990). One more time: Do female and male managers differ?. *Academy of Management Executive, 4* (3), 68–75.

———. (1993). *Women and Men in Management* (2nd ed.). Newbury Park, CA: Sage.

Proctor, J. & Jackson, C. (1994). Senior women managers and processes of change in the National Health Service. *Journal of Gender Studies, 3* (2), 197–204.

Ragins, B. R. (1989). Barriers to mentoring: The female manager's dilemma. *Human Relations, 42*, 1–22.

Ragins, B. R. & Sunstrom, E. (1989). Gender and power in organizations: A longitudinal perspective. *Psychological Bulletin, 105*, 51–88.

Rainsbury, E., Sutherland, J. & Urlich, R. (1996). Women's situation is a management issue. *Chartered Accountants Journal of New Zealand, 75* (3), 15–17.

Remy, J. (1990). Patriarchy and fratrairchy as forms of androcracy. In J. Hearn & D. Morgan (eds.), *Men, Masculinities and Social Theory* (pp. 43–54). London: Unwin Hyman Ltd.

Reuters. (1997, September 20). Home Depot settles discrimination suits [article on the World Wide Web]. Reuters Limited. Retrieved September 10, 1999, from the World Wide Web: http://builder.hw.net/news/1997/Sep/20/depot20.htx.

Rheem, H. (1996). Equal opportunity for women—The verdict is (still) mixed. *Harvard Business Review, 74* (4), 12–13.

Richards, W. (1996). Equal opportunities for women in Britain: The case of Opportunity 2000 and the National Health Service. *Review of Employment Topics, 4*, 91–119.

Rigg, C. & Sparrow, J. (1994). Gender, diversity, and working styles. *Women in Management Review, 9*, 9–16.

Rosener, J. B.(1990, November). The way women lead. *Harvard Business Review*, 119–125.

———. (1995). Women: A competitive secret. *Business Quarterly, 60* (2), 79–80.

Rosin, H. M. & Korabik, K. (1990). Marital and family correlates of women managers' attrition in organizations. *Journal of Vocational Behavior, 37*, 104–120.

———. (1991). Workplace variables, affective responses, and intention to leave among women managers. *Journal of Occupational Psychology, 64* (4): 317–330.

———. (1992). Corporate Fligh of women managers: Moving from fiction to fact. *Women in Management Review, 7* (3), 31–35.

Rubery, J. & Fagan, C. (1995). Gender segregation in a social context. *Work, Employment and Society, 9* (2), 213–240.

Rubery, J., Smith, M., Fagan, C. & Grimshaw, D. (1998). *Women and European Employment*. New York: Routledge.

Rubin, J. (1997). Gender, equality and the culture of organisational assessment. *Gender, Work, and Organization, 4* (1), 24–34.

Russell, C. (1995). Glass ceilings can break. *American Demographics, 17*, 8.

Rustad, M. (1982). *Women in Khaki: The American Enlisted Women*. New York: Praeger.

Saltzman, A. (1996, August). Life after the lawsuit. *US News and World Report,* *121* (7), 57–61.

Schein, V. E. (1973). The relationship between sex role stereotypes and requisite management characteristics. *Journal of Applied Psychology, 57,* 95–100.

———. (1975). The relationship between sex role stereotypes and requisite management characteristics among female managers. *Journal of Applied Psychology, 60,* 340–344.

———. (1990). The relationship between sex role stereotypes and requisite management characteristics revisited. *Academy of Management Journal, 32,* 662–669.

———. (1994). Power, sex and systems. *Women in Management Review, 9* (1), 4–8.

Schullery, N. M. (1998, July). The optimum level of argumentativeness for employed women. *Journal of Business Communication, 35* (3), 346–367.

Schwartz, F. N. (1989, January-February). Management women and the new facts of life. *Harvard Business Review,* 65–76.

Scott, J. W. (1986). Gender: A useful category of historical analysis. *American History Review, 91,* 139–158.

Seidler, V. (1994). *Unreasonable men: Masculinity and social theory.* London: Routledge.

Serepca, B. (1995). Sexual harassment. *Internal Auditor, 52* (5), 60–62.

Sheppard, D. (1989). Organisations, power and sexuality: The image and self-image of women managers. In J. Hearn et al. (eds.), *The Sexuality of Organization* (pp. 139–157). London: Sage.

Sly, F. (1996, March). Women in the labour market: Results from the spring 1995 Labour Force Survey. *Labour Market Trends,* 91–113.

Smith-Keller, L. (1992). Discovering and doing: Science and technology, an introduction. In G. Kirkup & L. Smith-Keller (eds.), *Inventing Women: Science, Technology and Gender* (pp. 12–32). Cambridge, UK: Polity.

Spencer, A. & Podmore, D. (1987). Women lawyers: Marginal members of a male-dominated profession. In A. Spencer & D. Podmore (eds.), *In a Man's World* (pp. 113–133). London: Tavistock.

Stanko, B. & Warner, C. (1995). Sexual harassment: What is it? How to prevent it. *National Public Accountant, 40* (6), 14–16.

Still, L. (1988). *Becoming a Top Woman Manager.* Boston: Allen and Unwin.

———. (1994). Where to from here? Women in management: The cultural dilemma. *Women in Management Review, 9,* 3–10.

Stroh, L. K. & Senner, J. R. (1994, December). Female top executives: turnover, career limitations and attitudes towards the work place. *Industrial Relations Association Proceedings.*

Stroh, L. K., Brett, J. M. & Reilly, A. H. (1993). Turned over, or turned off: A comparison of male and female turnover. Conference paper, Society of Industrial and Organizational Psychology, April.

Summerfield, R. (1984). *Women Workers in the Second World War.* London: Croom Helm.

Symons, G. (1992). The glass ceiling is constructed over the gendered office. *Women in Management Review 7* (1), 18–22.

Tangri, S. S., Burt, M. R. & Johnson, L.V. (1982). Sexual harassment at work: Three explanatory models. *Journal of Social Issues, 38,* 33–54.

Tannen, D. (1990). *You Just Don't Understand.* New York: William Morrow.

———. (1995). The power of talk: Who gets heard and why. *Harvard Business Review, 73,* 138–148.

Taylor, A. P. (1986). Why women managers are bailing out. *Fortune, 18,* 16–23.

Thibaut, J. & Kelley, H. (1967). *The Social Psychology of Groups.* New York: John Wiley and Sons.

Through a glass, darkly. (1996, August 10). *The Economist, 340,* 50–51.

Thurow, L. (1969). *Poverty and Discrimination.* Washington, DC: Brookings Institute.

Turner, R. & Killian, L. (1957). *Collective Behavior.* Englewood Cliffs, NJ: Prentice Hall.

United Nations (1995). *The World's Women.* New York: United Nations.

University of St. Thomas, Graduate School of Business. (1993). *No Offense?* London: The Industrial Society Press.

U.S. Department of Labor, Bureau of Labor Statistics. (1997, April). *Facts on Working Women* (No. 97–3). Washington, DC: U.S. Government.

Van Velsor, E. & Hughes, M. (1990). *Gender Differences in the Development of Women Managers: How Women Managers Learn from Experience.* Greensboro, NC: Center for Creative Leadership.

Vinnicombe, S. (1987). What exactly are the differences in male and female working styles? *Women in Management Review, 3* (1), 13–21.

von Prondzynski, F. & Richards, W. (1995). Equal opportunities in the labour market: Tackling indirect sex discrimination. *European Public Law, 1,* 117–135.

Wajcman, J. (1991). Patriarchy, technology, and the conception of skill. *Work and Occupations, 18,* 29–45.

Walby, S. (1986). *Patriarchy at Work.* Minneapolis: University of Minnesota Press.

———. (1988). *Gender segregation at work.* Milton Keynes, England: Open University Press.

———. (1990). *Theorizing Patriarchy.* London: Blackwell.

Walker, R. (1985). *Applied Qualitative Research.* Hants, UK: Gower.

Weil, P. & Kimball, P. (1996). Gender and compensation in health care management. *Health Care Management Review, 21* (3), 19–33.

West, C. (1988). *Routine Complications: Troubles with Talk between Doctors and Patients.* Bloomington: Indiana University Press.

Whiddon, S. (1999, May 19). Personal communication, Mary Kay Cosmetics.

White, B., Cox, C. & Cooper, C. L. (1992). *Woman's Career Development: A Study of High Flyers.* Oxford: Blackwell.

Williams, C. (1998). The glass escalator: Hidden advantages for men in the "female" professions. In M. Kimmel & M. Messner (eds.), *Mens' Lives* (4th ed.) (pp. 285–299). Boston: Allyn and Bacon.

Wills, P. E. (1977). *Learning to Labour: How Wworking Class Kids Get Working Class Jobs.* Farnborough, UK: Saxon House, Teakfield Ltd.

Wilson, R. (1999, December 3). An MIT professor's suspicion of bias leads to a new movement for academic women. *The Chronicle of Higher Edcuation, 46* (15), A16–A18.

Winn Dixie grocery chain settles discrimination suit for $33 million. (1999). *JET, 96* (10), 30.

Witz, A. (1988). Patriarchal relations and patterns of sex segregation in the medical division of labour 1858–1940. In S. Walby (ed.), *Gender Segregation at Work* (pp. 74–90). Milton Keynes England: Open University Press.

———. (1992). *Professions and Patriarchy.* London: Routledge.

Wolff, M. (1996). Glass ceiling may start with Ph.D. education. *Research-Technology Management, 39* (3), 7.

The World Almanac and Book of Facts. (1997). Mahwah, NJ: Kiii Reference Group.

Yancy Martin, P. (1996). Gendering and evaluating dynamics: Men, masculinities, and managements. In D. Collinson & J. Hearn (eds.), *Men as Managers, Managers as Men: Critical Perspectives on Men, Masculinities and Managements* (pp. 186–209). London: Sage.

Yin, R. (1989). *Case Study Research: Design and Method.* Newbury Park, CA: Sage.

Young, K. & Spencer, L. (1991). *Breaking down the Barriers: Women Managers in Local Government.* London: Local Government Training Board.

Zellner, W., King, R. W., Byrd, V., DeGeorge, G. & Birnbaum, J. (1994, April 18). Women entrepreneurs. *Business Week,* 104–110.

Zimmer, L. (1988). Sex and supervision: Guarding male and female inmates. *Contemporary Sociology, 17* (1), 42–43.

Index

About the Author

MARTHA E. REEVES teaches marketing and women's studies at The University of Georgia. She has spent more than ten years working in a variety of management and marketing positions in the United States and United Kingdom.